BOOK COLLECTING

SEUMAS STEWART

BOOK COLLECTING

A Beginner's Guide

With a Foreword by
John F. Fleming

New revised edition

A Sunrise Book
E. P. Dutton New York

This second, revised edition to the memory of
JOHN WAYNFLETE CARTER, CBE
(1905–1975)
most human of bookmen

For information contact:
E. P. Dutton, 2 Park Avenue, New York, N.Y. 10016

Library of Congress Catalog Card Number: 78=70256

ISBN: 0-87690-345-6

Published simultaneously in Canada by
Clarke, Irwin & Company Limited,
Toronto and Vancouver

10 9 8 7 6 5 4 3 2 1

Contents

Illustrations

Acknowledgements

Thanks are due to the following for their kind permission to reproduce illustrations in this book:

Associated Newspapers Group Ltd, London: Caton Woodville's illustration to Kipling's *The Absent-Minded Beggar*.

Routledge & Kegan Paul Ltd, London: Jessie M. King's drawing from Milton's *Comus*.

Frederick Warne & Co Ltd, London: illustration and text from Beatrix Potter's *Benjamin Bunny*.

The family of the late F. L. Griggs and Sir Basil Blackwell: the engraving from F. L. Griggs's *Campden*.

Thanks are also due to Sotheby Parke Bernet & Co, London, for permission to quote from Sotheby & Co's catalogue of June 22–3, 1970, and to Wheldon & Wesley Ltd, Hitchin, Herts, for the quotation from their new series catalogue No 135. The copy of H. M. Stanley's *In Darkest Africa* was kindly lent for illustration by Bookworms of Evesham, Worcs, and further help with illustrations was given by Eric and Grace Benton, Sibford Gower, Oxon.

Foreword

by John F. Fleming

The late Dr. A. S. W. Rosenbach, whom the press dubbed 'The Napoleon of Books', once wrote, 'The greatest sport, next to love, is book-collecting'. His friend Christopher Morley thought it a statement worthy enough to include in his edition of *Bartlett's Familiar Quotations*. It is true that any sport, if you are going to excel at it, requires deep interest and dedication. But in practically every sport the rewards are short-lived. They burn you out. Not so in the pursuit of The Book. It is a leisurely, dedicated chase that leaves you exalted, not exhausted, in body and spirit.

There is no explanation in the Annals of Medicine that explains the efficacious effect that the pursuers of the printed word enjoy, nor do they mention the reasons for the longevity of the book collector. The record is long and convincing.

This is in a way an extra dividend for the fledgling book collector who will want to follow the guidance and advice given in this book. There is a very wide range of subjects to collect here, and serious beginners are well advised how they may be able to value a book and escape the pitfalls of this fascinating game.

A rule one must remember: Examine and collate. Examine and collate again. Make sure your purchase is perfect. Even if you become a seasoned collector, don't take the word of anyone.

Many years ago, to be exact fifty-one years ago, an eminent

9

Rare Book dealer bought from a not-so-eminent Rare Book dealer a copy of the celebrated first edition of William Blake's *Poetical Sketches* for $3,000.00. It contained the bookplates of R. A. Potts. It is a small octavo of only 70 pages. Within easy reach of the famous book dealer's staff was the superb Blake *Bibliography* by Geoffrey Keynes, published by the Grolier Club a few years before. A very young but curious neophyte, just hired, wanted to find out why it was worth $3,000,000. He fumbled his way through the reference catalogue and found the card listing the Keynes *Bibliography*. He located the impressive tome and soon found the listing of the fourteen known copies. Under Copy 'K' he read : 'R. A. Potts copy. Sold at Sotheby's Feb. 20, 1913 (lot 71, £8-5s) in calf gilt. pp. 49–70 in fac-simile.' The great dealer was informed. No, he had not yet paid for it. A young 'white-haired boy' was born.

I am happy to admit this occurs rarely, but if one is vigilant he will escape monetary losses, and what is more important, a sense of despair. To me the game is so rewarding that a few mistakes over the decades are trivial.

The demand for the important printed volumes of the world has become universal, and the constant search by collectors and institutions throughout the world has caused a sharp quickening of prices, especially for certain books. Seumas Stewart has provided a scale of value groupings, which as he says are variable and liable to increase with the years. Experience will inevitably help in keeping track of such price fluctuations. What may never need alteration, however, is the very extensive array of facts and knowledge that Mr. Stewart has assembled for you on the great avocation of book collecting.

J.F.F.

New York City
June 1978

Preface

Chipping Campden, Gloucestershire, where the author lives
and dreams his bookish dreams, is a unique flowering in stone
of the English spirit. In this ancient Cotswold wool town,
tradition is embedded in the fabric of its time-worn buildings, but is still alive, as when the mummers enact their play
of St George and the Dragon, or the Morris men jingle
through the measures of the age-old dances that are the town's
very own.

From his front door, the author can look across the street
to the building where the fine books of the Alcuin Press were
printed, forty to fifty years ago. His kitchen garden abuts on
the old silk mill in which, early in this century, C. R. Ashbee
set up the Guild of Handicraft and produced the lovely limited
editions of the Essex House Press. A short walk from his home
takes him past the house where Graham Greene lived and
worked in the thirties, on to Burnt Norton which inspired one
of T. S. Eliot's *Four Quartets*. A longer walk leads him to
Middle Hill, once the home of Sir Thomas Phillipps, whose
enormous collection of books and manuscripts has not yet
been fully sorted out, more than a hundred years after his
death. On this walk he could take a detour to Dover's Hill,
still the venue of the yearly Cotswold Olimpick Games, begun
by Robert Dover in about 1612, praised in verse by Ben
Jonson and Michael Drayton in *Annalia Dubrensia*, 1636,
and described by William Somerville in his poem *Hobbinol*,
1740, and Richard Graves in his novel *The Spiritual Quixote*,
1772. Chipping Campden is real bookman's territory.

11

Though a Gloucestershire rustic from choice, the author is unrepentantly Scottish by birth and upbringing, so the many references to the Cotswolds in this book do not stem from chauvinism. International exchange of one sort and another is an important aspect of book collecting. That is why the pages that follow deal with books originating in Britain, Ireland, North America and Australia, as well as a few books in languages other than English, mentioned as works of reference or because of their historical interest.

Since the first edition of this book appeared there have been changes in the collecting world. Many newcomers have entered the lists, new trends have developed and world-wide inflation has pushed up prices. These changes are reflected in the new scale of values given and in the ensuing text, which has been corrected, enlarged and extensively rewritten, with many fresh illustrations. No essential information from the first edition has been omitted.

Scale of Values

Throughout this book, approximate prices are indicated by the grade letters shown below. The table is based, not too strictly, on the equations, £1 = $1.90 and $1.90 = $A1.50. A study of comparative book prices over the past five years shows that, despite the fluctuations in currencies, these figures give reasonable equivalents for prices within the countries concerned.

(A)	up to	£2,000	$3,800	$A3,000		
(B)	„ „	£1,000	$1,900	$A1,500		
(C)	„ „	£900	$1,710	$A1,350		
(D)	„ „	£800	$1,520	$A1,200		
(E)	„ „	£700	$1,330	$A1,000		
(F)	„ „	£600	$1,140	$A900		
(G)	„ „	£500	$950	$A750		
(H)	„ „	£400	$760	$A600		
(I)	„ „	£300	$570	$A450		

(a)	up to	£200	$380	$A300
(b)	„ „	£100	$190	$A150
(c)	„ „	£90	$170	$A135
(d)	„ „	£80	$155	$A120
(e)	„ „	£70	$135	$A105
(f)	„ „	£60	$115	$A90
(g)	„ „	£50	$95	$A75
(h)	„ „	£40	$80	$A60
(i)	„ „	£30	$60	$A45

Where prices are above the range of (A), or very low in (i), approproximate figures will be given in sterling and US dollars. If the book is of particular interest to Australian collectors, the figures will be in Australian dollars as well. The table is not suitable for exchange transactions.

13

I

The Quarry and its Anatomy

In common with all its fellows, this particular copy of this book stands in danger of judgement for as long as it exists. At some time, its owner or trustee of the day will decide whether he should keep it, make it over to somebody else by gift or sale, or send it to oblivion. Until it is dumped, pulped or incinerated, it will inevitably be a collector's piece, in transit, or as a member of some collection. So it is with every extant copy of every book ever produced. Collecting books is not a game with hard-and-fast rules about what is acceptable and what is not. The arrays of magnificent volumes that dignify the shelves of the world's great libraries are collections — so are the worthless heaps of mouldering books that lie in many a neglected attic.

No evolutionist would seriously suggest that we are descended from magpies. Nonetheless, we share their propensities for collecting and hoarding. If we start seriously to collect books we tell ourselves that it is because we want to gain knowledge from them, to enjoy their contents, to delight in their appearance, or to do all three at the same time. If we are sensible, we shall choose our books for those reasons, while being aware that the acquisitive urge that lies behind it all is much more primeval. We shall appreciate that every book is potentially a collector's item, but we shall select according to our inclinations and our financial means.

Since any kind of book is collectable, anybody who obtains books by legitimate means is by way of being a collector.

However, a book collector is generally supposed to be one who regularly and systematically acquires books according to his taste and discrimination and thereafter lovingly cares for them. Such a person may also be called a bibliophile. In him the magpie instinct has become one of mankind's most civilized pleasures. A particularly zealous bibliophile is sometimes called a bibliomane. Though this word is only a variant of 'bibliomaniac', the latter form is usually reserved for a different type of collector, the man (to date bibliomaniacs have been predominantly male) who has let instinct take over and compulsively amasses books in quantity simply because they are books. Content and aesthetic appeal are of no account to him.

Sir Thomas Phillipps (1797–1872) has, with some justice, been called the greatest book collector of all time. He was an undoubted bibliomaniac. Almost every scrap of paper with writing on it was fair game to him. His declared ambition was to own a copy of every book in the world. In this unattainable pursuit Phillipps turned many categories of then unregarded books into marketable commodities. As he was willing to buy such stuff as old parish registers and records, other collectors were soon persuaded to do the same. While many of his acquisitions were of no use to him or anybody else, time has shown that at least as many were worth saving for posterity.

Under twentieth-century conditions, not even the wildest bibliomaniac could be so all-encompassing as Phillipps, and no bibliophile would wish to be. Yet a little of Phillipps's obsessional spirit is harmless and may be beneficial if it gets into the bloodstream of the many book-acquiring sobersides. They come in several varieties. There is the reluctant book collector who buys thoughtfully but sparingly and is incapable of giving books his love and affection. His library is like a Dickensian orphanage rather than a happy home. There is also the collector who lacks any spirit of adventure. He toddles along the well-worn paths and will never deviate to buy something just for the hell of it. Let him be a collector of illustrated books : he will reject various delightful examples of the genre just because the artist's name is unknown to him and is without the backing of the authorities he always consults.

Book-collecting can be loveless, strait-jacketed, venal or obsessive; it is never a hobby. None but the meanest of its practitioners would ever call it that. At its best it is an exhilarating pursuit, a glorious bloodless sport. That is how it will be treated in this book.

Like all good sportsmen, the bibliophile tempers his enthusiasm with wisdom and caution. Though there are no set rules to be obeyed, there are agreed principles to be studied. As with the 'Advices' of the Society of Friends, they are not laid down as rules or forms to walk by, but so that they 'may be fulfilled in the spirit — not from the letter, for the letter killeth, but the spirit giveth life'. The most obvious principle is that junk should not be collected. But what is junk? Their contemporaries probably classed the few who collected railway timetables fifty years ago as maniacs, without the mitigating qualification of biblio. Now the maniacs are seen as pioneers who cheaply amassed things that are now scarce, dear and sought by many.

There have been changes even since the first edition of this book was published. Former outcasts have become respectable and the process is continuing. Among the piles of printed dross still with us, there is material to which an enterprising bibliophile could give a figurative kiss of life by systematically collecting it. Nevertheless, the best hope for much of the residue is in recycling.

Book-collecting is not necessarily a rich man's activity. The rare and fine are inevitably costly, but a respectable collection can be built up for a surprisingly small outlay. Furthermore, every wise addition to a coherent collection increases its value. If he falls on really hard times the bibliophile can choose whether to sell his books and remain heart-brokenly alive, or to keep his collection intact and starve among his treasures. Possible financial gain from his acquisitions is not the bibliophile's first thought, but he should keep it in mind.

When the magpie in him lures an ordinary book-lover into the realms of bibliophily, it should lead him naturally to the main sources of his quarry—the dealers in secondhand, out of print and antiquarian books. The number of shops run by such dealers is now increasing, though many of the fraternity still work from private premises, where they sell by appointment to view or by post. Many dealers owning shops also do an extensive postal trade. Through the post, collectors who live in remote places can compete for scarce items on an almost equal footing with rivals whose homes are in London, New York or other big centres.

The collector should have his name on the files of several dealers to increase his chances of obtaining the books he wants. Mail-order booksellers issue lists or catalogues of items they have for sale. Some lists are barely-legible mimeographed sheets, while some catalogues are finely printed, lavishly illustrated and thoroughly documented. As well as the various grades between, both types should be studied. The poorly produced sheet may come from an informed eccentric with a good stock, though it is more likely that it is from an unschooled dealer with little to offer the serious book buyer. All the same, it deserves attention. The toad, though ugly and venomous, wears yet a precious jewel in his head. The dubious sheet may contain a jewel going cheap.

The lush catalogue is only rarely an impostor. It probably comes from a firm of high standing, with a name that is as good as a guarantee of integrity and accuracy. Every item it contains will be listed in detail and the report of condition, if colourful, will be fair. Such catalogues are repositories of useful information and should never be lightly discarded. The only aspect that need worry the prospective buyer here is the pricing. Big firms are just as reasonable as smaller men and

17

are not given to profiteering. But their reputations depend on the range and quality of their stocks. To maintain these they must be prepared to pay top prices, so they rarely have bargains to offer.

The beginner-collector may still be unsure about choosing a specialist line and would prefer to concentrate first on, say, the hundred standard books he would most like to own, in pleasant but ordinary editions. He will find a useful guide in *An English Library* by F. Seymour Smith, and discover that unless his tastes are exceedingly out of the way, most of his favourites are available in one or other of the various series, often called libraries, issued by important publishers. Among such are Dent's *Everyman's Library*, which is published in the United States by E. P. Dutton, and the Oxford *World's Classics*. Many of the volumes in both series have special introductions written by important literary men or other authorities. For example, the *Everyman* edition of Isaac Taylor's *Words and Places* has an introduction by Edward Thomas, a writer of the early part of this century, whose works are eminently collectable. Volumes of this kind, bought in first editions of good condition, will more than retain their admittedly slight value over the years.

In examining the old, the new should not be lost sight of. From time to time expensive limited editions of books, aimed directly at collectors, appear among the new publications. These must be treated with caution. Many are worthy acquisitions, others are gilded glitter on the outside but unreadable within. There are ordinary first editions of major living authors to be considered as well. These should be grabbed hot from the press and checked less they carry a fatal 'second impression before publication' imprint.

A heart-and-soul collector soon passes the hundred best books stage and fixes on some speciality. All who claim to love English literature have read, or say they have read, or intend to read, James Boswell's *Life of Samuel Johnson*. The reading of it has produced many Johnsonians and fired not a few with the determination to obtain all they can by and about the great man. Badly-worn family copies of the *Life* seem no longer to be worthy of the subject; the new Johnsonians look for better editions—but which? The ten-volume edition of 1859, edited by Croker and Wright, with its useful additional material, might be had in reasonable condition for less than £20 ($38)—low in grade (i) in the scale of values, page 13—but a first edition could conceivably be had for £500 ($950)—grade (G). This may seem surprising as there are records of firsts being sold for twice that amount in the salerooms, but price is largely governed by state and condition. There are several special points looked for in a first edition of the *Life of Johnson*, 1791, one or more of which is often lacking. Furthermore, most of the firsts that come on the market are bound in leather. As originally issued, the book was in two volumes, bound in impermanent paper-covered boards, and a copy in these boards is accepted as the most desirable.

Having bought the best copy of the Boswell work that he can afford, the Johnsonian still has a lifetime's happy hunting ahead, for his idol was a more prolific writer than is commonly supposed. Of the first and early editions of his books, the *Dictionary* and the *Lives of the English Poets* will probably be the dearest, but some of the others will be harder to find.

Inevitably, the beginner will soon find himself involved in the technicalities of book production. If his concern is with modern books he might get by with only a little knowledge; if his chosen period lies anywhere from the beginning of printing in the fifteenth century to the early nineteenth century, he will have to give some time to the study of bibliography, which deals with the systematic listing and accurate description of books. Bibliography is really too wide a term. A mere list of books pertinent to a particular subject is also called a bibliography. Sadly, the word 'bibliology' has never been widely accepted in our language. It could be used for the systematic analysis and description of books, and 'bibliography' could be kept for book lists and their compilation.

Books in the form in which we know them pre-date the introduction of printing. Manuscript books, however, were often bound before being written, while printed books were, and are, invariably put through the presses, then bound. This may be stating the obvious, but there was a time when ordinary people had no idea how printed books were produced and were prepared to believe that printers were in league with the devil.

Basically, the making of a book consists of sewing together a number of sheets of paper of the same size and fitting the result with a hardwearing cover. Wooden boards (the words *beech* and *book* are said to be connected) were in early use, though covers of tough limp vellum may be as old. It is possible, but inconvenient, to make a book by stitching together whole single sheets. It is easier to use folded sheets. When all paper was hand made it was produced in sheets suitable for convenient handling. The largest books were made by folding these sheets in half and sewing them together at the folds, one by one. Smaller, not necessarily thinner, books could be made by folding the sheets yet again, and so on down the line, until a fat little book could be made from a single sheet folded several times.

A book composed of sheets folded once was called a *folio*, folded twice it was *quarto*, three times, an *octavo*, four times a *sexto-decimo*, and five times a *trigesimo-secundo*. Apart from *folio* these names are the ablative Latin ordinal numbers denoting the number of leaves produced. They are still used, but folio is often contracted to fo, quarto to 4to, octavo to 8vo, and the others are almost always written 16mo and 32mo (strictly 32do) and spoken of as 'sixteenmo' and 'thirty-twomo'. There are also 12mos and 24mos, achieved by particular methods of folding, best understood by taking a sheet of paper, folding it once, folding it again longways in thirds, then making one more fold for 12mo and a further fold for 24mo. Whatever the method used, each single sheet when folded makes a complete *gathering*. The *format* of a book, fo, 4to, etc, refers to the number of folds in a gathering, not to its size, since the original sheets, though matched for any given issue of a book, were not made to a single standard.

It is easy to visualize how a book in folio has to be printed. A single fold gathering will give two leaves, comprising four pages, which can be numbered 1, 2, 3, 4. To print for this sequence the type will have to be set up for pages 1 and 4 together, both being on the same side of the whole sheet. The type for pages 2 and 3 must then be placed together for printing on the other side. If pages 1 and 4 are impressed together on one side and the sheet is then turned to receive pages 2 and 3 in proper alignment, the sequence will be correct when the sheet is folded.

Printing in quarto will be more complicated. A sheet of paper folded in half, then folded again, will make four leaves in pairs, joined along the tops. If the eight resultant pages are numbered in order, then unfolded without cutting the paper, the outside will show page 1 on the lower right, with page 4 above it, upside down, and page 8 on the lower left, with page 5 above, also upside down. The inside of the sheet will show 7 on the lower right, with 6 reversed above. For printing both sides of a whole sheet in quarto, the groups of pages of type will have to be arranged together in two large frames in the order explained, one frame for either side of the full sheet. Similar experiments in folding and numbering will show the arrangements for printing in 8vo, 16mo and 32mo. Methods varied for 12mo and 24mo. In earlier times it was usual to print a 12mo so that the sheets could be cut before sewing and double gatherings made of them. In the nineteenth century, the sheets were usually folded whole.

A bookbinder who had to fold and flatten a large number of sheets into gatherings for sewing together could hardly be blamed if he became confused. To help him keep the right order, every whole sheet was given a mark called a signature. This was printed so that when the folds were made it would appear in the lower margin of the first page of each gathering. Quite often, the signature, with the right sequence of numbers added, was carried over several leaves. Usually the signature was a letter of the alphabet, with 'A' reserved for the gathering that contained the title of the book and other preliminary matter. This first gathering was liable to be folded differently from the others. In the earlier days of printing, the letters J, U and W were not used and K and Z, too, were sometimes omitted. Normally, the first gathering was A, the second B, and so on. The first leaf of the first gathering would be marked A or A_1, and if subsequent leaves were marked, they would be A_2, A_3, etc. Some printers used roman numerals and marked Ai, Aii, or Aj, Ajj. If necessary, a fresh start was made with double letters: AA or aa. Rarely, the Greek alphabet was resorted to, and a few books are known with such signatures as § and ¶. Some modern books have numerals instead of letters. Many have neither.

With a grasp of the system of signatures, it should be possible to tell the format of a book. A folio will have A on the first page, B on the fifth, C on the ninth and so on, in sequence. The quarto pattern will be A on the first page, B on the ninth, C on the seventeenth and similarly to the end. In an octavo, the signature will change after every sixteenth page, in a 12mo after every twenty-fourth. The principle will be the same for other formats. A whole gathering is often referred to as a signature, as: 'The book is an octavo, but has the last two signatures in fours.'

The first gathering may be atypical and other unexpected features may be met. During the nineteenth century, and perhaps earlier, 12mos were issued with three numbers of the signature of each gathering on every first, third and ninth page, in the order A_1, A_2 and A_3. In the few 12mos still produced, this strange order may still be used.

Another peculiarity arises when the single folded sheets of

folios, instead of being sewn as individual gatherings, were printed so that they could be put together in groups of three sheets, in three tiers, folded to give six leaves. The sequence of the first gathering was then A_1, A_2 and A_3 on consecutive leaves, but the next leaf, though part of the third sheet, was signed A_4 so that the topmost sheet had two signatures. This showed the binder that his set of three sheets was complete and that he could pass on to the B gathering, similarly signed. This complication can be clarified by folding three sheets as folios and numbering them as described.

Sometimes the watermark—the maker's trade sign on the paper—is a guide to format. Until fairly recently, almost every sheet of paper for printing had a watermark, put in the same place on each sheet : threequarter-way across and half-way down. By plotting this position on a sheet of paper and folding according to the needs of the various formats, it can be determined where and on what leaf the watermark will appear. Refined versions of this method have enabled experts to accomplish feats of detection, even when the watermark has been unconventionally placed.

Learning about these abstruse matters may come hard on the beginner, but he is sure to meet references to signatures and formats as soon as he starts to receive booksellers' catalogues and he should understand their importance. Once the format of a book is established, more can be found out. Old printers were sometimes careless in numbering pages. It is possible for a book to be complete, but with the page numbers suddenly jumping from, say, 166 to 187. If the format is known, the book is easily tested for completeness and the gap in the pagination demonstrated.

Book production has always been subject to last-minute changes. Censorship, libel laws or an author's cussedness have all brought about alterations in a book at a late stage in its journey to the buyer. If leaves are taken out after printing and folding and others substituted, we have what are called cancels. For a long time the word 'cancel' in this context could be confusing. There were no separate terms for the leaf that had to be removed and the leaf designed to take its place; both were cancels. Dr R. W. Chapman, an eminent bibliographer, came to the rescue in 1924 by devising the term *folium cancellandum* for the leaf that has to be scrapped and *folium cancellans* for its replacement. *Folium cancellandum* has been shortened to *cancelland* and *folium cancellans* to *cancel*. Anybody who wants to talk of 'a cancel and a cancelland' will note the awkwardness of the terms, but such is the bookman's love of the high-flown that he has not yet accepted 'cancel' or 'cancel leaf' for the leaf to be removed and 'substitute' or 'substitute leaf' for the replacement.

The substitution of a single leaf is easily noticed as it is almost invariably pasted to the marginal stump of its predecessor. It may be harder to detect where two or more leaves have been pasted in and the old stumps removed, but if the format and arrangement of signatures have been determined, the difficulty is not so great. The attitude of the collector who neither knows nor cares whether any of his books have cancels is understandable, but their absence or presence is a guide to the correctness of books.

Format gives a rough idea of size, so little harm is done in describing large modern books as folios and quartos when they are technically octavos; but this should not be done with old books. Early in the last century some books were issued in 8vo for the first edition, but in 12mo for the second. Certain 12mos were then of a size and shape comparable to those of a small modern 8vo, so if a bookseller describes such a 12mo as an 8vo, he may mislead his clients into thinking he has a first edition to offer.

Whatever their format, books vary in size according to the measurements of the individual sheets from which they have been made. There are large and small folios, large quartos and small quartos. However, it is with octavos that the sizes are usually named. The most important are:

royal 8vo	10 x 6¼in
demy 8vo	8¾ x 5⅝in
crown 8vo	7½ x 5in
foolscap 8vo	6¾ x 4¼in

Modern octavos do not necessarily conform to any of these, so when size has to be stated it is better to give actual measurements than to use this Procrustean nomenclature.

Once a book has been gathered and sewn, it still has to be given a cover. Wooden boards soon gave place to pasteboard, which was more convenient and, in certain circumstances, more durable. From the fifteenth to the nineteenth centuries the standard permanent binding was in pasteboard covers overlaid with leather, vellum or parchment. Unless they were also binders, printers delivered the completed sheets to a publisher-bookseller, who could sell the sheets as they were, have them sewn and given temporary covers, or arrange for them to be bound to his own or his customers' requirements.

Methods of binding varied in detail, but in general the sheets were folded into gatherings and pressed flat. They were then sewn along the spine—the part that normally shows when books are shelved—to five cords held taut and upright in a wooden frame. The number of cords could be more or less than five, but seldom was. Two or more blank leaves were sewn in at the front and back, or more often stuck on when the sewing was finished. The cords were cut from the frame so as to leave good loose ends on either side of the book, then the spine was glued and lightly hammered to give it a satisfactory roundness. The loose ends of cord were laced through holes made at the right places in the boards, tightened and glued down. Fraying the laced ends and smoothing them into the material of the boards was a refinement not always carried out. The leather, vellum or parchment was cut to size and pared thinly at the edges. The inside of the leather or other material was then thickly soaked in paste all over and carefully laid on the spine and the outside covers, the pared edges then being folded and stuck down round the inner edges of the boards. The leather was pressed firmly against the spine and worked over the ridges of the cords to make attractive raised bands. The leather was turned over at the head and tail of the spine to form strong caps. The two outermost blank leaves were pasted down to the inner surfaces of the boards, one at the front and one at the back of the book. These leaves are the paste-down endpapers and their immediate blank neighbours are the free endpapers.

Books often have striped ridges inside the tops and tails of the spines. These are the head- and tail-bands, placed there for additional strength. Except in craftsman-bound books, modern headbands, if present, are stuck on. Until the eighteenth century they were made of strips of some tough material, such as vellum, and sewn to the book. The striped effect was given by using alternate colours of silken thread to cover the vellum strips and stitch them down to the inner edges of the book. There are, of course, head- and tail-bands without stripes.

Once a book was bound it was titled on the spine and, perhaps, the front cover, and decorated. The titling could be done directly on the leather cover, or, when applied to the spine, on paper-thin leather labels called titling pieces. The labels were applied blank to the spines and titled in position. Individual brass letters with wooden handles were heated and impressed in the right places, one by one, to form the required words. The impressions were covered with glair (prepared raw white of egg) over which gold leaf was laid. The letters were then reheated and applied again to the impressions already made. When the superfluous gold leaf was rubbed away, the gold titling remained.

Decoration was done in much the same way, using brass tools with designs cut on them in relief. When the tools were impressed without subsequent gilding, the book is said to be blind tooled. Large designs were built up from the impressions of several tools, or stamped from a metal block in one operation. Occasionally, blind designs were applied freehand, without heat, using a bone or ivory graver. Metal dies, hammered cold on the leather, were also used.

Books were also decorated by inlaying or overlaying with thin pieces of leather, but almost never with parchment or vellum as these are less tractable materials. Overlaying was easier and cheaper than inlaying, though both methods were used to produce the panelled covers fashionable in the seventeenth and early eighteenth centuries. Silver or brass clasps were sometimes put on important books, and pieces of the same metals were used to reinforce and decorate the corners of the covers.

Gilding was a slightly later development, but blind tooling and stamping goes back to the period of the *incunabula*, the term used for books produced in the earliest days of printing, generally accepted as covering the years up to 1500. The singular form, *incunabulum*, is seldom used and *incunable* (singular) and *incunables* (plural) are widely accepted.

Some bookbinders of the seventeenth century were grieved to find that in cutting skins of leather for covers they were left with pieces too small for whole books, so they devised the half binding to use them up. Here the leather is put on the spine and a little way over the boards, with other triangular pieces to give strength to the corners. The intervening area is covered in paper or cloth. Paper only was used for early half bindings. Though an invention of the late seventeenth century, the technique was not popular until nearly one hundred years later. Books dated before about 1750 and described as being in contemporary half leather should be inspected with care. They may have been rebound at a later date. Quarter binding, where the leather is applied to the area of the spine only, without the protective triangles at the corners, is a later development. A half binding where the allowance of leather is unusually generous is sometimes called a threequarter binding.

A binder could finish his work and still leave the book

27

unopened, that is with the folds of its component gatherings still intact along the top and side. This should not be confused with the uncut condition, where the folds have been slit open, but the rough edges of the paper have not been trimmed. As both unopened and uncut books are likely to trap and retain dust, especially along their top edges, they were often trimmed and gilded at these vulnerable places; hence the description top edge gilt (t.e.g.), top and fore-edge gilt (t. & f.e.g.) and all edges gilt (a.e.g.). The trimming was done with a special implement called a plough, which could be set to take off the minimum or maximum of paper. Binders who cared more for money than craftsmanship took off the maximum. The parings, when sold to papermakers, provided a useful perk. A heavily trimmed book with its resultant narrow margins is not desirable; when it is in the condition described as shaved—where the plough has eaten into the text —it is a disaster.

Books with flat spines instead of raised bands are a development of the eighteenth century. Before sewing, grooves were sawn horizontally across the spines and the cords sunk into the grooves. The five-band convention was largely discarded; binders economized in time and money by sewing to three bands only. The smooth-back fashion was short lived, but when raised bands came back, many binders continued to sew to three sunken cords. They then stuck five false bands to the spine and worked the leather over them.

In Georgian times it became usual for booksellers to offer their wares in temporary bindings of thin boards, covered with greyish-blue sugar paper, a coarse, laid variety, long used by grocers in England and elsewhere for sugar bags. The spines were backed with similar paper of a different colour. A printed label was stuck on the spine, also called the backstrip. When the customer bought the book these makeshift covers were meant to be replaced by a permanent binding.

This practice persisted well into the nineteenth century. About 1820 books began to appear with their boards covered in cloth instead of paper. These were still looked on as disposable, but within a few years cloth bindings were accepted as permanencies rather inferior to leather bindings.

Coeval with the rise of cloth was the beginning of casing instead of binding. Strictly speaking, a bound book is one in which the cords to which the gatherings are sewn have been incorporated with the boards to make an integral whole. In casing, the gatherings are sewn to tapes (sometimes to cords), which are cut off close to the spine. A piece of mull (a kind of cloth gauze) is glued along the sewn spine, with overlaps on either side. The case, consisting of cloth-covered boards with a flexible cloth spine, is made separately and the book is attached to the inside of the case by glueing down the overlaps of the mull and, where they exist, the stumpy ends of the tapes. The endpapers are then brought over and pasted to the insides of the boards.

The first cloth covers were plain, but publishers soon saw that decoration would have an extra appeal. The first attempts were imitative of leather tooling, but soon a distinctive style of cloth decoration was evolved, making use of printed patterns, plain and coloured. The designs of bookcloths can provide clues to the dating of editions and have been the subject of much research.

The arrival of cloth did not mean the end of papercovered boards. They became accepted for cheap editions and lost their austerity. Sugar paper was replaced by glossy paper, often decorated in colour. Under the influence of the arts and crafts movement, plain paper boards were revived at the end of last century for finely printed books in limited editions. Sugar paper was again applied to the covers, but canvas or buckram was often used for the spines.

The Victorian age saw many novel experiments in book production. Wooden boards were brought back ('cedar from the Holy Land', 'oak from a tree felled by Mr Gladstone', etc); elaborate *papier maché* covers had their day; there were even books with their covers protected with wrought iron work. Sportsmen had books bound in the hide of some lately departed favourite horse, and big-game hunters made similar use of the skins of lions, zebras and other wild animals.

Instead of being sewn, some books, not just pamphlets, were held together by metal staples. Saddest of all, it was found that books could be made up by trimming the gatherings into separate leaves, gripping these together in a clamp and sticking the backs with a gutta-percha or rubber solution. This method was favoured when thick paper, difficult to sew, was used. The average life of the dried solutions was from fifty to sixty years, so that today most of the books produced by this method consist of bundles of loose leaves spilling out from pathetically impressive covers. The first of these Ozymandiases of the book world date from 1840; the last were put together not much later than 1900, by which time the transitory nature of the process had been revealed.

The dust-wrapper, or dust-jacket, was another innovation of last century. Dust-wrappers are known to have existed as early as 1832 but few examples have survived from before about 1885, as the first were only of plain paper, with or without the title of the book printed on the spine and front. Once they had served their purpose of keeping books clean until they reached the customers they were discarded. By the beginning of the present century they had become almost universal and were often illustrated to fit the contents, or they carried printed information about the book. As knowledge about early wrappers is vague, collectors look for them only on twentieth-century books. It is often argued that because they are not truly parts of a book they should be ignored, yet books in dust-wrappers are favoured by most serious collectors, who will always pay a bit more for them.

2

First Editions and their Problems

A collector who acquires first editions without further specification can soon fill all his available shelf space at little expense. First editions are not necessarily the glittering prizes of popular fancy. The world is full of them, for all books achieve a first edition, if no other. The non-manic collector does not look for first editions of any and every kind, only those that have special claims on his affections because they bring him closer to some well-loved author than do any subsequent editions, because they are the first appearances in print of new statements about a subject he holds dear, or because, as firsts, the print of the text and the plates of the illustrations, if any, are clear and unworn. It is not merely a first edition that he wants, but the first *state* of the first identifiable *issue* of the first *impression* (often called the first printing). With some books, later editions will be more desirable, because of particular features, but generally speaking the earliest available copies of the first printings will be the collector's main quarry.

If he is pursuing books that few others now want, his main expense will be of time—and he may not use up too much of that if the books were issued as large first editions. It is when he is hunting for scarce books in the company of many others that he will have to pay dear. Even if the books he wants are reasonably plentiful, they will still be costly if they are among the world's truly important or beautiful books.

When a book has been set up in type, a certain number of copies may be printed and published and the type stored away. If the first impression sells well, another batch of copies may be run off without a great deal of trouble. This second printing is still officially of the first edition, but it is not good enough for the true collector. He wants his copy to be of the earlier printing, not of the second or any subsequent impression. Where they are not definitely stated to be so by the publishers, later impressions often give themselves away by having corrections made to minor errors of fact, layout or spelling, or by showing signs of wear on the type and illustrations. Sometimes in the course of the first printing an important mistake is noticed in the earliest copies. The presses are stopped, the correction is made and work resumes. As the mistake is not serious enough to warrant the scrapping of the early copies, they are allowed to go forth like so many warty Cromwells, ready to find fame in the world of books as first issues. Their less maculate successors, though still of the first edition, are relegated to the ranks of the second issue.

The definition of a first issue implied in the foregoing is not universally acceptable. Many bibliographers regard variations that have arisen from corrections made before the impression was ready for publication as denoting different states of the same issue. Only corrections made at the point of publication, or after the commencement of publication, are taken as signs of different issues. Unless the full early history of a book is known, the distinction is obscure.

The beginner often starts out with no intention of ascending into the higher reaches of bibliophily where the rarefied air makes the going difficult, but sooner or later he finds he is up there with the others. Late issues, reprints and doubtful editions are no longer what he wants. Even from the heights, however, he realizes that compromise is sometimes necessary and can even be a good thing.

The machine that can scan books fed into it and give

precise rulings on state, impression and edition has still to be invented. The collector must rely on his own judgment and on the opinions of experts who may differ among themselves. He is not always clear about the nature of the thing he pursues, since some books granted the honour of first edition are known not to be the true printed firstlings of their author's mind. But in time he learns when to accept the rulings of the best authorities and when to take an independent line. Ideally he wants his copy of a desired book to be the very first one published, with palpable evidence that it has been made up entirely from the first sheets printed and has gone through the bindery ahead of all its fellows. As he cannot have this outside of his dreams, he strives to get as near perfection as expert advice, common sense and financial resources will allow. Desirable issues seldom fall like manna. Even relatively common books must be looked for with patience.

One of Richard Jefferies's earliest books is *The Scarlet Shawl*. Though not his best, it is one of his scarcest, yet the collector need have no difficulty in recognizing the prime issue if it comes his way. The first edition was published by the firm of Tinsley Brothers in 1874. Anybody having a copy bearing that date can claim to have a first, but the matter does not end there. Copies so dated can turn up in one of four different bindings, all in original publisher's cloth. One is a bright blue cloth, one a red smooth cloth, one a red cloth with slight ridges running diagonally and one a red cloth finely grained. This last is on the earliest binding and is the one over which the collector rejoices—but not before checking that it has the first issue inside. The points by which this is known are : top edges uncut; a leaf of advertisements for Tinsley Brothers' two-shilling novels placed before the half-title (the leaf carrying nothing but a short title, coming immediately before the full title-page); a dedication leaf following the title-page, with TRAININ misprinted for TRAINING at line 7, and, at the end of the book, another leaf of advertisements for Tinsley Brothers' new novels, etc.

The points of the first issue and of the earliest binding have been settled by the work of Michael Sadleir, who compared various copies of the first edition and reached definite conclusions. On the spine of the copy with the red cloth diagonally ridged, the name of the author is misspelt JEFFRIES. As this is the kind of error usually made at the outset and corrected later, it could suggest a first issue. But inside, the dedication is a cancel, with TRAINING correctly spelt, so this cancel betokens a later issue. The British Library copy, which he examined, is in smooth red cloth, and cannot be a first issue, since it has JEFFERIES correctly spelt on the spine, though stamped over the previous misspelling, which is not completely erased. Besides, the dedication in this copy is also a cancel. Though the blue-cloth copy examined by Sadleir had the uncancelled dedication leaf, other evidence pointed to its being the latest binding of all. The fine-grained red-cloth copy remains as the earliest. Detective work of this kind has not always yielded such good results and there are cases where the question of priority has never been satisfactorily settled, as will be seen when *The Posthumous Papers of the Pickwick Club* is discussed.

It is possible to travel over wide areas of collecting without meeting any knotty problems. Either greater care is now taken in preparing books for the press or printers are more reluctant to stop to correct minor errors, but points of priority of issue arise less often in present-day books. Entire first editions show no variation in binding or in text. This simplifies matters for the collector of modern books. He feels safe in assuming that a book published in the past three decades is a satisfactory first if it carries no statement to the contrary—as 'second impression before publication', 'second impression', 'second printing', 'second edition', 'new impression', 'new edition', etc. Caution is needed even here. Points have a way of lying hidden for years before emerging to discomfit the bibliophile.

Lady Audley's Secret by Mary Elizabeth Braddon well

demonstrates the kind of tangle that can entrap the first-edition hunter. Its earliest appearance in print was in *Robin Goodfellow*, a magazine edited by Charles Mackay. The first number of the magazine, with the first chapter of *Lady Audley*, was issued on 6 July 1861, but *Robin Goodfellow* was not a financial success and came to an end in September 1861, by which time only the first sixteen chapters of the novel had appeared. The authoress had better luck with *The Sixpenny Magazine*, which took over the novel, made a fresh start with the first chapter and finished the serialization in 1863. The first complete printing therefore spans *The Sixpenny Magazine* from Volume II to Volume IV. As soon as the serialization had ended, the first edition in book form was issued in three volumes, dated 1862. The second edition, likewise in three volumes, followed hot on the heels of the first and is also dated 1862. Mixed sets, with the first two volumes in the second edition and the third volume in the first, were also sold.

What does the collector do here? If he settles for the first edition in book form, ignoring all that went before, he is not very near the authoress's original thoughts, as the book is different in many respects from the early *Robin Goodfellow* chapters and the complete *Sixpenny Magazine* serial. Yet if he collects the *Sixpenny Magazines* he is lumbered with much extraneous matter—and if he goes back to the sixteen chapters in *Robin Goodfellow* he has only a fragment. As it happens, he would do well in this case to go for the first complete printing in the *Sixpenny Magazine*. Finding all the requisite numbers will keep him happy for a long time, but this is more likely to be achieved than the acquisition of a first edition in book form. *Lady Audley's Secret* is one of comparatively few Victorian three-volume novels really worthy of the bookseller's peculiar description of 'excessively rare in the first edition'. The likely saleroom price for a copy would be above £2,000 ($3,800).

This and a few others apart, the collector of Victorian

novels disregards serial issues first published in magazines. Though the serial is usually the true first edition, he prefers convenience to logic and goes after the first edition in book form. It will cost him more, but will take up much less shelf room. Anybody with unlimited space and no objection to his library looking like a wastepaper depot could collect these real first editions in magazines more cheaply than the later issues in book form.

Avoidance of serials does not extend to certain novels and other works that were first issued in parts—notably several of the novels of Charles Dickens (1812–70). This author can be regarded as the father of the *part issue*, though Surtees fans might not agree. Before Dickens's *Posthumous Papers of the Pickwick Club* was launched on the world, some quite insignificant stories, with or without illustrations, had been served up at the rate of one or two chapters a month, sewn in flimsy paper covers. They were no more than enlarged chapbooks, looked down on by booksellers and their customers alike. There was also a superior type of part issue for which some well known artist would provide the illustrations while a literary hack supplied a brief text which more or less linked the illustrations together. In 1831 Robert Smith Surtees (1802–64) launched, with a partner, a periodical, *The New Sporting Magazine*, which, though it contained other material, could be considered a series of part issues with fine illustrations and a superior text, by Surtees, describing the sporting adventures of a London grocer called Jorrocks.

The success of the Jorrocks series encouraged the publishing firm of Chapman & Hall to engage Robert Seymour in 1836 to draw the pictures for a part issue on a sporting theme. Seymour was well known and the publishers expected at least to equal the Surtees success. They engaged a young up-and-coming journalist to write the linking letterpress. Happily for literature, though less so for Seymour, the journalist was Dickens. From the start, he took the upper hand, so that the text became more important than the illustrations and more popular with the public than even the Jorrocks adventures. Soon the already melancholic Seymour became so depressed that he killed himself, so another artist had to be found to replace him. A man called Buss produced a few illustrations, but they were not satisfactory and the work of completing the illustrations fell to Hablot K. Browne, better known as Phiz.

In all, there were twenty parts of *The Posthumous Papers of the Pickwick Club* issued in nineteen numbers, the last being a double one. As published, every number was scantily clothed in a flimsy paper wrapper, with some advertisement leaves between the wrapper and the illustrated text. Because of the two changes of illustrators and increases in the number of copies printed as the work progressed, it is hard to decide what constitutes an authentic set of the first issues of *Pickwick* in parts. The Dickens bibliographers, J. C. Eckel—*The first Editions of the Writing of Charles Dickens*, revised edition 1932—and, more particularly, Thomas Hatton and A. H. Cleaver—*A Bibliography of the Periodical Works of Charles Dickens*, 1933—have gone far towards establishing the first issues, but some bibliographers still 'hae their doots'.

There are few known sets of the accepted first issue of *Pickwick* in parts, complete and in good condition, so only the wealthiest and most determined collector should aim so high. Good sets, bearing many, though not all of the requisite stigmata, are still expensive, perhaps (a) in the scale of values, but within the reach of the non-millionaire collectors. Those with little money to spare would be better advised to look for a good copy of the first edition in book form rather than accept a poor, defective set of the parts. As is the case with many books of the period, the plates of *Pickwick* are liable to suffer badly from *foxing*, a bookseller's word for the condition of being marred with brown spots and blotches. A badly foxed first is hardly worth accepting as a free gift.

Only a few years ago, a clean copy of the first edition (dated 1837) rebound in one volume in full or half leather, was of little value. It was so far removed from the original that the serious collector despised it and its only interest would have been as an example of a Victorian binding. In the lean years that are now upon us, however, it is the half a loaf that is better than no bread and it could be in the (h) price grade at least. A copy of the first book edition in original cloth would cost much more—grade (c) up to (a)—depending on whether it carried the points of an early issue. In acquiring his *Pickwick* first, the collector must do his bibliographical homework, or go to a thoroughly reliable dealer who will guarantee that any copy he may supply will be of an early issue.

There are booksellers for whom the date 1837 on the title-page is enough. At the sight of it they pencil 'first edition' on an endpaper together with a high price, leaving the customer to check for relevant points. They are not unscrupulous but they want to make as much as they can from what, as far as they can tell, may be a valuable book. If somebody with superior knowledge is able to give them a true evaluation they will be prepared to accept it and fix a price accordingly.

The examples of *The Scarlet Shawl, Lady Audley's Secret* and *The Posthumous Papers of the Pickwick Club* illustrate some of the difficulties facing the first-edition collector. Though chosen from the area of nineteenth-century fiction, they could be paralleled in any field. There is no easy single formula for distinguishing first editions as the bibliophile wants them. In many cases it can be done only after years of study or, more conveniently, by consulting the works of those who have already done the research.

Reliable and reasonably detailed bibliographies covering an enormous range of authors and subjects have been published in the course of the last two centuries. The novice should find out which are appropriate to his needs and try to consult them. This is not always easy. Some advanced collectors and specialist booksellers growl in their mangers at beginners. They will write or talk knowingly about 'Wade 161' or

'Chubb 432', without deigning to explain that the reference in each case is to a standard bibliography, Wade and Chubb being respectively Allan Wade's *W. B. Yeats Bibliography* and Thomas Chubb's *The printed Maps in the Atlases of Great Britain and Ireland: A Bibliography, 1579–1870.*

Knowing the name of an appropriate bibliography is not an 'open sesame' to obtaining a copy. Many of these works were published in small limited editions and are not in print. As dealers look on bibliographies as the tools of their trade and established collectors guard their copies with their lives, such books seldom come on the market. However, several of the most important older bibliographies are being reprinted by university departments or by firms with an interest in the antiquarian book trade. This is happening on both sides of the Atlantic. Constant watch should be kept for the announcements of reprints and, of course, for the publication of new bibliographies. Scarce bibliographical works may sometimes be consulted through local public libraries and, despite the tight-lipped exceptions, many booksellers will let customers look at their working copies—under strict supervision.

What of the collector who finds that there is no bibliography covering his particular need? He will have to work extra hard and become his own bibliographer as he acquires his books. If he has read this far, he will be able to avoid gross blunders in his purchases. The inevitable errors he makes will have to be put down as the price that must be paid for the acquisition of new knowledge. Where possible, he will write to publishers and librarians for particulars of the first editions of the books he seeks; he will studiously browse in bookshops and will try to make contact with everybody who might be able to shed the smallest ray of light on the subject of his collection. The bibliographer, amateur or professional, is a detective, seeking clues in likely and unlikely places.

There are lumpers and splitters among bibliophiles. To the lumper, a first edition is a first edition and he does not worry much about the complexities of states and issues. The splitter looks for refined gold twice gilded. His copy of a book must be earlier than any other and be in better condition. And how his heart leaps if he finds something that makes it unique! What joy if his is the only copy with an error in pagination in the third gathering! The lumper, with his eyes shut against all complexities, misses such delights but has a contented mind. The splitter knows no peace in pushing to the extreme his search for points. Genuine points have a value in establishing priority, but there are many that are not to be trusted. In the first edition of Joseph Conrad's novel *The Arrow of Gold* (1919), the title of the book is used as a running headline at the top of every page of the text. In some copies, the headline on page 67 reads THE RROW OF GOLD. The splitter seizes on this as evidence of first state, or first issue, arguing that the 'A' of ARROW must have been missing when printing started and put in later, when the mistake was discovered. This was accepted as a valid point for a time. Now it is established that the 'A' was in position when printing began, dropped out at a later stage, and was replaced before printing was completed. Copies with the 'A' missing can be regarded as no more than interesting variants.

It must be emphasized that book-collecting has no kinship with the eccentricities of philately. Errors and misprints have no value except as indicators of the priority or otherwise of an issue or edition.

Collecting variant copies of first editions can become an end in itself, though it is a somewhat arid pursuit for a bibliophile who really reads his books. Surely it is enough that he should have one first edition of every book pertinent to his collection, complete and in the best possible condition consonant with his means. Even the richest men in the world have little hope of buying certain early printed books in an absolutely complete condition, as no perfect copies are known to exist.

Such rarities apart, however, completeness should be

strenuously pursued. It is not too difficult to check for missing leaves in the text, but illustrations may present a more difficult problem. If they have been printed with the text and form part of the normal signatures, well and good. If, as is quite usual, they have been printed separately and tipped or bound in, it may be hard to ascertain that they are all present. Where a list of illustrations is given, or where they are accounted for in a printed note of directions to the binder (often found in eighteenth-century books and not uncommon in later books), there is no problem; where there is no list, the copy must be compared with a known complete copy, either by borrowing it, or by reading its description in a detailed bibliography.

A missing free endpaper or fly-leaf need not be all-important before the era of cloth binding. The lack is always regrettable, but hardly detracts from completeness. For acceptance, a leaf other than one carrying an illustration, map, diagram, etc should be part of a gathering, as explained in the previous chapter. This is rarely the case with an endpaper or fly-leaf. With cloth bindings, however, the goal is original condition, so absent leaves of any kind are a defect. Where called for, half-titles are a necessity. From about 1660, books issued in temporary covers, or none at all, generally left the printer's with a short plain title on the leaf immediately preceding the title-page proper. This was for protection and though often as not part of a signed gathering, it was not intended to be a permanent part of the book. Some book-binders retained the half-titles when they bound, others disposed of them. Today, the careful collector insists that where it is known to have existed, the half-title should still be present. This equally applies to all other printed matter bound with the book—advertisements, errata slips, etc.

Advertisements, mainly of other works from the same bookseller-publishers, occasionally appear in seventeenth-century books, but are hardly common before about 1750. They are sometimes printed on a leaf placed before the title-page and included in the first signature; more often they occur on a leaf or leaves at the end where, in the earlier examples at least, they form an integral part of the book. By the beginning of the period of publishers' cloth, they can be on leaves bound in with the book, but not numbered as part of it. They are considered essential to a book's wholeness and may serve as guides to priority. Where the advertisement leaves form a genuine part of the sewn book, showing an appropriate signature, we can accept an informed statement that the first issue has so many advertisement leaves, that the second issue has a different number and so on; but where the leaves are obviously a separate addition, there is always room for doubt. Nineteenth-century publishers were anxious to keep their advertisement lists up to date and would change them at any time. When copies of the first issue were being bound, the binder was not interested in marrying the first copies he handled with the earliest lists of advertisements. He might use the later lists first, then fall back on the earlier ones to finish off the issue.

Sometimes errors are noticed in a book after it has been printed and are corrected on a piece of paper pasted in after binding. Such a paper is called an errata slip and is a frequent cause of headaches. Perhaps a number of copies was delivered to the booksellers before the correction was made, in which case a copy without a slip would rank among the earliest. But in these circumstances nothing is easier than to manufacture an early copy by carefully removing the errata slip. If it is known that a certain book usually has an errata slip it is best to rejoice when one is present in a copy and to lose no sleep if it is lacking.

While a book in original sheets, unopened, uncut, unsewn and without covers is as near the primary state as it could be, it rates below a copy of the same book which has been sewn and bound in the original boards or cloth. Binding or casing is an important part of wholeness.

There is hardly such a thing as an original binding for a

book of the seventeenth century or earlier. What is looked for is a binding indentifiable as of the same period as the book. From the eighteenth century until 1820, plain boards with paper labels on the backstrips are desirable, but copies bound in leather are not looked down upon and, if they are well-preserved examples of good craftsmanship, are sometimes to be preferred. From the emergence of publishers' cloth to the present, leather rebinds are second-bests, again with the exception of the works of master craftsmen. Emphasis is on original bindings. Sometimes books are described as being in binder's cloth. This should not be taken to mean original cloth. It describes an individual copy of a book that has been rebound in cloth at some time.

The stage is past when ex-library copies of first editions were scorned even when in original cloth bindings and only grudgingly accepted if they belonged to the pre-cloth era. Such is the scarcity now of collectable material that the cloth 'ex-libs' have become respectable in sound, clean condition. Some collectors even claim special virtues for copies from early circulating libraries. However, books that have never had such library connections are to be preferred.

One of the main objections to ex-library books arises from the practice of Mudie's Library, the most important of the old circulating libraries, of pasting an unsightly yellow label at the top of the outside cover of every book made available to borrowers. When such a book had outlived its usefulness it was sold cheaply and in many instances the new owner would have a go at the label with a penknife and succeed in scraping off part of it, leaving a mess more objectionable than the original label. With care, these labels and fragments of labels can be removed, but faint traces will almost always remain. Some libraries used less disfiguring marks of identification, but the prejudice against Mudie's extended to all such library copies.

A book from a private library, with its one-time owner's bookplate, should be highly esteemed, especially, but not necessarily, if the former owner was a person of note. Book-plates are marks of provenance and should be honoured as such. Provenance is to the book collector as pedigree is to the genealogist. Every true bibliophile thrills with pleasure when he sees, neatly written on an endpaper, a list of the names of past owners of a copy of some rare work. If the book is now his, he can proudly add his name. It is commoner, however, to find that the men of the past were strongly possessive and scattered their names liberally in all sorts of inappropriate places—on the title-page, at the beginning of the preface, on the blank sides of illustrations and so on. This kind of dis-figurement is tolerated in books over 150 years old, but not in later works. So it is with handwritten marginal notes, underlinings, textual emendations and end-of-chapter com-ments. If these are old they are revered, if they are recent they are considered to be unwarranted arrogance, unless they can be proved to be in the hand of a person of eminence. A first edition of *Tom Jones*, heavily annotated in the handwriting of Dickens, or some other author who drew inspiration from it, would be quite a prize.

Manuscript inscriptions on one or other of the preliminary leaves of a book can be valuable marks of provenance, or serious flaws. Imagine how delightful it would be to own an edition of Thomson's *The Seasons* with this authenticated inscription :

To my dear friend John Keats in admiration and
gratitude, from P. B. Shelley, Florence, 1820.

Imagine, too, how depressing to have an otherwise fine first of Milton's *Paradise Lost* with this ball-point inscription scrawled on the title-page :

To Ada from Jess, with lots of love and candy floss,
in memory of a happy holiday at Blackpool, 1968.

In another couple of centuries the second inscription might have period charm. For the present it would be catastrophic.

Inscriptions on title-pages are acceptable if written by the author himself or by the illustrator. Nobody else should write there. Such *signed copies* have an obvious appeal as have *presentation copies*. A signed copy bears the author's signature, perhaps with a place and a date, as 'San Francisco, Apr. 18, 1906', but nothing else. If there is an added message —'with every good wish', possibly—it is an *inscribed copy* and if there is a statement that it has been given by the author to so-and-so, it is a *presentation copy*. A presentation copy can express various degrees of intimacy. Lowest in the scale is one which merely stamped 'Presentation copy'; then comes 'with the author's compliments', in the author's hand but unsigned; next, something like 'To W.M.T. from C.D.' where C.D. are recognizably the author's initials, written by himself. Beyond this, the individual must make his own scale of values. Is a copy of Yeats's *Countess Kathleen* more precious if it bears, in the author's writing, the legend 'to F. from W.B.Y.' than if it is inscribed 'To Florence from William'?

It should now be possible to summarize the most desirable condition in which the ordinary collector can hope to obtain his books, according to the period in which they were first published.

BOOKS PRINTED BEFORE 1501

As nearly complete as possible, ideally in contemporary bindings, with good provenance and, perhaps, with interesting marginal notes in a contemporary or near-contemporary hand; still very acceptable in good bindings of a later period.

BOOKS FROM 1501 TO 1701

Much as above, but with more emphasis on completeness and on contemporary bindings in really good condition.

BOOKS FROM 1701 TO 1820

Important changes were taking place during this period. In the earlier part, contemporary leather or vellum is desirable, but from about 1740 onwards, original boards should be looked for, as should half-titles, though the latter were introduced earlier. Boards, even in worn condition, become preferable to workaday leather from 1780 or thereabouts. Leather half bindings, uncommon in the seventeenth century, now come into their own and in good condition hardly rank below full bindings.

BOOKS FROM 1820 TO 1901

This period sees the beginning of publishers' cloth, though it is unusual before 1830. It is also the period in which part issues came to the fore and plain boards gave way to decorated and pictorial boards. Where applicable, first editions in part issue are the most acceptable, with original cloth in second place. The Victorian novel, as well as other important books, was often issued in three volumes and is known as a *three-decker* on this account. Some books of the period, having gutta-percha or stapled bindings, almost never show up in good condition.

BOOKS FROM 1901 ONWARDS

The period that is most immediately rewarding to the beginner. There are still hard problems on which he can sharpen his wits, but on the whole the task of identifying first editions is easier. It should be remembered that first editions can now be acquired as they are published.

Although this summary applies primarily to first editions it is applicable to all books of the given periods. The statements should be borne in mind too, by one-author collectors interested in acquiring every significant edition of works by their chosen favourite. This is different from collecting a range of variant copies of the same edition and can be a productive aspect of bibliophily. Two names spring to mind in this field—Izaak Walton and Gilbert White. Many editions of Walton's *The Compleat Angler* have appeared since it was first published in 1653, some noteworthy for the extra material supplied by the various editors and some for the quality of the illustrations. The first edition of White's *Natural History of Selborne* is dated 1789 and has similarly been enriched at the hands of different editors, through many editions.

3

General Literature to 1800

Sir Thomas Phillipps, who was as keen to snap up rejected drafts of trifling letters, parts of old newspapers and bills of account as he was to acquire important manuscripts and printed books, was the complete collector of literature, in the widest sense of the word. Normally, the interests of the bibliophile devoted to literature are limited to poetry, drama, fiction and that body of miscellaneous writing classed as *belles lettres*. He would still have to be something of a Phillipps if he ranged freely over this vast domain. More probably he would confine himself to one little corner of the territory for his serious collecting and perhaps keep in touch with the other localities through paperbacks and other cheap editions, or by borrowing from a public library. Most of his resources would be reserved for working in his chosen area.

Nowhere is the first edition more important than here, though other worthy editions are now receiving attention. Quirks of fashion alter the values of the works of some authors of the past hundred years. Some sink apparently for ever, others keep bobbing up and down. The collector of books published up to the end of the eighteenth century need have little fear of depreciation. Time has ensured a fairly steady scale of values here, with some spectacular advances in the past forty years. Just after World War I, a reasonable copy of Dryden's *Fables* in the first edition of 1700 would have cost about £2, or $8 at the exchange rate then prevailing. Today, a realistic price would be £70 ($135) or even more.

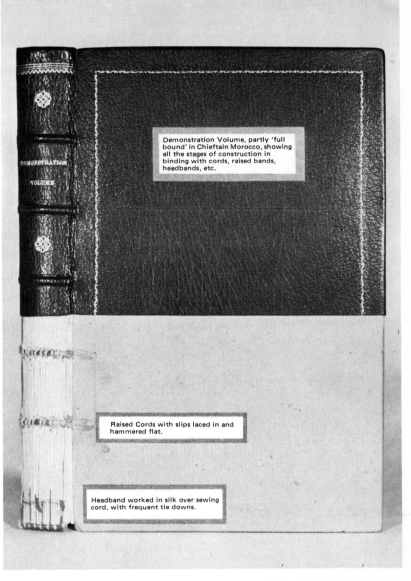

Demonstration Volume, partly 'full bound' in Chieftain Morocco, showing all the stages of construction in binding with cords, raised bands, headbands, etc.

Raised Cords with slips laced in and hammered flat.

Headband worked in silk over sewing cord, with frequent tie downs.

Plate 1 A demonstration book by Theodore Merrett of the Gloucestershire Guild of Craftsmen. It is in part fully bound in morocco leather. This view shows the gold-tooled leather on the spine and boards, the raised cords to which the sections have been sewn then laced to the boards and hammered flat, and the headband (in fact a tailband) worked in silk and sewn to the sections.

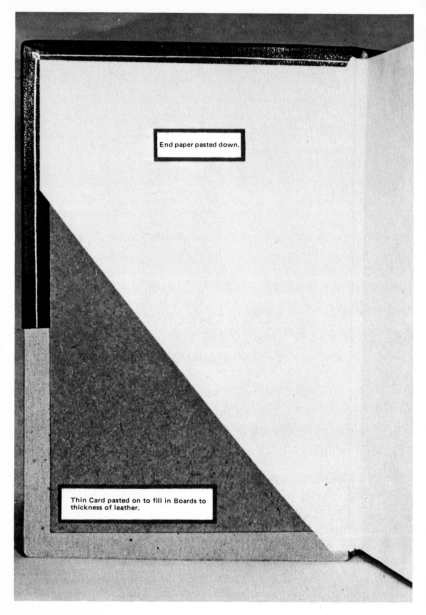

Plate 2   In the demonstration book this shows the endpaper pasted down over a rectangle of thin card to raise the board to the thickness of the surrounding leather.

So far, predictions that the rate of increase would level off have proved false.

The period 'up to the end of the eighteenth century' could go back to 4004 BC, the alleged year of the Creation. Postulants in bibliophily however, should accept as their first year of grace AD1477, when William Caxton issued the first book printed in England. Its title, *The Dictes or Sayengis of the Philosophers*, is mainly of academic interest, as the few surviving copies of the original are unlikely to be offered for sale. A facsimile edition of 1877 is the best that can be hoped for.

The first considerable work of English literature to be printed was *The Canterbury Tales* by Geoffrey Chaucer (1340–1400), which came from Caxton's press in 1478. A beginner should think twice before trying to buy a copy. If one in acceptable condition were offered for sale it would probably cost more than £50,000 ($95,000). The Caxton *Canterbury Tales* is an *editio princeps*, the term for the first printed edition of a work previously existing as a manuscript book, before the introduction of printing. It is also an incunable, as defined in the first chapter. It is better to gain considerable experience and plenty of spare cash before starting a collection of incunables, though not all are as dear as the Chaucer.

This does not rule out early authors for the tyro, only early editions. Caxton printed a second edition of *The Canterbury Tales* in 1482. Richard Pynson produced a third in 1492 and this was followed by Wynkyn de Worde in 1498. Pynson and de Worde were pupils and successors of Caxton. There are no more Chaucer incunables, but the editions of the *Tales* by Francis Thynne (1532) and of Chaucer's works by John Stowe (1561) and Thomas Speght (1598) are just as scarce and almost as expensive. Ordinary collectors can begin at 1721, when John Urry issued the first Chaucer in roman type —hitherto they had all been printed in black letter. Sadly, Urry spoilt the text by trying to modernize the language and rhythm. Copies of this edition would be in the price grade (g) to (f) (page 13), but students of Chaucer would do better with the five-volume edition prepared by Thomas Tyrwhitt and published 1775–8 (second edition in two volumes, 1798). It would cost no more than the Urry and is a landmark in Chaucerian scholarship. The best modern editions of Chaucer's works are those of A. W. Pollard, first published by Macmillan in 1898; of W. W. Skeat, first published by the Oxford University Press in 1894 and frequently reprinted; and of F. N. Robinson, also Oxford University Press, 1933 and later reprinted. These modern editions are not of outstanding interest to the advanced collector, but in a first printing each is a milestone in the progress of Chaucerian studies.

The next English printed book of note is *Le morte Darthur reduced in to englysshe by syr Thomas Malory*, 1485, also from Caxton's press. Though translated from French originals, *Le Morte D'Arthur* is a distinctly English production, which had a deep effect on subsequent literature and art. The first edition, two later editions by de Worde in 1498 and 1529, as well as the variants, *The Story of the Most Noble and Worthy Kynge Arthur*, printed by W. Copland in 1557, and *The Most Ancient and Famous History of Prince Arthur*, printed by W. Stansby for J. Bloom in 1634, are as far out of reach of the impecunious as are the early Chaucers. The first to come within the scope of the ordinary collector is *Le Morte D'Arthur*, two volumes, 1817, edited by Robert Southey. It is not adjudged as being of great merit and is grade (h). The three-volume edition of 1889–91, edited by H. Oskar Sommer, with an essay by Andrew Lang, is much better and might be grade (g). In 1947 there appeared the more definitive Oxford English Texts edition, probably in grade (i) and, if so, undoubtedly the best buy. Little is known about its author, Sir Thomas Malory (*fl*1470), but it is believed that he wrote the work in prison.

The Vision of Pierce Plowman is attributed to William

52

Langland, a contemporary of Chaucer. The evidence points to its having been written before 1400, but the *editio princeps* did not appear until 1550. A copy of this edition might be found in grade (D), but for ordinary purposes, the two-volume edition of 1886, edited by W. W. Skeat, in grade (i), should suffice.

Apart from the Gaelic bards of oral tradition, Scotland's first important poet was the Aberdonian, John Barbour (1316–95). His epic *The Bruce* predates *The Canterbury Tales*, but had to wait until 1616 for its first printing, by A. Hart of Edinburgh. Again Skeat is the editor of the best modern edition, published by the Scottish Text Society in two volumes in 1894. It should be available in grade (i). Other good editions are those of J. Pinkerton, Edinburgh, 1790, in three volumes, and John Jamieson, Edinburgh, 1820, in two volumes.

The greatest poets of the Middle Scots period were Robert Henryson (1430–1506), William Dunbar (1460–1520) and Gawin Douglas (1474–1522). Though all three looked to Chaucer as their master, they were not imitators but original poets. Only Dunbar saw any of his poems in print. Walter Chepman and Andro Myllar set up the first Scottish press in Edinburgh in 1507 and in the following year produced Dunbar's *The Ballade of Lord Barnard Stewart, The Flyting of Dunbar and Kennedy* and *The Twa Mariit Wemen and the Wedo*, all as separate items. First editions of these poems are unobtainable except by theft from the National Library of Scotland, but the titles can be found in *The Poems of William Dunbar*, edited by W. M. Mackenzie, Edinburgh, 1932, reprinted London, 1950.

Robert Henryson's first work to be printed (by Chepman and Myllar) was *The Traitie of Orpheus*, probably in 1508. His *The Testament of Cresseid* followed in 1593, printed by H. Charteris, Edinburgh. The first collected edition of his *Poems and Fables* did not appear until 1865, edited by David Laing and published at Edinburgh.

Gawin (Gavin) Douglas's first printed poem was *The Palis of Honoure*, from the London press of William Copland about 1553, the year in which Copland also printed the first edition of Douglas's verse translation of Virgil's *Aeneid*. If a copy of this book came on the market it would be grade (C) at least. The Edinburgh edition of 1710 by Symson and Freebairn and the four-volume edition of Douglas's works, edited by John Small, Edinburgh, 1874, would both be grade (h).

The more important contemporary English poets were Alexander Barclay (*d*1552), satirist and self-confessed doggerel writer, and England's first two sonneteers, Sir Thomas Wyatt (*d*1542) and Henry Howard, Earl of Surrey (*d*1547). Between 1557 and 1574, Richard Tottel or Tottell printed seven editions of the songs and sonnets of Wyatt and Surrey. Another edition came from J. Windet in 1585 and another from R. Robinson in 1587. All nine are (B) rising to (A) and above, for every one is different, with poems by other contributors as well, including Lord Vaux and Nicholas Grimold. The entire collection is sometimes known as *Tottel's Miscellany* and was reprinted under this name in 1717 and 1795. The reprints should be (g), or a little above. Wyatt is well served in the collection of his poems edited by Kenneth Muir and published by Routledge in 1949, but there is no recent authoritative edition of Surrey. A copy of the fifth edition of *The Songes and Sonnettes*, by Surrey and others, 1559, sold for £16,000 ($30,400) in 1975.

Wyatt and Surrey heralded a great upsurge of English letters. Sir Philip Sidney (1554–86) was a devotee of the sonnet, but no satisfactory complete edition of his works appeared until 1962 when his poems, edited by W. A. Ringler, were issued in The Oxford English Texts series—now a collector's piece. Early (never first) editions of his *Countesse of Pembroke's Arcadia* turn up at the important book auctions where they have risen to grade (E).

In poetry, Sidney's great contemporary was Edmund Spenser (1552–99), author of *The Shepheard's Calender*,

1579, and *The Faerie Queene*, the first three books of which appeared in 1590. Early editions are not for the humble, who should look for the ten-volume edition of 1880–2, edited by Dr A. B. Grosart, grade (g). No other non-dramatic poet of the period measures up to Spenser. Perhaps Michael Drayton (1563–1631) comes nearest. His best work is found in *Ideas mirrour. Amours in quaterzains*, 1594, but *Poly-Olbion or a chorographicall description of Great Britain*, two volumes, 1612–22, is a favourite with collectors who can afford grade (A) books.

Of the prose written up to the time of Spenser, little falls into our category of literature. Sir Thomas More's *Utopia*, though more of a philosophical work, should be admitted as the ancestor of such diverse books as *Gulliver's Travels*, *Erewhon* and *Brave New World*. More (1478–1535) wrote *Utopia* in Latin and had it published in Louvain in 1516. The first edition is rare, as is the first English translation, *A fruteful and pleasant worke of the best state in a publyque weale and the new yle called Utopia*, by Ralphe Robynson, 1551. Even the edition of this translation by the Rev T. F. Dibdin, in two volumes, 1808, is uncommon and would be (g).

The English theatre achieved its first full flowering in the sixteenth century. Thomas Norton (1532–84) and Thomas Sackville, Earl of Dorset (1536–1608), collaborated in writing *Gorboduc*, the first tragedy of importance in the English language, published in 1561. It is most easily obtained in Dent's two-volume *Everyman* edition of minor Elizabethan drama.

The earliest notable comedies are of the same period— Nicholas Udall's *Ralph Roister Doister*, probably 1566, and *Gammer Gurton's Needle,* 1575. The only copy of the original *Roister Doister*, in Eton College Library, lacks the title-page, though the name of the work and its author have been authenticated from other sources. Several copies of *A ryght pithy, pleasaunt and merie comedie: intytuled Gammer gurtons nedle* are known in the 1575 edition. William

Stevenson, a jovial cleric, is now accepted as the author. Apart from the reprint of the first edition, made in 1818 and now (f), *Ralph Roister Doister* is found in the *Everyman* minor Elizabethan drama. *Gammer Gurton's Needle* is given in the second volume of Robert Dodsley's *Select Collection of Old Plays*—twelve volumes in the first edition of 1744, but fifteen in the re-edited edition of 1874–6. Although a complete set of Dodsley in either edition would be (d), odd volumes should cost little more than £5 ($13) each. A reprint of the nineteenth-century edition was published in 1963 at £35 (then $100).

After Udall, poet-dramatists came thick and fast until Elizabethan drama reached its peak with Wiliam Shakespeare (1564–1616). It is impossible in a book of this scope to deal adequately with Shakespeare and what has been written about him, or to give much advice on a truly representative collection. The Shakespeare student could start with a one-volume edition of the works—*The Oxford Shakespeare*, maybe—then acquire facsimiles of the original editions such as Helge Kökeritz's facsimile of the 1623 First Folio and Sir Walter Greg's facsimiles of the earliest quartos. These are publications of the Oxford University Press.

The complexities of Elizabethan and Jacobean drama are so great that for further information the reader had best refer to *English Theatrical Literature 1559–1900,* published by the Society for Theatrical Research in 1970. This book is based on Robert W. Lowe's *A Bibliographical Account of English Theatrical Literature*, 1888, but has been revised by J. F. Arnott and J. W. Robinson to include material that has come to light since the original work was published. The book is, of course, invaluable to students of later drama.

But for the fact that he might have to pay £3,000, or over $5,700, for a really good complete copy, the Elizabethan scholar would be advised to obtain the *Palladis Tamia, Wits Treasury* by Francis Meres (1565–1647), a book acknowledged to be the first companion to English literature. Those lucky enough to have easy access to it say it is full of useful information about English authors up to 1598, the year in which it was published.

Among Shakespeare's younger contemporaries and immediate successors were the metaphysical poets. John Donne (1573–1631) is the chief metaphysician, but in his own time much of his verse circulated in manuscript, so the collector of rare first editions is well-nigh defeated from the start. There are, however, *Poems, with elegies on the author's death*, 1633, to be looked for in grade (E), and *Juvenilia* of the same year in the same grade. The most dependable text of the poems is probably that of Sir Herbert Grierson's edition, two volumes, Oxford, 1912.

George Herbert (1593–1633) is another important metaphysical poet, most of whose verse is contained in a single book, *The Temple*, published in the year of his death. Early editions might be (b). Richard Crashaw (1612–49), Abraham Cowley (1618–67), Henry Vaughan (1622–95) and Francis Quarles (1592–1644) are also grouped as metaphysicals. The last named is a favourite with collectors of old illustrated books. His *Emblems*, 1635, is a series of verses each based on a text from the Bible and followed by an epigram, illustrated by a wood engraving. George Wither (1588–1667) produced a similar *Collection of Emblems ancient and Modern* in the same year. Really good first editions of these emblem books would be in the (G) and (F) ranges.

Robert Herrick (1591–1674), one of the sweetest of English lyricists, links the metaphysicals and the Cavalier poets. His chief work is *Hesperides*, 1648, rare enough to have been sold for £4,700 ($9,000) in a first edition, but included in Humbert Wolfe's four-volume edition of Herrick, Cresset Press, 1928, in grade (h). The true Cavalier poets were Thomas Carew (1598–1639), Edmund Waller (1606–87), Sir John Suckling (1609–42) and Richard Lovelace (1618–58). Their first editions are (H), but other early editions would cost less. Most of their poems are in the *Everyman* edition of

57

Minor Poets of the Seventeenth Century.

Andrew Marvell (1622–78) is sometimes grouped with the Cavalier poets, but he was on the other side and wrote poems in honour of Oliver Cromwell. The first collection of his works was *Miscellaneous Poems*, 1681, an edition with an error of pagination, skipping from page 116 to 131, and probably (G). Not so long ago a first edition made a disappointingly low price at an English provincial sale. In the catalogue it was described as lacking pages 117 to 130, though it was in fact complete.

Part of Marvell's fame rests on his having been secretary to John Milton (1608–74). As would be expected, firsts of Milton's major poems are much desired. His *Paradise Lost*, 1667, in the first state of the first edition, could sell for £10,000 ($19,000), though worn copies in the later states might be had for a tenth of this amount. None of Milton's minor works is quite so highly prized, but none is cheap. Milton was also a pamphleteer. Items like his *Discourse shewing in what state the three kingdomes are in at this present*, 1641, though only of four leaves, would be grade (d). The best modern edition of his poems is the two-volume *Poetical Works*, edited by Helen Darbishire, Oxford, 1952–5.

A few collectors, aware of her significance, would be prepared to pay Miltonic prices for the poetical works of Anne Bradstreet (1612–72). Although born in England, she lived in Massachusetts from the age of 18. Her poems, published in England in 1650, were the first literary works of importance produced in New England. A limited edition of her *Alas All's Vanity* was published in New York in 1942 and should be grade (g).

A watershed in the history of English-language books has already been passed. In 1926 there appeared one of the great works of English bibliography : *A short-Title Catalogue of Books Printed in England, Scotland, & Ireland And of English Books Printed Abroad 1475–1640*, compiled by A. W. Pollard and G. R. Redgrave, with the help of others. Not every extant book from the period was recorded, but it is plain that the compilers' hope was not vain that their errors and omissions would not exceed five per cent. The work is usually known as the STC and the books it lists range from Caxton's translation of Le Fevre, *hEre begynneth the volume intituled the recuyell of the historyes of Troy*, printed by Caxton himself at Bruges, probably in 1475, up to the abundance of volumes published in 1640. Some collectors specialize in STC books, irrespective of subject.

Pollard and Redgrave's work was magnificently continued by Donald Wing (1904–72) of Yale University Library, who compiled *A Short-Title Catalogue of Books Printed in England, Scotland, Ireland, Wales and British America, and of English Books Printed in Other Countries 1641–1700*. The first three volumes were published at New York in 1945–51 and the index volume at Charlottesville, 1955. A second edition, with many more entries, the work of Wing's closing years, when his health was poor, is in course of publication. This massive bibliography is referred to as *Wing* for short and, covering a period of expansion in printing and publishing, it contains many more entries than the STC.

During the *Wing* era, the greatest developments were in prose. Francis Bacon (1561–1626) and Robert Burton (1577–1640) had already helped to set new standards. They are dealt with in a later chapter. However, *The Pilgrim's Progress* by John Bunyan (1628–88) should be considered now because of its effect on later writing.

Though it is an all-time best seller, copies of the first edition, 1678, in anything like acceptable condition are rare, as can be gauged from the fact that in 1947, when a well-documented copy, known as the Warner copy from one of its previous owners, was put up for sale by Sotherby's, the London auctioneers, it made £4,400 (about $12,570 at the rate then prevailing). If a comparable copy, in a contemporary binding and with only minor defects, were auctioned today, the price could be five times as much. There are many fine editions of this book to tempt the collector, but also thousands of tired copies of worthless editions, which depress booksellers' cheapest shelves.

The works of John Dryden (1631–1700) could hardly be more different from those of Bunyan, the tinker-pastor. Dryden was a classical scholar whose verse set the fashion for a hundred years. The beginner might feel safe in starting a Dryden collection, for some of his first editions are still fairly plentiful and in consequence not too dear—in the (i) to (d) grades.

Dryden wrote some plays, which are too wearisome for production today. In the Victorian era, the plays of his contemporaries and immediate successors were also unacceptable, not because of tediousness, but because their wit and humour were considered coarse. Nevertheless there has always been a demand for first editions of the so-called Restoration dramatists. Nineteenth-century gentlemen paid well for them and placed them in the darker recesses of their libraries. The leading Restoration playwrights, most of whose best work dates in fact from the reigns of William and Mary (1698–1702) and Anne (1702–14), are Colley Cibber (1671–1757), William Congreve (1670–1729), Sir George Etherege (1634–91), George Farquhar (1678–1707), Thomas Otway (1652–85), Sir John Vanbrugh (1664–1726) and William Wycherley (1640–1716). To these must be added Aphra Behn (1650–89), England's first woman dramatist and, some would claim, the first English novelist. As an indication of prices, the first collected edition of the plays of Cibber is (f) and firsts of individual plays are from (g) to (I).

Single plays of this period are often sold as *disbound*— a term that officially means that they have been plucked out of larger miscellaneous volumes. Some, however, were first issued as single pieces without an outer binding and might be better described as *unbound*.

Milton and Dryden apart, there are no giants among the *Wing* period poets, though several are of above average calibre, including Sir John Denham (1615–69), John Oldham (1653–83), Matthew Prior (1664–1721), Thomas Stanley (1625–78) and Thomas Traherne (1636–74). Traherne was known only as a writer of religious works until his poems were discovered at the beginning of the present century by Bertram Dobell, a scholarly bookseller, who edited and published Traherne's *Poems* in 1903 and *Centuries of Meditation* (prose) in 1908. These are sometimes rated (h), but should be obtainable for less.

The chief defect of Henry King (1592–1669) was in keeping too tight a string on his poetic gifts, so that he produced only one book of verse, *Poems, Elegies, Paradoxes and Sonets*. Growing appreciation of his work has tended to raise the first edition beyond grade (f).

After 1700 the bookman's world expands. No Herculean bibliographer could produce almost single-handed, as Wing did for his period, a short-title catalogue of the English-language books of the eighteenth century. Now the beginner can come into his own. There is a multitude of worthy literary items of the century waiting to be picked up at prices he need not fear to pay. Demand is keen at important metropolitan and provincial sales, but if the collector has time to investigate small sales in remoter areas, his efforts should not go unrewarded. He must, of course, know what he is about. He should be aware, for example, that the first collected edition of *The Spectator* was published between 1712 and 1715, in eight volumes. Though the set of part issues, dated 1711–12, is the true first, the collected edition is a high enough aim for the beginner, who will have done well to buy below grade (e). At the little sales, competition will be keenest for well known books. Items by good minor writers are the most likely to go cheaply.

Some school textbooks date the beginning of the English novel with the first publication, in 1719, of *Robinson Crusoe* by Daniel Defoe (1661–1731). This is wrong on two counts : novels were published in England in the previous century and Defoe, a shocking fibber, passed off *Robinson Crusoe* as a true story. Nonetheless, the old fraud wrote a masterpiece, so an authentic first edition, which includes *The Further Adventures*, would certainly be worth £5,000 ($9,500) in good condition. None of Defoe's other works is in quite the same class—a first of *The Life of Captain Singleton*, 1720, would probably be (a). As Defoe was a prolific writer of pamphlets, examples of his work in this direction may still be obtainable, some at (e) others costing much more. As in so many cases, the lower-priced items are not necessarily the most easily found.

Robinson Crusoe is often linked with the very different *Gulliver's Travels*, 1726. Jonathan Swift (1667–1745), the author, was one of the world's great satirists and a master of English prose. A decent copy of the first edition of *Travels into several Remote Nations by Lemuel Gulliver* may be (A) if it is classed as 'Teerink AA'. This esotericism denotes the first issue and refers to *A Bibliography of the Writings in Prose and Verse of Jonathan Swift, D.D.* by H. Teerink, first edition published at The Hague, 1937, and second edition, edited by A. H. Scouten, at Philadelphia, 1963.

The great English novelists of the eighteenth century are Henry Fielding (1707–54), Samuel Richardson (1689–1761) and the Irish-born Laurence Sterne (1713–68), alongside whom must be set the Scot, Tobias Smollett (1721–71). With these, prices may seem puzzling. A set of the nine volumes of the first of Sterne's *Tristram Shandy*, 1760–7, may reach (B), while the six volumes of Fielding's far greater *Tom Jones*, 1749, in comparable condition could be (C). Comparative scarcity accounts for the difference, though as the demand for Fielding increases, the gap narrows. While Fielding's *Joseph Andrews*, 1742, commands much the same price as *Tom Jones*, his *Amelia*, 1751, should be cheaper—perhaps (a). It is the commonest of the Fielding novels. *Tom Jones* was so successful that in anticipation of an immediate demand for a new book from the same pen, Strahan, the publisher, had 5,000 copies of *Amelia* printed—one of the largest first editions of the century.

Rivington and Osborne had no such high hopes when they began publication in 1740 of Richardson's *Pamela*. The first edition was small, which makes it a grade (A) book today. With *Pamela*, in which he had taken the novel out of the bawdyhouse and tavern into the drawing-room, Richardson became famous throughout Europe. His later novels, *Clarissa Harlowe*, 1747–8, and *Sir Charles Grandison*, 1753–4 were equally successful, but being printed in much larger first editions, they are priced well below *Pamela*.

Joseph Andrews, Fielding's first novel, began as a satire on *Pamela*, then the author went his own way, pausing in the parlour or tarrying in the tavern, but keeping his characters on the move, as did Cervantes with Don Quixote and Sancho Panza. The form was repeated in *Tom Jones*, where Fielding acknowledges his debt to Cervantes. This Quixotic pattern was taken up by other authors and influenced the English novel for a long time. It is not noticeable in Smollett's earlier novels, *Roderick Random,* 1748, and *Peregrine Pickle*, 1751, but is clear in *Sir Launcelot Greaves*, 1762, and *Humphrey Clinker*, 1771. Significantly, Smollett published a translation of *Don Quixote* in 1755—grade (g). The scarcest Smollett novel is *Sir Launcelot Greaves*, which could be grade (B), with the others varying from (I) to (E).

Other novelists took their cues from the masters. In 1752 came *The Female Quixote* from Charlotte Lennox (1720–1804), and in 1772 Richard Graves (1717–1804) produced *The Spiritual Quixote*. Other more or less Quixote-haunted novelists of the period included Henry Fielding's sister, Sarah (1710–68) with *David Simple*, 1744, Thomas Amory (1691–1788) with *John Buncle*, 1756, Henry Brooke (1703–83) with *The Fool of Quality*, 1766, and Mrs Elizabeth Inchbald (1753–1821) with *The Simple Story*, 1791. An investment of about £300 or $600 a year for ten years ought to be enough for a fairly complete collection of the minor Quixotic novels.

As he wrote only one novel, Oliver Goldsmith (1728–74)

cannot be classed as a great novelist, but his *The Vicar of Wakefield*, 1766, is a masterpiece, worth a (C) rating for the first issue of the first edition. The Dublin edition, also 1766, was pirated, but now has some curiosity value and could be rated (h). Goldsmith's friend, Dr Johnson, did not reach great heights with his one novel, *The Prince of Abissinia*, 1759, now usually called *Rasselas*, so it is no more than (I).

When the dilettante and antiquarian Horace Walpole (1717–97) wrote *The Castle of Otranto* in 1765, he started a craze for the Gothic novel with its paraphernalia of ghostly ruins and screams in the night. His best-known followers are Ann Radcliffe (1764–1823) with *The Mysteries of Udolpho*, 1794, Matthew Gregory Lewis (1775–1818) with *The Monk*, 1794, Mary Shelley (1797–1851) with *Frankenstein*, 1818, and Charles R. Maturin (1782–1824) with *Melmoth the Wanderer*, 1820. Her connection with the poet helps to make Mrs. Shelley's book grade (G), with Walpole's pioneer work in the same bracket. The others should be around grade (a).

Though they published their work in the nineteenth century, Maturin and Mrs Shelley were carrying on an eighteenth-century tradition. With *Frankenstein* Mrs Shelley also anticipated the much later flowering of science fiction, though she had a predecessor in Robert Paltock (1697–1767), whose *The Life and Adventures of Peter Wilkins*, 1751, has a kinship with the fantasies of Jules Verne. A first of this book would be (I).

The oriental interests of William Beckford (1759–1844) inspired his *Vathek*, a gloomy tale in an *Arabian Nights* setting. Beckford wrote it in French, but a Dr Samuel Henley got possession of the manuscript and translated it into English. It was in this form that the book first appeared, at the end of 1786. The French original was published in Paris and Lausanne the following year. Beckford understandably tried to suppress Henley's version, not very successfully, it seems. It was once thought to be a rarity, but as further copies kept coming on the market its value dropped. Now it has become truly scarce, but has gone out of fashion and might be obtainable at (a). The French edition, as the original work, could be (I).

Among the items that prudent executors would remove for unceremonious cremation from the libraries of outwardly respectable deceased bibliophiles, there was sometimes a first edition of John Cleland's *Memoirs of a Woman of Pleasure*, two volumes, 1748. This book is better known to us as *Fanny Hill*, obviously scarce in the first edition (though the gardener —or was it the gamekeeper?—sometimes kept a copy instead of putting it on the bonfire) and is still liable to be sold *sub mensa*, so is difficult to evaluate. In 1971, a modern French edition was sold at the Swann Galleries, New York, with the description, 'loose as issued'. This referred to the illustrations and was not a statement of the obvious.

Mention has already been made of *The Spectator*, a new venture in journalism, started by its chief contributors, Joseph Addison (1672–1719) and Sir Richard Steele (1672–1729). It popularized the light essay, which flourished from then on. Goldsmith was a master of the medium and many of his best essays are in *The Citizen of the World*, two volumes, 1762. Prices continue to fluctuate, so it may still be had in acceptable condition at (d). Dr Johnson also practised the essay, but his great gift to English language and literature was his *Dictionary of the English Language*, two folio volumes, 1755. Really good copies are (A) or (B), but a defective copy, at much less, is still worth acquiring.

The two greatest British poets of the eighteenth century could hardly have been more dissimilar. One was a withdrawn, waspish little man, unprepossessing, but educated and urbane. The other was an extrovert, well-built and handsome, but ill-schooled and rustic.

Alexander Pope (1688–1744), the first of the two, was quite prolific. A nice selection of his commoner firsts might be built up without spending a fortune. The first collected edition of his works, 1717, in a good contemporary binding, should be

(d) and small items, such as *Of the Characters of Women*, 1735, might be (g). The most sought-after and dearer Pope items are better left to the experienced buyer.

Robert Burns (1759–96), the other member of the pair, published less than Pope. *Poems, Chiefly in the Scottish Dialect* was brought out at Kilmarnock in 1786 and this is the edition that every Burnsite dreams of owning. As the original binding was of thin paper, the mortality rate has been high. Only a few copies in original condition exist, so a really good rebound copy would be worth at least an (A) grading. The second edition of Burns's poems was published at Edinburgh in 1787 and is far commoner than the Kilmarnock edition. In the first issue of the second edition, 'stinking' is written for 'skinking' in *To a Haggis* on page 263. This issue is (H) and the second is (d).

Later editions of Burns are less valuable. There has been a burst of interest in two items that contain the first printings of many of Burns's best songs: George Thomson's *A Select Collection of Original Scottish Airs for the Voice*, Edinburgh, 1799–1818, and James Johnson's *Scots Musical Museum*, Edinburgh, 1787– 97. They should be (d), complete.

William Cowper (1731–1800) and Thomas Gray (1716–71) are next in importance as poets. Cowper did not produce a large number of separate editions of his poems, so presents the collector with no great undertaking. In the first issue of the first edition of his *Poems*, 1782, however, there is a preface and no cancels. In later issues the preface is suppressed and there are cancels at E_6 and E_{16}. Prices could be between (G) and (I) according to issue. Apart from the exiguous firsts, several later editions of Cowper are worth attention.

Gray was a considerable poet whose popular fame rests on his *Elegy Wrote in a Country Church Yard* [*sic*], 1751. The earliest issue of the first edition shows how a collector's point, though detracting from the literary merit of a book, can add to its cash value. The phrase 'kindred spirit' was one of Gray's gifts to the English language. It occurs in the *Elegy* at the

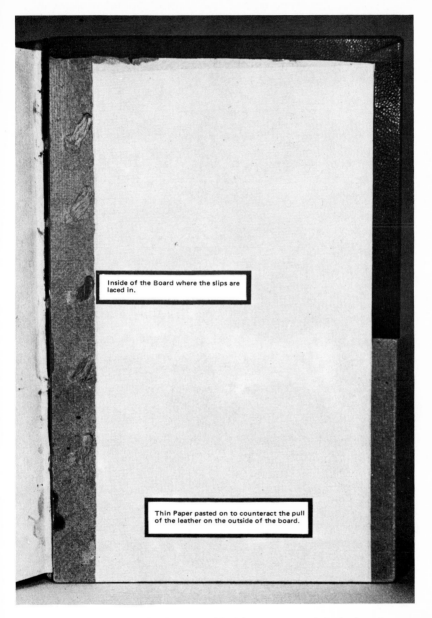

Inside of the Board where the slips are laced in.

Thin Paper pasted on to counteract the pull of the leather on the outside of the board.

Plate 3 This shows the back cover with thin paper pasted to the board to counteract the pull of the leather. The method of lacing the cords to the board can also be seen.

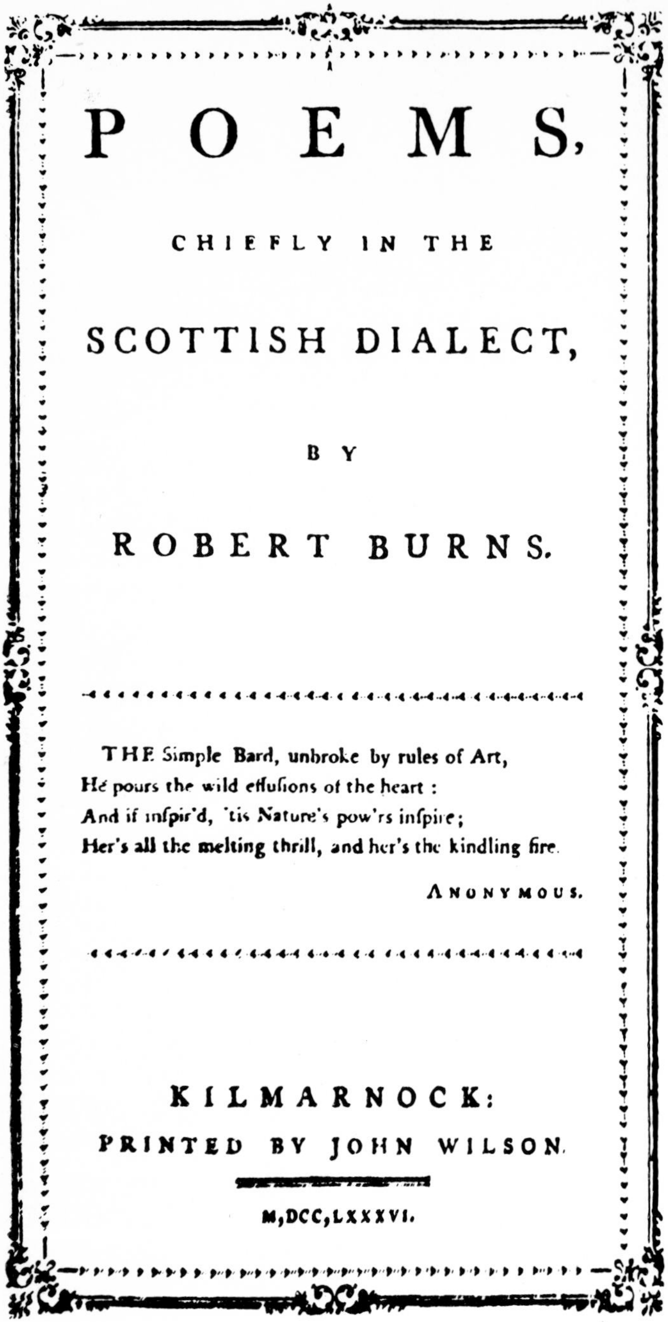

POEMS,

CHIEFLY IN THE

SCOTTISH DIALECT,

BY

ROBERT BURNS.

THE Simple Bard, unbroke by rules of Art,
He pours the wild effusions of the heart :
And if infpir'd, 'tis Nature's pow'rs infpire;
Her's all the melting thrill, and her's the kindling fire.

ANONYMOUS.

KILMARNOCK:

PRINTED BY JOHN WILSON.

M,DCC,LXXXVI.

Plate 4 The Burnsite's dream possession: the title-page of the Kilmarnock edition – the first of Robert Burns's poems.

fourth line of the twenty-fourth verse. It is not found in the first issue, where the feebler 'hidden spirit' takes its place. Yet the collector intent on priority will pay about four times as much, perhaps into grade (B), for the unmemorable version as for the other.

The eighteenth century offers the collector a whole army of lesser poets. James Thomson (1700–48), who wrote *Rule, Britannia!* as well as two long poems, *The Seasons*, 1726–30, and *The Castle of Indolence*, 1748, and William Collins (1721–59) are among the best, along with that man-of-all-letters, Oliver Goldsmith. John Dyer (1699–1758) and Thomas Chatterton (1752–70) both deserve mention.

Three dreary versifiers enjoyed a popularity that lasted into the next century : James Beattie (1735–1803), who wrote *The Minstrel*, 1771–4, Robert Blair (1699–1746), whose path of glory led to *The Grave*, 1743, and Edward Young (1683–1765), who gave us *The Complaint, or Night Thoughts*, 1742–5. Their works are more fun to collect than read. Firsts of Blair and Young are of far less value than the later editions illustrated by William Blake. When their surnames are put together, Thomas Tickell (1686–1740), Richard Savage (1697–1743) and Stephen Duck (1705–56) make an interesting trio.

Hawkeyed seekers may pick up firsts of these minor poets for less than the (h) or (f) grades into which they usually fall. One way of acquiring their works is to look for them in John Bell's *The Poets of Great Britain, from Chaucer to Churchill*, Edinburgh, 1777–92. The complete set consists of 109 volumes, usually described as 12mos, but actually 18mos. A set would be (H) in the salerooms, but odd volumes might be found in bookshops at £2 ($4) each. Similar later collections of poetry lack the period feel and smell of the Bells.

Eighteenth-century drama was largely a matter of bombast and ostrich plumes—the latter being the accepted headwear for tragediennes. Some of the comedies are enjoyable, but most of the tragedies are tragically dull. Even Sheridan, who ridiculed overblown drama in *The Critic*, 1779, was as boring as his contemporaries when he adapted Kotzebue's *Die Spanier in Peru* as *Pizzarro*, 1799. Much of the drama of this period is collected for its historical rather than its literary merits and there is still plenty of material to be had. Unbound copies of individual plays were sold to audiences during the run of the play and may now appear with added paper covers. Sometimes the covers are pasted on, sometimes the book or booklet has been resewn to include the added covers The stickler for original condition can have an endless debate with himself about whether resewing contravenes his rules.

Names to look for are John Gay (1685–1732), George Lillo (1693–1739), Edward Moore (1712–57), Henry Fielding, David Garrick, the actor (1717–79), Samuel Foote (1720–77) and Arthur Murphy (1727–1805). Helpful books for the collector are *A History of Early Eighteenth Century Drama*, Cambridge, 1925, and *A History of Late Eighteenth Century Drama*, Cambridge, 1927, both by Allardyce Nicoll. If it were more generally available, *Some Account of the English Stage, 1660–1830*, ten volumes, Bath, 1832, would be recommended. It was the life's work of the Reverend John Genest (1764–1839) and its price on publication was five guineas (£5.25) the set. There were few buyers, even when the price was lowered to 30s (£1.50). Today it is (H).

The literary man may settle for collecting only the two great dramatists of the century, Oliver Goldsmith and Richard Brinsley Sheridan (1751–1816). Goldsmith's theatrical fame rests on *She Stoops to Conquer*, 1773, and *The Good Natur'd Man,* 1768. First editions of these are (a). Considering their popularity in his own times, Sheridan firsts are not abundant. *The School for Scandal*, undated, but published at Dublin in 1780, is the Sheridan high spot. Only a rash prophet would suggest a price for the next copy, acceptable in all its parts, that may be offered for sale. Rashly, £3,000 ($7,700) is suggested. The other Sheridans would be priced much as the Goldsmiths.

4

General Literature from 1801

The world's great age did not begin anew on 1 January 1801. However, it is convenient to accept the date as marking the start of the Romantic Revival, since it is so much a part of the early nineteenth century. In their enthusiasm for its fresh lyricism, our immediate predecessors glossed over certain absurdities in this new romantic movement. They mocked the oriental extravagances of the Brighton Pavilion while swallowing them whole in Coleridge's *Kubla Khan*; they scorned the revived Gothic of a Pugin church while revelling in the archaisms of *The Ancient Mariner*.

The man of taste of the late twentieth century makes different evaluations. He acknowledges the greatness of the chief writers of that time, but for him the lesser lights are esteemed as much for their social and historical interest as for their literary merits. This diminishes the collector's zeal only slightly, so the demand for books by the neo-romantics has lessened only a little in the past few years and the easing of prices is hardly noticeable. No serious devaluation need be feared.

Robert Southey (1774–1843), Poet Laureate and brother-in-law of Coleridge, is now among the least regarded of the romantics, but the high cost of some of his firsts is likely to be maintained. His seldom seen *Omniana*, 1812, in two volumes, original boards, should be (e), with the two volumes, in similar state, of his *Annual Anthology*, Bristol, 1799–1800, reaching (I). His other first editions should be cheaper.

Southey had nearly 1,400 volumes of his own library covered in flowery chintz and titled on the spine with distinctive paper labels. These he called his 'Cottonian Library' from the real collection of that name, now part of the British Library. Not every old book covered in chintz is from this source, but anybody who found one with the right provenance would have a rare treasure.

Southey, William Wordsworth (1770–1850) and Samuel Taylor Coleridge (1772–1834) formed the trio known as the Lake Poets. Several other writers were associated with them, particularly Thomas De Quincey (1785–1859), Charles Lamb (1775–1834) and, through Lamb, Charles Lloyd (1775–1839). Lloyd, a Quaker from Birmingham, is relegated to the footnotes in histories of English literature, but his name can still cause a stir in the salerooms. The first edition of Coleridge's *Poems on Various Subjects,* Bristol, 1796, contained four poems by Lamb. The next edition, in 1797, had an extension to the title reading: 'to which are now added poems by Charles Lamb and Charles Lloyd'. The following year, Lamb and Lloyd together produced *Blank Verse*, a small collection of their poems.

The Coleridge and Lamb poems of 1796 would probably be (G) in boards, the second edition (I) and the Lamb and Lloyd *Blank Verse* (a). Yet an acceptable first of Lloyd's own individual *Poems on Various Subjects*, Carlisle, no date, but 1795, could well be (F). The beginner must hope that as this is not a well-known book, copies may still be lurking in odd corners waiting to be seized by the lucky hunter. There are misprints on pages 26, 47 and 57 in the first state of this book.

Coleridge's collaboration with Wordsworth produced the *Lyrical Ballads*, 12mo, Bristol, 1798. The first issue in its original binding is out of reach of the average collector, though a good rebind is possible at (G), which would also be the grading of the second issue in original state. The chances of bargains in Coleridge and Wordsworth firsts are slim. A rebound copy of Coleridge's *Christabel; Kubla Khan*, 1816, in fair condition, might be (f), but fine, in original wrapper it could be (G). A reasonable rebind of Wordsworth's *The Excursion*, 1814, might be (h), and of his *An Evening Walk*, 1793, possibly (B).

George Gordon, Lord Byron (1788–1824), John Keats (1795–1821) and Percy Bysshe Shelley (1792–1822) are the next trio of romantic poets to be considered. Byron saw himself as a classicist rather than a romantic. Though radically inclined, he never quite uncurled his aristocratic lip, and his poetry contains more sardonic wit than warm human sympathy. His verse enjoyed great popularity in his lifetime, so several Byron first and early editions are quite common— a complete set of *Don Juan*, sixteen cantos, 1819–24, may be only (e). On the other hand, a choice copy of *The Waltz; An Apostrophic Hymn*, 1813, written under the pseudonym of Horace Hornem, could be (A).

Keats, burning himself out with hectic creative energy, epitomizes the Romantic Revival. His first book, *Poems*, was published with Shelley's help in 1817 and proved a failure. Today it would be (G). His next publication, the following year, was *Endymion*. This is desired even more. The first issue of the first edition, identified by an erratum leaf of one line of print, could be (C) in original state and (E) as a very good rebind. *Endymion* was savaged by the critics of *Blackwood* and *The Quarterly*. However, *Lamia and Other Poems*, 1820, the last of his works to be published before his death, was highly praised in the *Edinburgh Review*. A first of this collection sold for £2,500 ($4,750) at a London sale in 1975. It had been rebound, but by Cobden-Sanderson, a master craftsman, so this probably enhanced rather than detracted from its price.

The death of Keats brought from his friend, Shelley, *Adonais, An Elegy on the Death of John Keats*, 1821. This is one of the greatest poems in the English language and grading the first edition as (B) is like defacing Michaelangelo's 'David' with an outsize price label. But the collector must learn there is little sensitivity in the marketplace. Shelley's unactable drama, *Prometheus Bound*, 1820, has 'miscellaneous' misspelt as 'miscellaneus' on the contents page of the first issue of the first edition. The presence of this point doubles the value over the second issue, putting it in grade (H), or higher.

The Irishman, Tom Moore (1779–1852) is certainly a romantic. He did almost as much for non-Gaelic Irish song as Burns did for Lowland Scots song. His *Irish Melodies* appeared as a series between 1808 and 1834 and a set could be (G). The collector who wanted to build one by buying piecemeal would have an exceedingly long haul. Moore's *Lalla Rookh*, 1817, a best seller in its day, can be bought very cheaply, even in Dublin.

George Crabbe (1754–1832) stands outside the Romantic Revival. His early classicism developed into a highly individual realism, best seen in *The Borough*, 1810, which could be (f) or (e). Sir Walter Scott (1771–1832) was once a popular poet. His verse romances, *The Lay of the Last Minstrel*, 1805, *Marmion*, 1808, *The Lady of the Lake*, 1810, are gey dreich and dreary for modern readers, but Scott is enjoying a slight revival and booksellers are blowing the dust from their firsts of these poems and trying them midway up (i).

Charles Lamb, already viewed as a poet, is better known as an essayist. He was more or less the inventor of the essay in which the writer says nothing in particular, but says it very well. Lamb wrote many of his essays for the *London Magazine* under the name of Elia and the first collection in book form was published at London as *Elia, Essays Which Have Appeared under That Signature in the London Magazine*, 1823. This should be (I). Now comes a complication. The second collection, *Last Essays of Elia*, was published at London in 1833. This volume and the 1823 *Elia*, uniformly rebound, are sometimes sold together as the two first editions. But the 1833 London edition of the *Last Essays* is not truly the first, 'for the collection was published at Philadelphia,

Pennsylvania, in 1823. Ought the collector to go for uniformity and disregard the alien, or should he make a strict point of priority? This problem arises with other authors and bibliophiles are still arguing about it.

One of the most desired Lamb items is *The King and Queen of Hearts*. As first published in 1805, this is a dainty 16mo, in blue wrappers with fifteen illustrations. It is very scarce, but the American composer Jerome Kern (1885–1945) owned a copy that, as far as is known, is unique. It has the date 1805 printed on the wrappers, and this has been found on no other. When the Kern copy was sold at New York in 1946 it fetched $1,000 (then only £250). The finder of a similar copy today could expect its value to be at least $3,000 (£1,580).

William Hazlitt (1778–1830), Thomas De Quincey and James Henry Leigh Hunt (1784–1859) may be considered together as talented essayists and miscellaneous writers. Firsts of their writings should be acquired between (i) and (b).

Sooner or later, the collector will have to contend with Thomas J. Wise, whose baleful influence on bibliophily was at its height at the beginning of the present century. Wise, who began his working life as a London clerk, developed a taste for collecting books. In his young day, the unchanging bookman pursued the unreadable book much on the principle that if it was old it was good, if modern it was worthless.

Not having much money, the young Wise had to hunt on foot while others could ride but he soon realized that his quarry was right at hand. In a few years he had not only formed an enviable collection of then modern authors, but was profitably encouraging others to follow his example. He stressed the importance of condition and popularized systematic bibliography. Soon he was the accepted authority on nineteenth-century English books.

Unusually in a bibliophile, he was a vain and venal man. He had a genuine facility for finding rare editions but when they were not to be found he manufactured them. As a master forger he made money from his fakes. Vanity was also a spur which pricked him to the production of items that set collectors' eyebrows on high on both sides of the Atlantic. His forgeries were editions of authentic works. He never tried to fabricate new material in an established author's style.

Hardly a collectable poet of the nineteenth century escaped his attentions, from Tennyson to Swinburne. His knowledged masterpiece is the reputed Reading edition of *Sonnets by E.B.B.*, supposedly 1847, by Elizabeth Barrett Browning (1806–61). This is so fine and rare that at Sotheby's in 1976 £1,800 ($3,400) was paid for the John Carter copy (see below). This is a much higher price than any genuine Mrs Browning first would make. Such is the value put on Wise forgeries by collectors that forgers have forged some of the forgeries. Incredible as it may seem, some of these doubly spurious efforts have been sold at prices rivalling those of the true Wise forgeries.

John Carter and Graham Pollard, two of England's most accomplished bibliographers, finally blew the gaff on Wise in 1934 with the publication of their joint book *An Enquiry into the Nature of Certain 19th Century Pamphlets*. No direct accusations were made, but the finger was clearly pointed at Wise, by that time a frail old man. He died peacefully in 1937.

Since Wise's day, some of his chosen victims have not advanced in popularity. The only genuine Mrs Browning items in much demand now are her first book, *Essay on Mind*, 1826, and the first edition of her *Poems*, 1844, in two volumes, with eight pages of advertisements dated 1 June 1844 at the beginning of volume I, and an additional leaf at the end. These two items could be (a), but interest seems to be waning. The position is much the same with Robert Browning (1812–89). The Wise forgeries are more valuable than the genuine firsts. A single-volume edition of *Bells and Pomegranates*, 1841–6, may be (a), but his late firsts, usually bound in maroon cloth and published by Smith, Elder & Co, may be found at £2 (say $4). These husband-and-wife poets provide a cheap and interesting subject for the beginner to collect. Ironically, he will have to turn for help to Wise, whose bibliographies of the Brownings are still standard.

Alfred, Lord Tennyson (1809) is placed rather as the Brownings are. The Wise forgery of *Morte D'Arthur, Dora and Other Idylls*, allegedly 1842, is perhaps the dearest Tennyson book, in grade (E), while the genuine first issue of *In Memoriam*, 1850, with 'the' for 'thee' on page 2, line 13, and 'baseness' for 'bareness' on page 198, line 3, may be only (g). Here again is a good subject for the beginner, though if too many people are inspired by this to collect, prices will increase.

The nineteenth century saw the rise of the American poets, with William Cullen Bryant (1794–1878) in the van. Bryant's first book, *Poems*, 1821, published at Cambridge, Massachusetts, should be (a) and a first issue of his *A Forest Hymn*, no date, but 1860, is (i). John Greenleaf Whittier (1807–92), the Quaker poet, can be collected inexpensively save for his *Snowbound*, 1866, in the first issue, which has the last page of the text numbered '52' (it is unnumbered in the second issue). This should be (H). A first issue of *The Song of Hiawatha*, 1855, by Henry Wadsworth Longfellow (1807–82), would be in the same grade. His *Belfry of Bruges*, 1845–6, in original wrappers, might be (e), but his other firsts should be cheaper.

Though American, these three poets belong partly to the English tradition. The first issue of *The Song of Hiawatha* has the American form of the past tense of 'dive' on page 96, line 7. Longfellow quickly amended this, so the second issue has the English 'dived' instead of the American 'dove'.

Walt Whitman (1819–92) would have been less eager to make that kind of change. His is a much more strongly American voice. A few Whitman items are within reach of the indigent, but most are dear. The slim *Leaves of Grass*, first issue (with no extra pages of press notices) 1855, is in the

$4,000 (£2,100) range. Later editions do not decline much in value, for Whitman kept adding poems until his original 94-page quarto had grown to nearly 400 pages in the eighth edition.

Emily Dickinson (1830–86) belongs to much the same period as Whitman, but little of her poetry appeared during her lifetime. It was not until the publication of the three series of her *Poems* at Boston, Massachusetts, in 1890–91–96, that a proper appraisal of her genius could be made The three series together are (H), with *The Masque of Poets*, Boston, 1878, published while she was still alive, as a rising (g).

Collecting first editions of the poetry of Edgar Allan Poe (1809–49) is no common man's exercise. Their bibliography is complicated and they are desperately expensive. Only twelve copies of his *Tamerlane and Other Poems*, 12mo, Boston, Massachusetts, 1827, are known, so a copy of his unpretentious book in paper wrappers could cost up to $40,000 (over £21,000).

If poetry thrived in the nineteenth century, the novel boomed. Maria Edgeworth (1767–1849) bridged two centuries with *Castle Rackrent*, 1800 and *Belinda,* three volumes, 1801, both probably (a) in fine original condition, and was a herald of greater writers. In 1811, *Sense and Sensibility*, three volumes, by Jane Austen (1775–1817), appeared. Sir Walter Scott published his first novel, *Waverley*, in 1814. Both are esteemed authors, with Jane Austen as the more popular today. A good first of *Waverley* in boards could make the (a) grade, but really fine Jane Austens in original bindings with half-titles can over-top (A). At the beginning of the century, *Waverley* might have been the dearer of the two. A Scott collector could hope to find good firsts of the other Waverley Novels at (h) on average.

Most of the Dickens novels could be found in the same grade, though the part issues would be much higher, as would be *Great Expectations*, 1861, always difficult in a first issue.

Dickens is finding favour with more and more collectors, so prices will rise.

William Makepeace Thackeray (1811–63), still lagging in popularity, could be collected more cheaply than Dickens, except for his *Vanity Fair*, 1847–8. Quite presentable leather-bound first editions of this novel are not above grade (i); a first issue in the original 19/20 parts could well be grade (A).

As Dickens and Thackeray were best-selling novelists whose works were issued in large first editions, most of their books tend to be cheaper than those of the other Victorian 'greats'. Everything by the Brontë sisters, Charlotte (1816–55), Emily (1818–48) and Anne (1820–49), would be from (e) to (H). The novels of George Eliot (Mary Ann Cross, born Evans, 1819–80) and Anthony Trollope (1815–82) would command similar prices, though not quite rising to Brontë heights.

Among the later Victorians, Thomas Hardy (1840–1928) has a large following of collectors, who are willing, it seems, to pay up to grade (a) for the cream of his work. George Meredith (1828–1909) has fewer followers and his books are mainly (h) or below. This is also the case with R. L. Stevenson (1850–94).

A particular joy in the field of Victorian fiction is the hunt for books by the minor authors. Here Michael Sadleir was the pioneer. The most authoritative work on the subject so far is his *XIX Century Fiction, a Bibliographical Record Based on His Own Collection*, two volumes, Constable & Co Ltd, London, and University of California Press, Los Angeles, 1951. This magnificent work gives details of the books in Sadleir's private collection, with some added information on books that he had been unable to find. The photographs of some of his choice items are provocative of bibliomanic lust. Also illustrated and definitively named for the first time are the various types of cloth favoured by Victorian binders.

There are apparently 3,761 items listed, but the real total is 2,770, for the numbering skips from 2,009 to 3,000 in the midst of descriptions of the novels of W. Clark Russell. Professor Lee Wolff of Harvard University drew attention to this slip in *The Book Collector* in 1965. Such an error hardly detracts from the usefulness of *XIX Century Fiction*, though it is not and was never intended to be an infallible guide.

In describing the *Mrs Brown* series by 'Arthur Sketchley' (George Rose, *d*1882), enormously popular as yellowbacks a hundred years ago, Sadleir hopes his is a correct and comprehensive survey. Later checking shows his information is not quite accurate. He dates *Mrs Brown on Cetewayo* as 1879. This must be wrong as Cetewayo, the African chief, did not come to England till 1882. He also gives this title as number 34 in the series. Some copies show the number 33. His number for *Mrs Brown on Home Rule* is 36 and for *Mrs Brown on Jumbo* 35. Some copies bear the numbers 31 and 32 respectively, so Mrs Brown is still unruly.

There is plenty of scope for the collector who aims at surpassing Sadleir. This has already been done by Professor Lee Wolff, with well over 6,000 items to his credit and an ultimate unattainable goal of 42,000. One of the difficulties is that some nineteenth-century firsts never occur in a condition fit for shelving. The collector has then to decide for himself whether to accept a ruin or make do with a fine later edition. Many are now accepting the latter remedy, so second editions are becoming dearer and scarcer.

It is hard to give guidance on the prices of Sadleir-type books. Competition is fierce for the more worthy of them. J. Sheridan Le Fanu's *Guy Deverell*, three volumes, 1865, may be (a) while the obscure Mrs J. C. Bateman's *The Netherwoods of Otterpool*, three volumes, published anonymously, 1858, may still be waiting in a junk shop at little more than £1 (say $2), though this is less likely than it would have been a year or two ago. Interest in this kind of fiction is developing. Some book dealers put extravagant prices on the most trashy of old novels and award them what they hope will be magical letters—NIS (not in Sadleir). Sadleir was a man of discrimination and his followers should remember that; otherwise they will spend their declining years contemplating shelves full of dowdy old books whose faded titles are their most readable features.

Sadleir's interests were mainly in books published in Britain, so his followers have tended to neglect North American fiction of the same period. The major writers, of course, are collected, so much so that Poe's prose works are as precious to the bibliophile as his poetry is, and matched as to price. A first of Nathaniel Hawthorne's (1804–64) *The Scarlet Letter*, 1850, would be (a). The novels of Stephen Crane (1871–1900) are mostly grade (g), though his rare *Maggie: A Girl of the Streets*, New York, 1893, by 'Johnston Smith', is now (A). Henry James (1843–1916) firsts are about (g), with a few rather higher, and those of 'Mark Twain' (Samuel Langhorne Clemens, 1835–1910) also (g), with some reaching (B). The books of Herman Melville (1819–91) rise to (I), while *Uncle Tom's Cabin*, 1851–2, by Harriet Beecher Stowe (1811–96) could be (C). A few other American novelists, such as J. Fenimore Cooper (1789–1851) and Bret Harte (1839–1902), have been collected for a long time, never cheaply; but many American writers are just emerging from comparative obscurity.

Among these can be listed William G. Simms (1806–70), Sylvester Judd (1813–53), Josiah G. Holland (1819–81), Maria S. Cumins (1827–66), Helen Hunt Jackson (1831–85), Frank R. Stockton (1834–1902), Thomas B. Aldrich (1836–1907) and Paul L. Ford (1865–1902). Books by some of these authors are more easily obtainable in recent limited editions than in firsts, but the originals are to be had, though widely scattered over North America and Europe—there has long been two-way traffic in novels. The collector will have to spend more money in finding them than in buying them when found. As American universities are now paying more attention to minor native writers and increasing the demand, prices will not remain low.

A section of Sadleir's collection was given over to yellow-backs—cheap editions of novels (and sometimes non-fiction) published in England in garish pictorial boards, throughout the second half of the nineteenth century. They have their American equivalents, Harper's *Black and White* series for example, which are at last being collected. Some are unrewarding trash but the best are worth keeping. As they bring no dignity to a library, the lordly type of bibliophile leaves them alone, so they are rarely over-priced.

Frankly, most yellow-backs and their kin look cheap and nasty, but they are not the worst products of their period. The growth of literacy generated an indiscriminate demand for reading matter that was met in part by the meanest products of an era of crude commercialism. This aspect of the time led to the escapist aestheticism of poets like D. G. Rossetti (1828–82) and A. C. Swinburne (1837–1909), and the pessimism of James Thomson ('BV') (1834–82). Swinburne in particular has declined in favour, though his *Atalanta in Calydon*, 1865, seems to have held its own and is grade (e), the same as the first collected edition of Rossetti's *Poems*, 1870, and Thomson's *City of Dreadful Night*, 1880.

Three widely different writers typify the literary and social conflicts of the last years of the Victorian era : Oscar Wilde (1854–1900), Bernard Shaw (1856–1950) and Rudyard Kipling (1865–1936). Wilde's witty epigrammatic style is at its best in such plays as *The Importance of Being Ernest* and *An Ideal Husband*, both first published in 1899 and probably (h). A representative selection of his other work could be got together by buying in grade (i). Most Shaw firsts, all delightful examples of his paradoxically clever and opinionated criticisms of society, can be bought cheaply. Shaw collectors look for signed copies, which are much more costly.

Kipling's inescapable jingoism used to discourage liberal-minded collectors. Now even they are realizing that Kipling did more than bang the big drum. He was a born storyteller with his own particular insight into human motives. His stock has risen in the last decade and with it the prices of his firsts and of sets of his works. It is no longer true that the Wise forgery of his *The White Man's Burden*, 1899, is the dearest of his works. His other early publications are on a par at grade (b). His early *Schoolboy Lyrics*, 1881, has moved to a little above grade (A). Later Kipling firsts are still cheap. They are plentiful as firsts go and some of them are in fact collections of short works first published at a much earlier date. The collector saves his money to buy the scarce early items.

Authors do not obligingly stop writing at the end of one century to clear the decks for a fresh crew in the next. A collection of twentieth-century literature has to include writers who spanned the two periods. These may include Sir J. M. Barrie (1860–1937), Robert Bridges (1844–1930), George Moore (1852–1933) and George Russell ('AE') (1867–1935). None of these should set problems of expense—ordinary first editions of their works should not be above £10 ($19) and sometimes quite far below.

Barrie is one of the authors of the period whose works have dropped in value. In the early thirties first editions of his *Tommy and Grizel*, 1900, sold for about $4.50, which is $45 (over £23) in today's terms, at a conservative estimate. Similar copies could be bought today at $2 (just over £1). Barrie's best work seems to be more in demand in North America than in Britain. As much as $110 (£50) has been paid in New York of late for *The Little Minister*, 1891, but this is untypical. Those who find they can still read Barrie with enjoyment can collect at little cost.

Joseph Conrad (Teodor Josef Konrad Korzeniowski, 1857–1924), E. Arnold Bennett (1867–1931) and H. G. Wells (1866–1946) are all accepted as worthwhile writers who bridged the centuries, but collecting their works comes easy on the purse. There are expensive items, like Conrad's *'Twixt Land and Sea Tales*, 1912, (a), Bennett's *The Old Wives' Tale*, 1908, (g), and Wells's science fiction novels (see Chapter

6). For the most part, however, these writers' books are far down in grade (i), providing good digestible literary fare at low cost.

Once the century was under way, English writing began to take new directions. James Joyce brought out *The Day of the Rabblement* in Dublin in 1901. This book, little more than a pamphlet, is Joyce's rarest work and could be (E). In the same year, George Douglas Brown (as George Douglas) issued his *The House with the Green Shutters*, in which, with his opening paragraph, he emptied a pail of slops over the gooey Scottish novelists of the sentimental 'kailyaird' school. An undervalued book, it may be had as a first in top condition for about £10 ($19).

Change was well under way by 1911, the publication year of *The White Peacock* by David Herbert Lawrence (1885–1930). Like most of Lawrence's novels, its form is conventional. Lawrence was an innovator in the things he said rather than how he said them. The price range of D. H. Lawrence firsts is particularly wide—from about £6 ($11.50) to grade (a). The first unexpurgated English edition of his *Lady Chatterley's Lover*, published by Penguin Books in 1960, is an accepted collector's piece, still found in some bookshops at under £1 ($1.90).

The development of the novel continued through the century and a number of important novelists emerged. The prices of many of their firsts are hard to assess, as supplies dry up and the demand grows greater. Joyce's *Ulysses* in the Egoist Press edition, Paris, 1922, is moving to (G). The novels of Virginia Woolf (1882–1941), in the (h) grade not so long ago, range from (g) to (b). Grade (h) is no longer safe for the important American novelists who flourished in the first half of the century. These include Theodore Dreiser and F. Scott Fitzgerald. Their most esteemed books are (f) and higher. Ernest Hemingway, whose assertive masculinity appeals to wide sections of the American public, is in particular demand, with some of his novels reaching (a).

Perhaps the standing of E. M. Forster is not so high as it was, but he wrote beautifully and his body of writing is small enough to be collected in its entirety on a modest budget. *A Passage to India* might prove to be the dearest at (h). The collector who gives most of his spare time to shopping around would have to spend little more than is asked for current new novels to collect firsts of many front-rank twentieth-century novelists—Sinclair Lewis, Edith Wharton, Aldous Huxley and Richard Aldington, to name only a few. Many Irishmen at home and abroad are enthusiastic collectors of their modern novelists and do not object to paying highly for their books. But the Scots still seem to underrate their writers, so the great trilogy by James Leslie Mitchell (as Lewis Grassic Gibbon), *Sunset Song*, 1932, *Cloud Howe*, 1933, and *Grey Granite*, 1934, is frequently sold for less than £5 ($9.50) a volume.

Some oddities among twentieth-century fiction are attractive. The writings of Frederick Rolfe (Baron Corvo) come under this heading and are now (h) or (g), though the first issue of *Hadrian the Seventh*, 1904, with the thirty-two page catalogue at the end, is dearer. If not an oddity, Ronald Firbank was a highly individual writer. His high spot is *Odette d'Antrevernes*, in wrappers, 1905, in grade (g).

The end of the century is not far away. Perhaps now is the time for another Sadleir to come forward and collect and classify the minor novelists who have been published from 1901 to date. Perhaps he is already at work. There are certainly collectors beavering in this area, harvesting their firsts of Warwick Deeping, Ethel M. Dell, P. C. Wren and others while they are still cheap. We can only hope that in time one or other of them will produce a definitive *XX Century Fiction*.

Faced with the problem of collecting novels of the twentieth century, Sir Thomas Phillipps would have solved it by attempting to acquire them all. This is not practical today, but there are several good reasons for collecting forgotten novels of our time. Some could turn out to be neglected masterpieces; some, though otherwise flawed, may tell a good story; some may reflect certain social attitudes now obsolete; and some may be so outrageously bad as to be genuinely funny. Many, alas, will have no merit at all, being so much 'styte'. This Scots monosyllable has no direct equivalent in English. It means, though with greater force, 'unmitigated tosh doubly distilled' and no non-manic collector wants to be burdened with that. The beginner who wants minor twentieth-century novels will have to clear the way ahead by carefully selecting his quarry, which means reading or dipping into a wide selection of novels until he finds a writer worth pursuing. He can be fairly sure that when he hits on an author who appeals to him, somebody else will have done the same at roughly the same time. His early purchases, costing only a few pence, or cents, will be made with little difficulty, but when he comes to look for the author's scarcer items he will be aware of competition from somebody else—and possibly from others who have subsequently jumped on to the same bandwagon.

Since there is as yet no twentieth-century Sadleir to guide him, he will largely be working in the dark. Authors who have had bibliographies of their works compiled cannot be classed as neglected, though they may not be widely collected. For information about the largely forgotten, the sixty numbers of *Book Collecting & Library Monthly* should be consulted if possible. This periodical, published in London and latterly in Brighton, ran from May 1968 to April 1973 and had a select circulation in Britain and the United States. Its editor, B. Hutchison, was himself a collector of minor twentieth-century books and he supplied in his magazine a great quantity of essential information on novels of his period, including check lists of titles. A complete run of the publication would be an investment that would pay dividends. It is worth looking for in grade (i).

The novice in this field might even discover another Amanda McKittrick Ros, of whose novels Angus Wilson once wrote in *The Spectator*: 'They have probably given more dishonourable pleasure than any works in the English language.' The only editions of Mrs Ros's novels that can be looked for with confidence today are the reprint of the 1897 Belfast edition of *Irene Iddesleigh*, 1,250 copies, Nonesuch Press, 1926, and the 1935 edition of *Delina Delaney*, Chatto & Windus. The 'dishonourable pleasure' comes from the author's unique handling of language and her naive use of incredible situations. When the eponymous heroine of *Delina Delaney* first visits Columba Castle:

> The different shades of a lustrous lounge seemed to spurn at her in sparkling silence; the embossed seats of brilliant brilliancy that rested quietly here and there throughout the room almost taunted her girlish timidity with their blooming laugh of rosebud scorn.

When, later, Lord Gifford examines the corpse of the villainess, Lady Mattie, Mrs Ros in all seriousness makes him exclaim:

> O God, it is true! This is my cousin, Lady Mattie Maynard! She had six toes on her right foot!

Our century has seen a steady decline in the ordinary reader's interest in poetry, yet it has been an age of remarkable poets. The four greatest are probably W. B. Yeats, T. S. Eliot, Ezra Pound and C. M. Grieve (better known under his pseudonym, Hugh MacDiarmid). Of the four, Yeats and Eliot are the most consistent. Yeats's mannered dreaminess rarely dissolves into whimsy and Eliot's preoccupation with desiccation seldom turns to aridity. Pound and Grieve, magnificent at their best, can weary with the dull hum of the axes they have to grind. Those who would collect these four are seeking the best and must pay. The dearest are Eliot and Yeats, some of whose works in ordinary firsts are grade (a), but Pound and MacDiarmid are heading in the same direction.

With £80 or $155 available, it should be possible to obtain the one significant book of Gerard Manley Hopkins (1844–89). Though a nineteenth-century poet, he did not become known until his *Poems*, edited by Robert Bridges, was published in 1918. Since then, Hopkins's effect on English poetry has been all-pervading. Those acknowledging their debt to him include W. H. Auden, Stephen Spender and C. Day Lewis, the late Poet Laureate.

During his formative years, the US poet, Robert Frost, lived in England where his first obtainable book of poems was published—*A Boy's Will*, 1913. The first issue is (G). Though Frost shares Hemingway's insistence on masculinity, he is a nature poet of the highest order who had a vitalizing effect on Edward Thomas (1878–1917), an almost major English poet, hard to collect, though not dear in ordinary first editions—perhaps averaging $16 (just over £8). Thomas was one of several promising poets killed in World War I.

The best of these was Wilfred Owen (1893–1918). His *Poems* edited by Siegfried Sassoon, was first published in 1920 and is (f). Sassoon was himself a poet of the 1914–18 war. His *Counter Attack*, 1918, would now be (h). Rupert Brooke (1887–1915) is the legendary World War I poet. His most celebrated book is *1914 and Other Poems*, 1915, but the rarest is *Lithuania*, 1915. A copy in the original wrappers sold in 1968 in New York for $6,750 (about £2,700 then), but the price has now eased. Robert Graves began as a poet of World War I, but has continued to produce work of an impressive quality. His early firsts are (e) on average.

By the end of the nineteenth century the distinctively American poetic voice had fully matured. Edwin A. Robinson (1860–1935), the poet of Tilbury Town, is typical of the period. His early *Children of the Night*, Boston, 1897, is (B) in a limited edition. Ordinary firsts are (g). This would also be the grading for the works of Carl Sandburg (1878–1967), though his near contemporary, William Carlos Williams (1883–1963), stands rather higher. For some strange reason, that fine poet Vachel Lindsay (1879–1931) is not a first favourite with collectors and is grade (i).

Dylan Thomas (1914–53), who started to write verse in the thirties, became a great literary figure just after World War II. While he had considerable talent, future generations may not grant him quite the position he holds today, when his earliest works are grade (I).

Other important poets of the first half of the century include Edwin Muir (1887–1959), Walter De La Mare (1873–1956) and John Masefield (1878–1966). Roy Campbell (1901–57) also wrote verse. Sir John Betjeman, the present Poet Laureate and still cheerfully productive, would not claim to be the greatest of poets, but his verse is wonderfully evocative of England and the English scene. Among younger writers there are almost as many different schools of poetry as there are poets. Some show great promise, others seem merely to be making private noises in public. Time will tell which are worthy of the bibliophile's attention.

It required his suicide at Minneapolis to bring to the fore John Berryman (1914–1972), a poet whose best work has been considered comparable with that of T. S. Eliot. Berryman's *Homage to Mistress Bradstreet*, 1956, is sought at (g).

5

Fine Books and Illustration

A collector who has gathered together a reasonable number of books may still have a feeling of dissatisfaction. He has done moderately well in his way, yet everything is rather impersonal. His ordinary first editions have brought him near to his favourite authors, but not near enough. This is when he begins to think of presentation copies, signed copies and limited editions associated with their progenitors.

Since the late nineteenth century, the extra desirability of books bearing their authors' signatures or produced in limited editions issued in advance of ordinary firsts, has been emphasized by the leading bibliophiles. Gradually the difference in price between ordinary firsts and those that are signed or limited has increased.

In May 1976, a copy of Bernard Shaw's *The Millionairess*, privately printed in 1935, sold at Hodgsons, London, for £190 ($360). It would not be too difficult to pick up the ordnary first edition of this play, issued in one volume with two others in 1936, for £2 ($3.80). The price difference here is perhaps abnormally wide, because Shaw in ordinary editions is undervalued, but it illustrates—dramatically, it could be said—the financial problems the collector has to face when he graduates to limited, signed or association items.

It was with an eye on the requirements of collectors that the production of limited first editions, signed by their authors, developed in the eighties and nineties of last century. The practice is, of course, much older. An edition of the *De*

Rerum Naturae of Lucretius, published at Leyden in 1725, carries a notice, signed by the editor and printer, that only 800 copies were printed. A poem, *The Rival Lapdog and the Tale*, printed for W. Smith and G. Greg, 1730, would appear to be the first English book in a numbered and signed edition.

From the end of the nineteenth century onwards, signed limited editions are often printed on superior paper and specially bound. They may also be large-paper copies, which means that while the text takes up the same space as in ordinary copies, the pages have much bigger margins. This is an affectation that grew out of the tastes of a vanished race of bibliophiles. When books of an earlier age left the printers, they had been given wide margins so that once the binder got to work he could trim them down with the plough (see Chapter 1) without cutting into the text. The best book-binders did the least trimming, so bibliophiles preferred copies with good margins, particularly in the case of books published in the sixteenth and seventeenth centuries by the Elzevirs, a family of Dutch printers. The family gallicized the name to 'Elsevier' when printing books in French, as in *Le Pastissier François, Amsterdam, chez Louis et Daniel Elsevier*, 1655. This latter form is now widely used elsewhere, but British bibliophiles still favour 'Elzevir'. One well-known early book in English bearing the family imprint, a *Confession of Faith*, 1649, has a third form—'Elsever'. A 'tall Elzevir' became a byword among booksellers. In his book, *The Library*, 1881, Andrew Lang wrote: 'In Elzewirs a line's breadth of margin is often worth a hundred pounds . . . No Elzevir is valuable unless it be clean and large in the margins.' Niggardly margins are unpleasing to the eye. Those that are excessively wide are no better. Yet there are still special editions produced where generosity in this respect is not related to artistic proportions.

Some limited editions of the late nineteenth and early twentieth centuries have most unsatisfactory bindings. While the ordinary editions were cased in honest cloth, their betters

91

were dressed up in boards covered with sugar paper and given undyed canvas backstrips. This looks impressive, but wears badly. The canvas, usually with a fragile paper titling piece, discolours easily and the sugar paper soon becomes rubbed and scored.

Limited editions were especially popular in the twenties. The most clueless of poetasters had their meretricious verses issued at their own expense, with a printed note on a fly-leaf stating that this was the first edition, limited to x copies, signed by the author. Misguided persons sometimes collect these cheaply and end up with nothing that they, or anybody else, will ever want to read except as a penance for mistaken industry.

Contemporaneous with the development of the limited edition was the growth of the private press. In theory, if not always in fact, books from a private press are printed without the use of elaborate machinery, the type being set by hand. The owners of the press may also print for commercial publishers, but their main concern is to produce whatsoever books they choose, as finely and beautifully as they can. Some so-called private presses are really publishers who supervise the production of fine books without themselves doing any printing. Private-press work is almost invariably in limited editions, as it is hardly practical to adapt hand printing to large-scale production.

The first British private press of note was the Strawberry Hill Press, started by Horace Walpole in 1757. The most desirable work of this press is the 1757 edition of the *Odes* of Thomas Gray, whom Walpole patronized. In original condition, this book would be (G). Other early private presses were the Lee Priory Press, founded in 1812 by Sir Samuel Egerton Brydges (1762–1837) and the Auchinleck Press, begun in 1815 by Sir Alexander Boswell (1775–1822), son of James Boswell, Dr Johnson's biographer. Sir Thomas Phillipps gave himself more material to collect by starting his Middle Hill Press in 1822. Though his printers produced some worthy books and pamphlets, the craftsmanship was not always of a high standard. The products of the Daniel Press, founded in 1845, were better, but the beginning of the modern private press was in 1891. In that year, William Morris (1834–96) launched the Kelmscott Press, which set new standards of excellence in English book production. Nowhere is this seen to better advantage than in the Kelmscott edition of Chaucer, with designs by Sir Edward Burne-Jones and published in 1896. The edition was limited to 425, with forty-six copies bound in princely style by T. J. Cobden-Sanderson at the Doves Bindery. These latter are now worth from £5,500 to £6,000 ($10,400 to $11,400) or more each. Cobden-Sanderson joined with Emery Walker to form the Doves Press in 1899 and produced more beautiful books, in a specially designed type. The partnership lasted until World War I. When it was broken, Cobden-Sanderson—in a fit of pique, they say—threw the lovely Doves Press type into the River Thames, whence it has never been recovered.

The Eragny Press was founded in 1894 and in 1895 C. H. St J. Hornby set up the Ashendene Press, which turned out magnificent work until the thirties of this century. The Vale Press was started in 1896, and in 1898 C. R. Ashbee, founder of the Guild of Handicraft, a community of craftsmen, employed some of the Kelmscott pressmen to develop the Essex House Press as part of the Guild's activities. Ashbee designed an extraordinary type, called Endeavour, for his press. It heavily exaggerates the characteristics of the Kelmscott types, but is surprisingly effective in the right context.

Other famous private presses of later foundation are the Shakespeare Head, Nonesuch, Gregynog and Alcuin, with the Golden Cockerel (1921) as the best known of all. Most of these presses have done great service to Spenser, Shakespeare, Milton, Bunyan, Keats, Shelley and writers of like calibre. As illustrators, Eric Gill and Robert Gibbings gave a unique quality to the Golden Cockerel productions and were followed

93

by Sir William Russell Flint and Buckland Wright, whose bosomy ladies effectively decorate the later Golden Cockerels.

In the United States, the Grolier Club of New York played a major role in the revival and development of fine printing and binding. This unique association of dedicated book-lovers and publishers was founded in 1884 with a membership limited to one hundred (later enlarged). It aimed to collect and exhibit outstanding works of the past while issuing new books to serve as examples of the best that modern skill and taste could produce. There was no Morris or Cobden-Sanderson to provide the club with masterpieces. Nevertheless, the early publications achieved a distinction of style and quality that had a galvanic effect on commercial book production. As it was the club's first publication, the 1884 reprint of *A Decree of Starre-Chamber 1637* commands attention and may be (g), but it was the third publication, in 1886, that showed what the club could do. This was an edition of Washington Irving's *History of New York . . . by Diedrich Knickerbocker*, with illustrations by George H. Boughton, Howard Pyle and Will H. Drake. Even better was the Grolier edition of Bishop de Bury's *Philobiblon*, 1889. An inexplicable slackening in demand for these books has brought them within the reach of every collector and ensured that they will be good investments. Later products of the club have been of particular interest to bibliophiles and include the Geoffrey Keynes *Bibliography of William Blake*, 1921, grade (b) and Luther S. Livingston's *Franklin and His Press at Passy*, 1914, (c).

The Grabhorn Press of San Francisco is an outstanding example of a private press in the United States at least indirectly influenced by the Grolier Club. Typography is a subject dear to the hearts of the principals of this press and the student of printing should look out for such Grabhorn products as *Nineteenth Century Type . . . cast by United States Founders now in the Cases of the Grabhorn Press*, 1959, and *The Compleat Jane Grabhorn: A Hodge-Podge of*

Typographical Ephemera, 1968, both (g). The Grabhorn Press has issued many books of a different sort, such as the notable 1930 edition of Whitman's *Leaves of Grass* (H).

The collector who concentrates on private-press books rather than first editions must be prepared to pay highly for the cream. The Ashendene *Don Quixote*, a large folio of 1913, of which 145 copies were printed, would be (F); the special Doves Press version of Milton's *Areopagitica*, twenty-five copies on vellum, 1907, would be (I); the Golden Cockerel *Endymion* by Keats, would be (b), and the Gregynog's famous *Shaw Gives Himself Away*, 1939, also (b). Some lesser productions of these presses are not so expensive, but none is cheap.

Fine printing characterizes the work of the best private presses. Unhappily, the bulk of ordinary British books has not been noted for this. The early English and Scottish printers never reached the standards of their masters on the continent of Europe, though past critics have been too hard on Caxton. The irregularities found in his printing were intended to give the pages the appearance of manuscript and were not the result of bad workmanship. However, the first folio edition of the plays of Shakespeare is typographically unworthy of the great dramatist. The same could be said of the early editions of many of our important writers. John Day (1522–84) was the oustanding printer of his time. It is a matter for regret that his best-known work, the first English edition of John Foxe's *History of the Acts and Monuments of the Church* (Foxe's *Book of Martyrs*), 1563, grade (D) or more if complete, was printed before Day had cast his improved roman and italic types in the 1570s.

No printer of great note appears on the scene until William Caslon (1692–1766), who began by engraving designs on guns. Between 1720 and the year of his death, he cut many founts of type of different kinds, good enough to be sought after by foreign printers. The edition of the *Opera Omnia* of John Selden (C), printed in 1726, is probably the best example of Caslon's craftsmanship.

Chronologically, John Baskerville (1706–75) is next in importance. He served many trades until he turned to printing in his mid-forties. He concerned himself with the whole craft, the quality of paper and ink as well as layout and choice of type. The types he cut were better than anything that had previously been achieved in England. His *Virgil* of 1758 was the first of several masterpieces. It may be only grade (h) in ordinary leather, but some copies were specially bound and these, if not worn, can be (H). Baskerville Bibles, produced in the 1760s and 1770s, are among the few eighteenth-century Bibles of any value—perhaps (f) or (e).

The Foulis brothers, Robert (1707–76) and Andrew (1712–75), of Glasgow, were the first producers of fine books in Scotland. Their printer, Alexander Wilson, designed types rather similar to those of Baskerville, giving the books from the Foulis press a dignity unique in Scottish printing. The Foulis *Horace*, 1744, and *Homer*, four volumes, folio, 1756–8, are outstanding. A fine set of the *Homer* would be (H), but one or two minor Foulis books could be (i).

John Bell (1745–1831) was not a publisher of the first rank. He made an important contribution to European typography, however, when he published his edition of Shakespeare, 1773–5. It was the first considerable work to dispense with the long 's' which so closely resembles an 'f'. Bell and others had eliminated the unnecessary form in earlier books, but it was the Shakespeare which contributed most to its general abandonment.

At the close of the eighteenth century a greater contrast between the thick and thin strokes of printed letters became fashionable and brought about what are called modern-face types, in which the contrast is strongly marked. R. B. McKerrow (*An Introduction to Bibliography*, 1927) suggests 1815 as the date when modern face became really common and declares that the period 1815–44 was perhaps the worst of all from the point of view of type design.

In 1844, Mrs Hannah Mary Rathbone had a book published anonymously by the Chiswick Press for Longman, Brown, Green & Longmans: *So Much of the Diary of Lady Willoughby as Relates to Her Domestic History, & to the Eventful Period of the Reign of Charles the First*. It was written in the archaic language that the title suggests, and to maintain the illusion of antiquity, Charles Whittingham, principal of the Chiswick Press, had a special fount of type cut for the book. He chose Caslon's type as his model, retaining the long 's'. He was so pleased with the result that he used this revived Caslon again in the same year to print an edition of Juvenal for the publisher, William Pickering (1796–1854). Pickering, most of whose books were printed by Whittingham, approved of the new type so it was used again and again— to particularly good effect in Pickering's edition of Milton, eight volumes, 1851. *Lady Willoughby's Diary*, with a second volume published in 1848, may cost £20 ($38) and the Juvenal would be in the same grade. The Milton could be (h), but frequently appears in a fine binding, which adds to the price. The name of the Chiswick Press has continued to be linked with fine printing up to the present.

Following the Whittingham example, types of the Caslon style largely replaced the thick-and-thin modern faces by the middle of the century. Rather confusingly, revived Caslon and similar types are referred to as old-face and old-style although they superseded modern faces. Between the times of Whittingham and Morris, satisfactory developments in book production were few.

Printing in more than one colour goes back to the earliest days. In Germany, Johann Fust and Peter Schoeffer printed a psalter at Mainz. It is the first book to carry a date (1457) and is also the first book with colour printing. This was confined to initial capital letters, executed in red and blue. The letters were cut on wood, and either two blocks were used, one inked in blue for the letter and one in red for the surrounding decoration, or a single block was employed with the two different coloured inks applied to the appropriate areas at the same time.

Probably a two-block system was used for the first English book printed with added colour—*The boke of Hawking, hunting and blasing of arms*, St Albans, 1486, said to be by Dame Juliana Barnes, Bernes or Berners. The coloured illustrations are of coats of arms. A facsimile of this book, edited by William Blades, was published in 1901 and copies might be (h). Notwithstanding this early venture, colour printing was little used until the eighteenth century. Illustrations were mainly black and white.

As with printing, the story of the English illustrated book is uninspiring in the early stages. Illustrations were almost invariably printed from wood blocks. Some have a touch of inspiration and others possess a quaint charm, but none is a work of genius.

The process of reproducing illustrations from engravings on copper plates was known in the first half of the fifteenth century though it is seldom seen in English books before the middle of the seventeenth. Wenceslaus Hollar (1607–77) was a Bohemian who lived in England after the restoration of Charles II. He produced illustrated books that are now highly valued—his *Animals of the Chace*, thirty plates, 1646–7 may be grade (F). He was followed by David Loggan, famous for his bird's-eye views of the ancient English universities: *Cantabrigia Illustrata*, no date, but 1688, and *Oxonia Illustrata*, 1685. Really fine copies merit an (F), but examples where the plates are foxed could be a lot cheaper. Both books are too often savaged by breakers, about whom more later.

The first great English book illustrator is William Hogarth (1697–1764). He did a series of engravings for the three parts of *Hudibras*, a long satirical poem by Samuel Butler (1612–80). The first editions of the parts appeared in 1663, 1664 and 1678, but the first Hogarth edition was 1726. It has been somewhat neglected and should be grade (h). Hogarth's other important series of book illustrations was for an edition of *Don Quixote*, (i) unaccountably cold-shouldered.

Hogarth's inclination towards caricature was developed by many of his successors, but a more refined influence came from Hubert-François Bourguignon (1699–1773), whose *nom-de-guerre* was Gravelot. A Parisian, he lived in London for fifteen years and illustrated many English books, including a 12mo edition of Dryden's *Dramatick Works*, six volumes, 1735, and, with F. Hayman, the mixed sixth and third edition of Richardson's *Pamela*, four volumes, 12mo, 1742. Gravelot's elegant style is never insipid.

Though the work of Francis Hayman (1708–1776) shows the influence of his friend Hogarth, it more closely resembles that of Gravelot. His engravings may be found in Smollett's *The Adventures of Roderick Random*, second edition, two volumes, 12mo, 1748, and Christopher Smart's *Poems on Several Occasions*, 4to, 1752, as well as in other books of the time. As a first edition, the Christopher Smart would be (b), possibly; but Hayman illustrations are to be found in quite cheap items. There is a delightful rococo touch to the engravings of Anthony Walker (1726–65). He contributed headpieces and vignettes to several publications, but his work is at its best in his seven illustrations for William Somerville's poem, *The Chace*, in the fourth edition of 1757 (i).

The spirit of Hogarth is manifest in the work of Thomas Rowlandson (1756–1827). When the German–English publisher Rudolf Ackermann (1764–1834) projected his *Microcosm of London*, three large volumes of coloured illustrations of public buildings and places, he commissioned an architect, A. C. Pugin (1762–1832), to draw the buildings and Rowlandson to supply the foreground figures. The arrangement worked well. The dignity of Pugin is balanced by the liveliness of Rolandson. *The Microcosm*, published in 1806–8, is a much sought work and a regular victim of the breakers. It is now (A). Rowlandson's most popular work is his series of coloured aquatints for the *Tours of Doctor Syntax*, three long poems by William Combe (1741–1823), who is not otherwise remembered. The three tours were first published in 1812, 1820 and 1821, and ran into many editions, with the Rowlandson illustrations. A sound set of the three firsts would be (G), but later sets of mixed editions might be had in the (b) or (c) grades. As was more or less standard practice at the time, the Rowlandson books were coloured by hand. Colour-printing improvements were still to come.

Rowlandson's mantle fell on George Cruikshank (1792–1878). Most people know him as the illustrator of Dickens's *Oliver Twist*, but he was a prolific artist whose work spans many years. No better examples of his illustrations are to be found than those in the English translation of the Grimm Brothers' *German Popular Stories*, published in two volumes, 1823–6, with twenty Cruikshank plates. Together, the volumes are probably (d), if entirely free from the foxing which so often disfigures them. Cruikshank collectors can start more humbly. Plenty of books with his illustrations may be had under £5 (say $10).

Hablot K. Browne (1815–82), who usually signed himself Phiz, was Dickens's chief illustrator. His work has still the Hogarthian element of grotesque, but lacks Cruikshank's fierce concentration. He worked for many others besides Dickens, so his illustrations are easily found in Victorian novels of differing standards. John Leech (1817–64), who did the pictures for Dickens's *A Christmas Carol*, 1843, had a similar style and also illustrated most of R. S. Surtees's hunting novels; his work is industriously collected by the English sporting fraternity, who, attracted by the hand-coloured plates, pay to (d) and beyond for first editions.

After Cruikshank, Browne and Leech, some of the guts went out of book illustration, as can be seen by comparing the original illustrations for Dickens's *Our Mutual Friend*, 1864–5, by Marcus Stone, with those of *Oliver Twist* or *David Copperfield*. Samuel Palmer (1805–81) did some good work, but is more famous in other artistic fields, as is Birket

Engraving techniques used for book illustration:
Plate 5 (above)   The Stag– perhaps the most decorative of the wood engravings in Thomas Bewick's *The General History of Quadrupeds*, Newcastle, 1790.

Plate 6   A steel engraving in vignette form, after J. M. W. Turner, from Samuel Rogers's *Italy*, 1838.

"A gentleman in kharki."

Plate 7 This striking illustration by Caton Woodville is the centrepiece of the three folded leaves which make up the first separate edition of Rudyard Kipling's 'The Absent-Minded Beggar', published by the 'Daily Mail' in 1899 (see the Glossary of terms used in book collecting, under 'first printing' – p. 261).

Foster, who produced some pleasant rustic pictures for equally pleasant rustic books.

The great era of the topographical engraving was the first half of the nineteenth century. Francis Grose (1731–91) made a tour of England and Wales in the latter part of the eighteenth century and as a result published his *Antiquities of England and Wales*, 1773–87, lavishly illustrated with copper engravings of old churches and other buildings. A tour of Scotland in 1789 brought him the friendship of Burns (they were both fond of bawdry and the bottle) and produced *The Antiquities of Scotland*, which incidentally contains the first printing of Burns's *Tam o' Shanter*. Grose died while working on a similar book for Ireland, but it was duly produced in the year of his death. A complete set of the *Antiquities*, in ten volumes, should be (H).

Grose's success set a pattern frequently followed in the next century, further encouraged by the invention of steel engraving, capable of giving finer gradations of tone than copper. Between 1803 and 1814, John Britton (1771–1857) and E. W. Brayley (1773–1854) issued *The Beauties of England and Wales* in eighteen volumes full of topographical engravings. Complete sets are now (g). Britton on his own, or with other collaborators, produced several other similar books. William Beattie and W. H. Bartlett were associated with similar works covering Scotland, Switzerland and other more distant parts of the world. Between 1845 and 1852, R. W. Billings (1813–74) published his *Baronial and Ecclesiastical Antiquities of Scotland* in four volumes, which would be no bad bargain if they were in the (e) grade. One of the most attractive books of topographical illustrations is William Daniell's and Richard Ayton's *Voyage Round Great Britain*, eight volumes, 1814–25, containing 308 hand-coloured aquatints. This could cost over £5,000 ($9,500).

Conservationists in the book world fear that many of these volumes containing topographical illustrations will soon become extinct. It is still profitable for 'specialists' to remove

103

the plates, mount them and sell them individually. As an undiscerning public prefers its twopence coloured to its penny plain, profits are enhanced if original black and white engravings are given a discreet lick of watercolour. There can be little harm in removing the plates from a book that is hopelessly incomplete or beyond repair, but to ravish sound copies is little short of criminal. Those who are against conservation argue that the plates are almost always the only features of the books worth preserving, the texts being dull, out of date or inaccurate. By selling the illustrations individually they are spreading around the pleasurable aspects of the books. No doubt the pros and cons will continue to be advanced till there are no such books left intact.

The greatest English book illustrators of all were William Blake (1757–1827) and Thomas Bewick (1753–1828). Even the best of the botanical illustrators, who will be dealt with later and achieved more spectacular results, are not quite in the same class. Blake was poet, artist, engraver and mystic all in one. If his draughtsmanship was sometimes defective, this was more than compensated for by the visionary power that shines through everything he did. Only those who have seen the originals can fully appreciate the enchanting beauty of his *Songs of Innocence*, 1789, or the grandeur of his twenty-one *Illustrations to the Book of Job*, prepared and published in 1826, when he was an old man. Original editions of Blake's major works are liable to rise above £4,000 ($7,600) in the salerooms. The best of the coloured facsimiles, produced at various times are (f) or above. Copies of Blair's *The Grave*, 1808, and Young's *The Complaint, or Night Thoughts*, 1797, with Blake illustrations, may be graded (a) and (F) respectively.

Thomas Bewick, was more mundane than Blake, though there is nothing cloddish in the execution of his celebrated woodcuts, despite the earthy nature of some of the subjects. Apart from his *British Birds* and *Quadrupeds* (see Chapter 9), his best-known book is his edition of Aesop's *Fables*, Newcastle, 1818. A satisfactory copy might be had in grade (b). Not every woodcut in the Aesop is the work of Bewick, for he had several pupils who learnt to engrave in his style and worked with him before setting up for themselves. None ever developed the same feeling for the medium that the master possessed. Bewick and alleged Bewick plates are found in many books of the late eighteenth and early nineteenth centuries. They are among the rewards of the diligent hunter.

Bewick confined himself to black and white, although he was convinced that satisfactory colour printing from wood was a possibility. It was left to George Baxter (1804–67) to show how it could be done. Three-colour printing from metal plates was practised by James Le Blon as far back as 1720, but his was a laborious and expensive process, scarcely applicable to ordinary book illustration. Baxter, following up experiments by others, tried to print from wood blocks using a watercolour medium. After further trials, he adopted oil colours and found them more rewarding. He then combined the use of metal plates for the basic drawing, with wood blocks for the area of colour.

His first important achievements in book illustration were two coloured prints in *The Feathered Tribes of the British Islands*, 1834, by Robert Mudie. He did some more book work, but later concentrated on producng individual prints. He granted licences to other firms to use his process, one of them being Kronheim & Co of London, who did much colour printing for books, sometimes by cruder processes than Baxter's.

If the Mudie is too dear in grade (f), pleasure can be more cheaply bought in collecting less important books with Baxter, Kronheim or sometimes Le Blond (no connection with the Le Blon mentioned earlier) coloured illustrations.

While Baxter was experimenting, others were trying to produce illustrations in full colour by lithography, in which the prints are taken from a special type of stone. At first it was difficult for lithographers to get subtle gradations of tone, but this was no disadvantage as far as Owen Jones (1809–74) was concerned. He was interested in reproducing flat designs in colour, so chromolithography, as colour lithography is called, suited his purposes admirably. Jones, who became superintendent of works for the 1851 Exhibition in London, worked in association with H. Noel Humphreys (1810–79) to produce many beautiful illuminated books, some of them bound in carved wood, some in charmingly absurd *papier maché*.

The great Humphreys-Jones work is *Illuminated Books of the Middle Ages*, 1849, splendidly coloured and gilded, and (H) in top condition. Jones's *Grammar of Ornament*, 1865, may be (a), but later editions, usually loose within their covers because of perished gutta-percha bindings, or else rebound, should be available upwards from £12 ($23). Later chromoliothographic refinements made possible the reproduction of many handsome colour plates in the better books of about a hundred years ago. In some methods of lithography, where oil colours were used (oleolithography), the colours took a long time to dry, which caused the illustrations to remain sticky after they were bound into the book, so that they adhered firmly to the neighbouring leaves of the text. All such books should be inspected carefully. If text and illustrations are stuck together there is no known way of separating them without doing irreparable damage.

Randolph Caldecott (1846–86) was an artist who often availed himself of the opportunities of colour printing. Between 1878 and 1885 he produced a series of sixteen picture books for children, full of bright illustrations. A good complete set would be (f), though prices are showing an upward trend. He had something of John Leech's zest, but his characters are more genial—they are sleek-headed men, such as sleep o' nights.

When Caldecott died he had just begun to illustrate a series of books for Macmillan, the publisher. His work here, in black and white, was continued and developed by Hugh Thomson, an artist who delighted in the costumes and settings of the Regency. His illustrations have more grace than vigour and are to be seen at their most charming in more than one edition of Jane Austen.

Though the development of book illustration in North America followed much the same lines as it did in Britain, there are some divergences. F. O. C. Durley (1822–88) was the counterpart of Hablot Browne, but his younger contemporaries and immediate successors maintained his kind of vigour when they illustrated life and events around them. Winslow Homer (1836–1910) was, among greater things, an early pictorial journalist. His folio of two portraits and sixteen tinted lithographs, *Proceedings at the Reception in Honor of George Peabody*, Boston, Massachusetts, 1856, is a fair sample of his work in this sphere and is grade (b). The sense of history in the making was well maintained by Frederic Remington (1861–1949) who followed. His *Pony Tracks*, New York, 1895, is only one of several books that he produced around the turn of the century, all of them collected and worth looking for in the (f) to (b) grades. Howard Pyle (1853–1911) and E. A. Abbey (1852–1911) were contemporaries of the Ulsterman, Hugh Thomson, and drew in a similar style. One of Pyle's most successful books was *The Merry Adventures of Robin Hood*, New York, 1883. The subject gave full scope for his talents and the book is justifiably grade (g). His folio edition of Goldsmith's *She Stoops to Conquer*, New York, 1887, is not far up grade (i), though it deserves a place in every collection of North American book illustration. Perhaps it has suffered by comparison with the later (undated) and admittedly more elegant Hugh Thomson *She Stoops*, which sells readily on both sides of the Atlantic in (f) in the limited edition.

Working at the same time as Thomson was Aubrey Beardsley (1872–98), whose cool passion is in such contrast to Thomson's slightly artificial charm. Beardsley accomplished much in his short life, beginning with illustrations in the Pre-Raphaelite manner for an edition of Malory in

1893–4, probably grade (H) in the original twelve parts. His work ended with some illustrations for Ben Jonson's *Volpone*, 1898, grade (g). As an interpreter of end-of-century decadence, through his skilful economy of line blended with a wealth of two-dimensional decoration, Beardsley had no equal. His work yearly increases in value.

Sir Max Beerbohm, a product of the same age, was a clever penman in a different way. His caricatures of the great people of his day are never savage, but always amusingly to the point. He was much more than a cartoonist and apart from his books of drawings he produced many essays, short stories and a bizarre novel, *Zuleika Dobson*, 1911. No wonder Bernard Shaw dubbed him 'the incomparable Max'. His books of drawings are in grades (i) and (h), but a fine first of *Zuleika* would be (g).

Towards the end of last century, when it became possible to reproduce line drawings without first cutting them on wood, encouragement was given to a new race of topographical illustrators, among the best of whom were E. H. New and F. L. Griggs. New was an Evesham man, brought up in the shadow of the Cotswolds. Something of the mellowness of Cotswold stone is apparent in his fine drawings.

F. L. Griggs (1876–1938) was born and spent his early years in Hertfordshire, but he too fell under the Cotswold spell and made his home in Chipping Campden, loveliest of the small Cotswold towns. He trained as an architect, but in taking to pen-and-ink drawing he was influenced by Samuel Palmer. His illustrations can be seen in such books as a 1902 edition of *The Sensitive Plant* by P. B. Shelley, *A Book of Cottages and Little Houses* by C. R. Ashbee, 1906, and *The Villages of England* by A. K. Wickham, 1932. Collectors have only recently woken up to Griggs, so many of the books he illustrated may not be available cheaply for much longer. His *Ernest Gimson: His Life and Work*, Shakespeare Head Press, 1924, and *Campden*, same publisher, 1938, are now both (a).

In the twenties, when Griggs was turning from book illustration to the production of some of the finest etchings of the century, a new school of wood-engravers was springing up, led by Eric Gill, Robert Gibbings, John Farleigh and others. They brought a novel emphasis to the technique of white line on black, first devised by Bewick. English wood-engraved illustration reached a peak in the thirties, then declined. No other form of engraving marries so well with clean, well-defined type. The illustrators and typographers of today seem incapable of turning out books with the unassertive dignity of those of that heyday of wood engraving.

Though the best examples are to be seen in limited editions by the Golden Cockerel and other private presses, there are plenty for the modest collector to work on. A first edition of Bernard Shaw's *The Adventures of the Black Girl in Her Search for God*, 1932, should cost no more than £5 ($9.50) in brilliant condition. Unfortunately, it was issued in paper boards, which have not stood the test of time. Worn copies should be avoided.

Line drawing is the basis of much modern illustration and has many competent exponents. One of the most pleasing illustrators in line was John Minton, who would undoubtedly have developed his technique had he lived. He is easily and cheaply collected. Most of the books he illustrated are still found on the ordinary shelves of secondhand booksellers. They include H. E. Bates's *The Country Heart*, 1949 (not later editions), Reginald Arkell's *Old Herbaceous*, 1950, and Elizabeth David's *French Country Cooking*, 1951.

An earlier and highly individualistic exponent of line drawing was Jessie Marion King (1876–1949). She was a disciple of Charles Rennie Mackintosh (1868–1928), the great Scottish art nouveau architect and designer. Some of her illustrations are sometimes excessively sweet and 'twee', but all have the weird fascination of the art nouveau. In describing himself as a lover of 'Jessie at her dottiest', Sir John Betjeman is referring to her technique of sprinkling her drawings with tiny leaves, pebbles, blossoms or anything that

109

would display her Hopkins-like love of dappled things. The essential Jessie M. King is to be found in a 1906 edition of Milton's *Comus*. Much of her work was done for quite obscure little books, published by the Glasgow firm of Gowans & Gray, and T&N Foulis, of Edinburgh and London. Since the first edition of this book was published, with its mention of Jessie King, she has become much more widely collected. The *Comus*, bought for £6 ($11.50) in 1972, would now be a bargain at £25 (just under $48).

A really inviting private library is one where the variety of books is immediately apparent. There are rows of modern volumes, immaculate in their dustwrappers, books of last century in cloth that still looks fresh, some items in original boards, mostly protected in cases, and some rather battered books of all periods, well, rather than badly worn—for much-used books wear differently from those that are the victims of neglect. There will also be some books more or less handsomely bound in leather.

Leatherbound books are still bought indiscriminately for their decorative qualities and there are still those who imagine that such library furniture can be had by the yard for a small outlay. Today, status seekers pay highly for any sort of rubbishy printed matter contained within attractive calf or morocco leather.

In face of the competition, the serious collector of fine craftsman bindings has to pay a small fortune for the items he wants. Beginners are warned that this branch of bibliophily is full of boobytraps.

However, it is possible to secure some pleasing leather or half-leather bindings of the eighteenth and nineteenth centuries, containing readable matter within grade (i). A few of these bindings may have binders' tickets on the front pastedown endpapers—little labels with legends like 'Bound by LYON, *WIGAN*'. Here is a challenge to the inquiring mind. The collector can have fun by consulting old trade directories and pestering local librarians to gain more information about those old bookbinders.

A collector whose chosen period is the nineteenth century will inevitably have on his shelves something of a review of the history of publishers' cloth; he can make himself an amateur of cloth bindings as well as following his main line. The earliest authentic examples of original cloth bindings are probably on some volumes of Pickering's Diamond Classics, issued in calico about 1822.

Brander Matthews, in his *Bookbindings, Old and New*, London and New York, 1896, states: 'I have among my Sheridaniana the third edition of Dr Watkins's *Memoirs of the Public and Private Life of the Right Honourable Richard Brinsley Sheridan*, printed for Henry Colburn in 1818, and both volumes are clad in glazed calico . . . The date of the biography is that of the binding.' Despite this statement, the matter is open to doubt. Brander Matthews's copy may have lain unbound in the publisher's warehouse for several years before being sent for retail in calico. John Carter studied the subject of cloth bindings from many angles and consulted the records kept by publishers of the early nineteenth century. He refused to date the introduction of cloth further back than 1820, declaring that 'inferences of early date drawn from books themselves can only be made with extreme caution'— *Publishers' Cloth, 1820–1900*, New York and London, 1935.

Anybody with a genuine interest in fine bindings will not be content to treat the subject purely as ancient history. The paper dust-wrapper has largely destroyed the incentive that gave us brightly designed covers on ordinary books, but there are still craftsmen at work who can clothe books in leather and gold as well as could any of the masters before them. It should be a duty and pleasure for the true bibliophile to have at least one of his books bound by a capable binder, not as a job of restoration, but as a tribute to some admirable modern book. A fine morocco or calf binding will be expensive, but if the work is entrusted to the right person, it will be a thing of beauty and a joy for ever—or for at least three hundred years.

111

6

Adventure, Detection and Children's Books

The universal love of a good story made inevitable the creation of the novel. When it arrived, and for many years after, the reading public was prepared to wait while the novelist put down his knitting, as it were, and discussed the beauties of nature, the vanities of human wishes or almost anything else that came into his head. In time authors became aware that some of their readers did not welcome digression, but wanted the strands of narrative to be kept on the move to produce a compact, well-knit whole. So emerged the 'rattling good yarn'—the kind of adventure story which, free from digression, drives the reader along at a spanking pace from beginning to end. Novels which tell, as Othello did, 'of moving accidents by flood and field, of hair-breadth 'scapes i' the imminent deadly breach' are as old as the medium itself. Defoe's *Robinson Crusoe* and *Captain Singleton*, though pretended true stories, are outstanding examples. But they move at the pace of stately baroque carriages, which may lumber and jolt, but never get up enough speed to rattle. Collectors of these and of the later eighteenth-century picaresque novels which they foreshadowed would regard themselves as workers in the main stream of literature. The collector of adventure novels is usually one concerned with the tighter-knit writings of a later period.

The growth of the adventure novel was no sudden thing

and no dates can be given. The shape of things to come may be discerned in *Lorna Doone* by R. D. Blackmore (1825–1900). This novel had plenty of action, even if some parts get bogged down in the Exmoor clay. The first edition, published in 1869 in three volumes, was accepted to begin with as no more than a good average historical novel, yet the terseness of the writing at the 'exciting bits' seems to have had an effect, for its first appearance coincides with the English novel's departure from long-windedness. He who wants to read *Lorna Doone* in his own copy of the first edition must expect it to be (H).

The development of the railways played a part in the rise of the short direct novel of adventure. Bookstalls were quite early established at the larger railway stations, where intending passengers could buy books to while away their journeys. Many of the novels sold were single-volume reprints of the bulky three-deckers, but not all of these were suitable for railway journeys. With a growing demand for fairly short, light novels, authors arose to satisfy it. The first efforts were, for the most part, poorly written, but the quality gradually improved.

By the end of the 1880s, the rattling good yarn was showing well above the horizon. The appropriately named *Dawn* by H. Rider Haggard (1856–1925) was published in 1884 and his *King Solomon's Mines* appeared the following year. *She* and *Allan Quartermain* date from 1887 and thereafter the Rider Haggard output was well maintained. The points of some of his first editions are tricky, and first editions are between the (h) and (b) grades according to relative scarcity, with prices rather higher in England than in North America.

The year 1894 brought a new phase with *The Prisoner of Zenda* by Anthony Hope (Sir Anthony Hope Hawkins, 1863–1933). This was the original Ruritanian romance, for Hope invented the kingdom of Ruritania for this novel. He repeated his success with the sequel, *Rupert of Hentzau*, in 1898, leaving the stage ready set for a host of imitative stories. *Rupert of Hentzau* is easy to identify in a first edition, but *The Prisoner of Zenda* should have the misspelling 'imposter' on line 7 of page 112, the misprint 'hree' for 'three' on the last line of page 296, and there should be only seventeen titles in the list of books advertised at the end. Both novels have much the same value as firsts, being (h).

With *Monsieur Beaucaire*, New York, 1900, Booth Tarkington developed another type of historical romance, deriving from Alexandre Dumas *père*, but slimmed down. One of its most important subsequent practitioners was Baroness Orczy (1865–1947) with her Scarlet Pimpernel novels: *The Scarlet Pimpernel*, 1905, *I Will Repay*, 1906, *Eldorado*, 1913, and *Sir Percy Hits Back*, 1927. The Booth Tarkington novel may be grade (h), but the Orczys should be below £10 or $20 each.

Though his early work has affinities with Stevenson and Kipling, John Buchan (1875–1940) soon developed a stiff-upper-lipped style of his own, emergent in *Prester John*, 1910, and fully matured in the Richard Hannay novels: *The Thirty-Nine Steps*, 1915, *Greenmantle*, 1916, and *Mr Standfast*, 1919. These are only a few from Buchan's large output, now popular with collectors and showing a marked rise in price in the past few years. The scarcer titles are (h).

Since Rousseau's day, the noble savage has had many literary manifestations. In 1914 he was given a Nietzschean twist by Edgar Rice Burroughs, who created a wild white superman as hero of *Tarzan of the Apes*. Though not a work of great literary merit, the book is a favourite with collectors of popular fiction and the first edition is (h). The later Tarzan books are (i). Mention should be made of the phenomenally successful *Ben Hur*, New York, 1880, by General Lew Wallace (1827–1905). This novel brought together religion and adventure as never before. However, first editions are not rare and could still be found below grade (h).

The picaresque novel, which flourished in the eighteenth century, is well exemplified in the works of Smollett and can be regarded as a form of adventure fiction even if it is hardly within the 'rattling good yarn' classification. Captain Frederick Marryat (1792–1848), however, with his rather purified picaresque tales, is almost in the 'rattling good' classification. Some of his works offer a challenge to the collector. In 1951, Sadleir wrote that several of Marryat's firsts were almost undiscoverable in any condition. Now the position has worsened and only the indomitable spirit of the hardened collector prevents him from writing off for ever such rarities as *The Naval Officer*, three volumes, 1839. If a copy, complete in original boards and in acceptable condition, were auctioned in any of the well-known salesrooms it might rise above (A). Of Marryat's works, *Diary of a Blasé*, Philadelphia, 1836, *Jacob Faithful*, Philadelphia and Baltimore, 1833–4, and *Stories of the Sea*, New York, 1836, have American first editions in advance of the first English publications.

In his two novels of the sea, Michael Scott (1789–1835) shows a literary kinship with Marryat. Both novels were first published anonymously, *Tom Cringle's Log*, two volumes, Edinburgh and London, 1833, and *The Cruise of the Midge*, two volumes, Edinburgh and London, 1836. As a first edition, each occurs in two different bindings, of which the priority has never been established. Michael Scott is not in demand now. Michael Sadleir's copy of *The Cruise of the Midge* sold for only £20 ($38) in 1975 and the price has not advanced much further since then.

This summing-up of adventure fiction touches only the fringe. The field is almost unlimited and there is much readable material still available at almost shamefully low prices.

Detective stories may be so crammed with adventure that the books that contain them are likely to crack at the joints, but they are put in a separate class by most collectors. The first acknowledged detective story is Edgar Allan Poe's *The Murders in the Rue Morgue*, 1841. This masterpiece of its kind—as fabulously expensive as the other Poe items—did

115

not set an immediate trend in North America.

Soon the detective story was independently created in England. London's real-life detective force came into being in 1845, when twelve policemen were seconded for plain-clothes work. Five years later, the good journalist Dickens wrote about the force in his magazine *Household Words*, but did not at once grasp the fictional possibilities. In 1852, however, Mr Bucket, the detective, appeared in Dickens's *Bleak House*, which nevertheless cannot be greeted as England's first detective novel since the main interest is not in a crime and its solution. Towards the end of the fifties, there came a spate of railway yellow-backs dealing with the reminiscences of former detectives, authentic and otherwise. The first of these recorded by Sadleir is *Recollections of a Detective Police Officer*, 1856, by 'Waters' (William Russell, alias also 'Lt Warneford'). Sadleir lists many similar books from that year onwards.

The first English full-length detective novel of consequence was *The Moonstone*, three volumes, 1868, by Wilkie Collins (1824–89). Naturally the first edition is assiduously hunted down. The first issue, distinguished by the misprint 'treachesrouly' on page 129 of volume two, is (H). After Collins's success, the detective novel of quality became established in England. Dickens's *The Mystery of Edwin Drood*, 1870, would probably have resolved itself into a first rate example had the author lived to complete it.

It took some time for the form to recross the Atlantic. Allan Pinkerton (1819–84) helped by publishing at Chicago in 1874 *The Expressman and the Detective*, for which he drew on his own experiences as a private agent. This book is (g). Within three years, the American output of detective fiction was rivalling the English. In 1878, America produced the first of a long line of women crime writers, Anna Katherine Green, with her *The Leavenworth Case*. She had an extensive literary career, for her last novel, *The Step on the Stair*, was published at New York in 1923. In 1879, another woman writer in the medium emerged. *Shadowed by Three* by Lawrence L. Lynch was published at Chicago in the same year. The masculine ring of the author's name is false. Lawrence L. Lynch was the pseudonym of Mrs M. van Deventer. The works mentioned in this paragraph should be grade (g) or below.

Early efforts lack the refinements of the later whodunnits. The man who brought a new dimension to the detective novel was Sir Arthur Conan Doyle (1859–1930), creator of Sherlock Holmes. Holmes stole quietly on the scene between the pages of *Beeton's Christmas Annual 1887*. This annual is graded (D) because it contains the first printing of the first Holmes story, *A Study in Scarlet*. The next year, this appeared as a book, in wrappers, as scarce as the annual and also (D). None of the other Holmes books commands so high a price. Some of the others could be graded thus: *The Adventures of Sherlock Holmes*, 1892, (a); *The Memoirs of Sherlock Holmes*, 1894, (c); *The Hound of the Baskervilles*, 1902, (f).

Fergus W. Hume (*d*1932) also contributed to the whodunnit revolution in writing *The Mystery of a Hansom Cab*, first published at Melbourne in 1887. The 5,000 copies of this paperbound edition were sold out in three weeks and a second edition was equally successful. Hume then parted with the rights to a syndicate called 'The Hansom Cab Publishing Company', which took the book to London, where the first English edition of 25,000 copies, in black-and-white pictorial wrappers, was issued in 1888. As Hume had no connection with the syndicate, all he received for the English and American rights was £50. He came to London in 1889 and after 500,000 copies of the original editions had been issued, he brought out a revised edition (Jarrold & Sons, no date), which sold well and can sometimes be found on bargain shelves. Though it is not regarded as a collector's edition it is important in that the author's preface gives the true history of the book for the first time.

One of the mysteries of this mystery is that no copies of

the first Melbourne edition or of the first London edition ever appear on the market. The earliest known London edition is marked 'seventy-fifth thousand' and is grade (f). It may be that this is in fact the first London edition and that 'seventy-fifth thousand' was printed on it to boost sales.

The success of Sherlock Holmes encouraged the appearance of whole packs of eccentric sleuths, but the public had to wait till 1907 before an investigator appeared who could have discussed crime with Holmes as an equal—R. Austin Freeman's Dr Thorndyke, who made his debut in *The Red Thumb Mark*, first published in black paper wrappers and in black cloth, the front cover in both styles bearing a red thumbprint. Copies in either form are rare, making it almost impossible to predict the price of the next copy to come to light.

The twentieth century saw detective fiction become popular as never before. G. K. Chesterton (1874–1936) struck a new note in 1911 with *The Innocence of Father Brown*, grade (h). This would also be the rating of *Trent's Last Case*, 1913, by E. C. Bentley (1875–1956). Some other Trent cases appeared in the *Strand* magazine during 1914, but did not appear in book form until 1928, in *Great Short Stories of Mystery, Detection and Horror*, edited by Dorothy Sayers (1893–1957). In 1936 there appeared the full-length *Trent's Own Case* by Bentley and H. Warner Allen. Because it was not published until long after the other Trent stories, it is often overlooked. Firsts are uncommon, but should be found for under £8 ($15.50).

Dorothy Sayers was a brilliant writer in the medium and her aristocratic amateur detective, Lord Peter Wimsey, is back in favour. Though still fairly low (i), prices of her firsts are rising. *Whose Body?*, the first Peter Wimsey novel, was published at New York in 1923 and takes priority over the first English edition.

Edgar Wallace (1875–1932) was probably the most prolific writer in English in the twenties. Though his name is

118

Plate 8 'Jessie at her dottiest': an Art Nouveau illustration by Jessie M. King from an edition of Milton's *Comus* published by Routledge, London, and Dutton, New York, in 1906 (see p. 110).

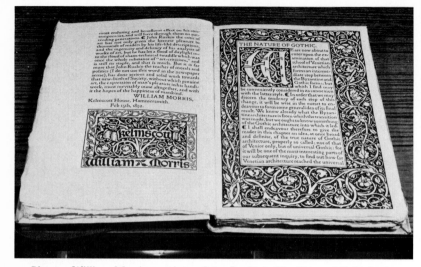

Plate 9 William Morris as printer: John Ruskin's *The Nature of Gothic* in the Kelmscott Press edition of 1892. The page on the left shows the end of Morris's introduction and the Kelmscott colophon. On the right is the first page of Ruskin's text, decorated by Morris.

Plate 10 Beatrix Potter's *The Tale of Benjamin Bunny* at pages 14 and 15. In this copy the text has 'muffetees' misspelt 'muffatees' at p. 15, line 10. This is accepted as evidence of the first issue of the first edition, Warne, 1907 (see p. 131). © Frederick Warne & Co, London.

associated with detection, he wrote comparatively few whodunnits, but many thrillers. To say that his work is uneven is putting it mildly, but the sheer volume of his output has obscured the genuine merits of his best books. A collector could give himself a lifetime's work in trying to acquire all that Wallace published and making up his own mind about the best. He would have the help of *The British Bibliography of Edgar Wallace*, 1969, by W. O. G. Lofts and Derek Adley. But Wallace was also popular in the United States (he created and provided the film script for *King Kong*), and there is little bibliographical help to be had for the US publications.

From being an intellectual exercise tricked out with thrills and horrors, the detective story has recently become more of a study in violence. Collectors must decide for themselves whether the bulk of detective fiction from the fifties onwards should be grouped with the earlier whodunnits.

Though they were not specifically addressed to the juvenile market, almost all the adventure novels above and some of the detective stories can be enjoyed by older children. So, too, can certain other novels, hard to classify but best considered as fairy tales written from an adult angle. Among these are *Vice Versa*, 1882, and *The Brass Bottle*, 1900, by F. Anstey (Thomas Anstey Guthrie, 1856–1934); *The Sword in the Stone*, 1939, and *Mistress Masham's Repose*, 1947, by T. H. White (1906–62) and J. R. R. Tolkien's Hobbit stories, comprising *The Hobbit, or There and Back Again*, 1937, *The Fellowship of the Ring*, 1954, *The Two Towers*, 1954, and *The Return of the King*, 1955. Most of these would be low in grade (i), but the Tolkiens are becoming expensive. *The Hobbit* is moving into (a) and the others may well be (h).

Modern fantasy has largely turned away from the faerie. The *sidh*, the good folk, the elves, trolls, nymphs and fauns have been replaced by aerial octopodes, predatory parsnips, venomous Venereans (Venusians to 'nice' people, but not to nice Latinists) and other unromantic things from outer space.

Do what we will, science fiction is 'in' and is attracting many collectors.

As one of the earliest and most accomplished writers in the field, H. G. Wells is first on many collectors' lists. His *The War in the Air*, 1908 is (I), with *The War of the Worlds*, 1898, apparently moving into the same grade. Other titles, such as *Tales of Space and Time*, 1900, *The Time Machine*, 1895, and *In the Days of the Comet*, 1906, are heading for (b). The North American, H. P. Lovecraft, who owes something to Poe, also commands attention. His *The Outsider and Others*, Sauk City, 1939, is (e) in the ordinary edition and (a) in the limited. The books of Robert E. Howard, another American, are moving upwards. His *Skull-face and Others*, Sauk City, 1946, could not be safely graded much below the Lovecraft books.

The SF pulp magazines from the United States are enjoying a vogue. Good long runs of *Amazing Stories*, New York, 1926 onwards, and *Astounding Stories*, New York, 1930 onwards, go for $600 (about £320). At this price they must have most of their original pictorial wrappers intact, for these have considerable pop-art appeal.

Had the monsters of SF been known to Mrs Sarah Trimmer (1741–1810), she would soon have sent them off with fleas in their ears. Exposing children to the evils of fantasy was a crime in her eyes. She described *Cinderella* as one of the worst stories for children ever written, depicting the vilest of human passions—jealousy, vanity and a love of dress. This was the view of many serious-minded people of her generation. To them, fairy stories were pernicious rubbish printed on broadsides and in chapbooks and peddled by low persons.

In *The History of the Robins*, 1786, Mrs Trimmer showed what she thought was suitable to the juvenile mind. She allowed birds to converse as humans, strictly to instil moral lessons. Mother Robin reproves her young with: 'Are these the sentiments that subsist in a family which ought to be bound together by love and kindness? Which of you has cause to reproach either your father or me with partiality? Do we not, with the exactest equality, distribute the fruits of our labours among you?'

As a period piece, this book, even in grade (g), would be a welcome addition to the library of a serious collector of children's books, but a modern child would not sacrifice a day's pocket money for it. So with masses of the juvenile literature of the eighteenth century. Dr John Aikin (1747–1822) and his sister, Mrs Anna Letitia Barbauld (1743-1825), jointly wrote *Evenings at Home; or, The Juvenile Budget Opened*, three volumes, 12mo, 1793–4. Despite the cosy title, this is another pompously edifying work, mostly made up of dialogues between an earnest tutor and his two pupils. The tutor has a way of luring the boys off on country walks to lower their resistance, then pumping them full of knowledge. 'When you have cooled yourself,' he tells them on one expedition, 'you may drink out of that clear brook. In the meantime, we will read a little out of a book I have in my pocket.' The poor tired bairns have no defence. Curiosity value, not sadism, puts this book in the same grade as the Mrs Trimmer.

Maria Hack (1777–1844) was a Quaker lady who abhorred fiction. Her four-volume *Winter Evenings; or, Tales of Travellers*, 1818, is in the same price grade as the previous two books. It achieved a comfortable family atmosphere, but it was as 'improving' as the others and was also cast in dialogue form, with a mother telling stories of travel to her two children. When little Lucy asks why almost all the pretty books she reads are about things that never happen, Mamma supposes that people who write books for children think that that they will be better pleased with fiction than with truth. Lucy (little prig!) replies; 'They are mistaken then, Mamma.' Mamma approves with; 'I am glad you think so, my dear Lucy: I wish you may always be distinguished for the love of truth.'

Despite the criticisms of light juvenile fiction contained in these educative works, it hardly existed and there was almost no light verse other than the nursery rhymes of oral tradition. Isaac Watts (1674–1748) with his *Divine Songs for Children*, 1715, moralized for the good of the souls of boys and girls and left for present-day collectors a book that has sold for £4,600 ($8,500) in the first edition. Ann (1782–1866) and Jane (1783–1824) Taylor followed Watts's example with *Original Poems for Infant Minds* and *Rhymes for the Nursery*, 1806, the latter containing 'Twinkle, Twinkle, Little Star'. Both books are (I).

Liberation came in the middle of the nineteenth century in the persons of W. M. Thackeray, Edward Lear (1821–88) and Charles Lutwidge Dodgson (1832–98). The first to strike his blow for juvenile freedom was Lear, with the publication of *A Book of Nonsense*, 1846. The first edition did not bear Lear's name but was attributed to Derry Down Derry. This edition is truly rare. The next copy in good condition to appear on the scene might fetch £900 ($1,710), or possibly more. Lear's later children's books, *More Nonsense*, 1872, and *Laughable Lyrics*, 1877, equally devoid of improvement, are not so scarce and might be (f).

Thackeray broke with the moralizing pattern in *The Rose and the Ring*, 1855, by adapting the English theatrical tradition of burlesque to a children's book. As is required of fairy stories, virtue is rewarded and vice punished, but the characters are not a bit goody-goody. A clean first in the original pictorial boards should not be above (h).

C. L. Dodgson, universally known as Lewis Carroll, was the greatest liberator of all. More clearly than any of his contemporaries, he grasped that children could be written to as though they were sentient beings. He entered their dream world and saw with their eyes. He mocked the pious stuff that had been presented to the young in the name of literature, for Carroll knew what he was about when he wrote his parodies. In *Alice's Adventures in Wonderland*, 1865 (but 1866), Watts's song about 'How doth the little busy bee?'

becomes 'How doth the little crocodile?' and the Taylor sisters' twinkling star is transformed in the Mad Hatter's 'Twinkle, twinkle, little bat'.

One of the grimmest children's books of all time appeared in 1828. It was called *The Child's Guide to Knowledge: Being a Collection of Useful and Familiar Questions and Answers on Everyday Subjects, Adapted for Young Persons, and Arranged in the Most Simple and Easy Language*, by A Lady. In the course of its long innings the work was 'considerably improved'. By 1873 it had reached its forty-seventh edition. A new edition appeared in 1880 'with considerable additions by Barbara R. Bartlett'. The original authoress was a Mrs R. Ward, about whom little is known. It is clear she was a down-to-earth lady. In the original preface she explains:

> It has not been thought advisable to introduce any woodcuts or engravings, which might take off the attention of children, for whom this little book is professedly designed; and the authoress trusts that the simplicity of the language in which the information is conveyed renders *picture* illustration unnecessary; she believes, indeed, that they would not add to, but rather detract from the usefulness of the work.

The long catechism begins by asking 'What is the World?' and answering, 'The earth we live on'. The next question is, 'Who made it?' with the answer, 'The great and good God'. Then follows:

Q. Are there not many things in it you would like to know about?
A. Yes, very much.
Q. Pray then, what is bread made of?
A. Flour.
Q. What is flour?
A. Wheat ground into powder by the miller.

So the interrogation continues, page after unrelieved page. Lewis Carroll must have known this work and may have had to learn the answers by heart as a child. If so, he was revenged in *Through the Looking-Glass*, 1872. In chapter nine, Alice has to suffer an examination by the Red and the White Queens, who want to know if she can answer useful questions. By putting Q. for the Queens' questions and A. for Alice's answers, this dialogue results:

Q. How is bread made?
A. I know that! You take some flour—
Q. Were do you pick the flower? In a garden or in the hedges?
A. Well, it isn't *picked* at all, it's ground—
Q. How many acres of ground? You musn't leave out so many things.

Tracing such connections between different books is one of the bibliophile's delights and helps to explain why a first edition of a tiresome book like *The Child's Guide* may be in grade (g), along with a first of *Through the Looking-Glass*, which, though in greater demand, is more easily found.

The true first edition of *Alice in Wonderland* is as scarce as icicles in Hades. No sooner was it published than the author had the copies recalled, as he and his illustrator, John Tenniel (1820–1914), were dissatisfied with the printing and presentation. It is not known how many copies escaped the recall, but they were very few. When found, a copy of this 1865 edition is a plum. In fine condition it could change hands at over £6,000 ($11,400). The best the ordinary collector can hope for is a copy of the second edition, 1866, generally known as the first published edition, grade (b).

John Ruskin (1819–1900) wrote an imitation Grimm's fairy tale, *The King of the Golden River*, 1851, which is less tendentious that most children's stories of the time. A first edition might be had at (h), though copies sometimes sell well above this. Nathaniel Hawthorne's *Wonder Book for*

Girls and Boys, Boston, Massachusetts, 1852 (reddish cloth binding) and *Tanglewood Tales*, Boston, Massachusetts, 1853 (with advertisements dated August 1853), could also be (h), though they too vary in price.

Influenced by his friend, Lewis Carroll, George Macdonald (1824–1905) produced *Dealings with the Fairies*, 1867, *The Princess and the Goblin*, 1872, and *The Princess and Curdie*, 1883. They should be collectable in (i).

Meanwhile, the mind-improvers were fighting a rearguard action. Margaret Gatty (1806–73) published her *Parables from Nature* between 1855 and 1871. These were after the style of Mrs Trimmer's *History of the Robins*, but more relaxed. Charlotte Yonge (1823–1901) wrote a series of pleasantly uplifting novels for children, beginning with *The Heir of Redclyffe*, in 1853. Firsts are harder to find than their placing in (i) would suggest, though her rather overrated *The Instructive Picture Book*, 1857, may be (g) because of its coloured plates.

Juliana Horatia Ewing (1841–85), struck an uncertain balance between edification and amusement. Her *The Brownies and Other Tales*, 1870, provided the myth on which the junior section of the Girl Guides is founded; her *Jackanapes*, 1883, enjoyed a popularity above its deserts. Most of her books were attractively produced in pictorial boards and are interesting to collect. Copies can be had for £5 ($9.50) each, or less.

Louisa M. Alcott (1832–88) deserves the attention she receives from collectors everywhere. *Little Women*, part 1, 1868, part 2, 1869, and *Little Men*, 1871, may be sentimental, but they are still among the best books ever written for older children—or older girls at any rate. *Little Men* may be (e), but the two parts of *Little Women*, both published at Boston, Massachusetts, could each be (H) in superlative condition. The second part of *Little Women* is known as *Good Wives* in Britain.

Captain Thomas Mayne Reid (1818–83), son of an Irish

Presbyterian minister, American citizen and English gentleman, could himself have been the romantic hero of some Victorian boys' story. He was packed off to North America as a young man and had a varied career as schoolmaster, actor and journalist before volunteering in 1847 for service with the American army in the Mexican War. He served with distinction and resigned at the end of the fighting with the rank of captain. After further adventures he came to England, where his first novel, *The Rifle Rangers*, was published in two volumes in 1850. Thereafter, he devoted himself to writing, returning to America for a time, but ending his days in England. Most of his work was written for boys, but changing fashion and his habit of holding up the action to enlarge on some point of natural history have put him out of favour. His books and magazine stories offer good hunting in the grades (i) to (d).

His influence on boys' fiction is noticeable in some of the American Dime Novels of the sixties and seventies of last century, published by Irwin P. Beadle & Co, New York. They were issued twice a month in paper wrappers and were not without a certain distinction in their writing. Authors included Edward S. Ellis (1840–1916) and Horatio Alger (1832–99). Though good runs sell for rather less than those of the later science fiction magazines, they are catching up and, being scarcer, may soon become the dearer.

George Alfred Henty (1832–1902) was a later Captain Mayne Reid in some respects. He too had an adventurous life as a war correspondent before settling to write his books for boys. No matter in what place or era he set his tales, he always ensured that his heroes were British or, when he wrote about ancient Egypt for example, proto-British lads. Most of his books were published in pictorial cloth and most first editions can be recognized by being dated on the title-pages, though this is not a totally reliable guide. First editions hover between (i) and (h).

The Frank who was the hero of the series of 'Frank' books

128

written by Charles A. Fosdick (1842–1915) under the pen-name of Harry Castlemon, was the North American counterpart of the typical Henty protagonist. Such titles as *Frank before Vicksburg*, Philadelphia, 1865, and *Frank Nelson in the Forecastle*, Philadelphia, 1876, are most elusive. A desperate searcher might pay up to (f) for them. Gilbert Patten (1866–1945), who wrote as Burt L. Standish, had a less martial Frank as his hero. His Frank Merriwell was an upright athletic schoolboy, featured in *Frank Merriwell's Daring*, New York, 1908, *Frank Merriwell's Victories*, New York, 1910, and many others. They should be found in their original wrappers at under $10 (£5.25) each, but reawakened interest may change the position.

In a different way, Kate Greenaway (1846–1901) was also a liberator. The pictures of children that she drew for her own books and those of others captivated late-Victorian mothers and encouraged them to dress their young offspring in sensible, loose-fitting clothes somewhat in Regency style. Most of the Greenaway books were painstakingly printed in colours by Edmund Evans and no collection of children's books is complete without at least one example. They can be found ranging from (i) to (g). Walter Crane wrote and illustrated children's books rather after the Greenaway manner. His *Flora's Feast*, 1889, and *Queen Summer*, 1891, approach grade (h).

The Greenaway-Crane period was also shared by Andrew Lang (1844–1912). He wrote some original stories for the young but is better known as the editor of a series of fairy books, named from the colours of their cloth bindings. Lang rifled the world's stores of folk-tales for his collections, so if his florid style does not suit every modern child, his material is invaluable to the folklorist. *The Blue Fairy Book*, 1889, was the first, followed by the *Red*, 1890, *Green*, 1892, *Yellow*, 1894, *Pink*, 1897, *Grey*, 1900, *Violet*, 1901, *Crimson*, 1903, *Brown*, 1904, *Orange*, 1906, *Olive*, 1907, and *Lilac*, 1910. There were other books in the series, not necessarily fairy-tale collections. Perhaps an average of £10 ($19) a volume would be a fair price.

Lang was one of the several Anglo-Scottish writers for children working in the nineteenth and early twentieth centuries, all of whom suffered in some degree from the whimsicality that is the other side of the dour Scottish coin. J. M. Barrie was one of the worst sufferers. This did not prevent his play *Peter Pan* (first produced 1904) from being an enormous success. When *Peter Pan and Wendy*, the story of the play, was published in 1911 it met with almost equal success, but is hardly collected now. However, *Peter Pan in Kensington Gardens*, 1906, extracted from Barrie's mawkish *The Little White Bird*, 1902, is a different story in every sense. Illustrated by Arthur Rackham, it would be grade (g) in the ordinary edition, (I) in the limited edition signed by the artist.

Kenneth Grahame (1858–1932), another Anglo-Scot, published *The Golden Age* in 1895. Though about children, it is hardly a children's book. *Dream Days*, 1899, is better and contains *The Reluctant Dragon*. But best is his *The Wind in the Willows*, 1908, which is (d).

The last of the Anglo-Scots to be worthy of mention is A. A. Milne (1882–1956), who dramatized *The Wind in the Willows* as *Toad of Toad Hall*, in 1929. He is best remembered for the Pooh books; *Winnie-the-Pooh*, 1926, and *The House at Pooh Corner*, 1928. When clean, in dustwrappers, they are grade (h).

Edith Nesbit (Mrs Hubert Bland, 1858–1924) had ambitions as a poet, but found her vocation in juvenile fiction. Her first major work was *The Treasure Seekers*, 1899, which introduced the Bastable family. Their adventures continued in *The Would-be-Goods*, 1901, *The New Treasure Seekers*, 1905, and *Oswald Bastable—and Others*, also 1905. The Bastables have many surprising adventures, but are never involved with the supernatural, as are E. Nesbit's other family, the children (no surname given) in *Five Children and It*, 1902, *The*

Phoenix and the Carpet, 1904, and *The Story of the Amulet*, 1906. Good copies of all the Nesbit firsts—she wrote many other children's books—should be had in grade (i).

Very young children were catered for as never before with the appearance of the Peter Rabbit books by Beatrix Potter (1866–1943). The first was *The Tale of Peter Rabbit* and a whole series followed, ending with *Cecily Parsley's Nursery Rhymes* in 1929. They were charmingly illustrated by the author. First editions, ordinary and limited, are hard to find in acceptable condition. Some of the ordinary ones may cost over £20 ($38). *The Fairy Caravan*, 1929, *Sister Anne*, US edition, 1932, and *Wag-by-the-Wall*, 1944, followed the main series, but are not so good.

Arthur Rackham's work as an illustrator of children's books and others is enjoying an ever-increasing reputation. Imposing volumes, full of well-produced coloured plates by him, were specially issued for the Christmas gift market for many years. The would-be connoisseur could buy limited signed editions bound in vellum, with perishable silk ties. Prices paid for these are reaching (H) and there is no sign of their toppling. However, Rackham is not in the Blake or Bewick class and care is still counselled.

7

Biography, History, Travel

One of the best biographies in the English language was written by Mrs Elizabeth C. Gaskell (1810–65). A novelist herself, she became friendly with Charlotte Brontë, and when Charlotte died in 1855, Mrs Gaskell began work on *The Life of Charlotte Brontë*, published in two volumes in 1857. The first edition, in the original dark-brown cloth with wavy graining, could be grade (d) and the second edition, which followed almost immediately, might be (h). Both contain material that was suppressed in later editions. Until recently, publishers were reluctant to reprint the full first edition text.

Brontë collectors will certainly want this book, as any specialist in a particular author will want the best available biography of his subject. Few authors have been as well served as Charlotte Brontë, although one woman writer is as well known from her biography as from her own works— Mary Wollstonecraft (1759–97), wife of William Godwin and mother-in-law of Shelley. Mary Wollstonecraft, a leader of the women's liberation movement of her day, was almost as radical as the present members of the movement. Godwin wrote his wife's biography, which was published in 1798 under the title *Memoirs of the Author of 'A Vindication of the Rights of Woman'*, the title within the title being that of Mary's own greatest work. The biography seems to have acquired a renewed importance and, in original boards, could be (H) in the first edition. Some more recent editions were entitled *A Memoir of Mary Wollstonecraft*.

The most famous biography of all, *The Life of Samuel Johnson* by James Boswell (1740–95) has already been dealt with. It is often forgotten that Johnson had a previous biographer in Sir John Hawkins (1719–89), Johnson's literary executor. Hawkins's *Life of Samuel Johnson* was published in 1786, five years before Boswell's. A less monumental work, it contains some of Johnson's *obiter dicta*, including his refreshing pronouncement that a tavern chair is the throne of human felicity. The Hawkins version is (e).

Johnson himself was an important biographer. His *Lives of the English Poets*, though full of typical prejudice, is a great piece of literary criticism as well as a summary of the careers of fifty-two poets. The true first edition was published at Dublin in three volumes, 1779–81, but is rated no higher than the first London edition, the four volumes of which were all issued in 1781. Though copies have exceptionally made grade (E), they might still be found at (H).

Another famous biography is *The Life of Sir Walter Scott*, by J. G. Lockhart (1794–1854). This work, published in seven volumes in 1837–8, is a bit like the Scott Monument in Edinburgh—massive and doggedly romantic. As Lockhart was Scott's son-in-law, the tone is somewhat adulatory, but it is a grand work for all that, at last receiving the attention it deserves. A first, with the errata slip for volume one, could be (g).

Earlier, Lockhart wrote a *Life of Robert Burns*, issued in 1828 as the twenty-third volume of *Constable's Miscellany*. Though unusual in the first edition, it is little collected and is grade (i). Biographies of Burns can be numbered by the score, but the great poet still waits the ideal biographer who will be neither sentimental nor denigrating in his view of a complex genius who wished to be democrat and gentleman, respectable husband and miscellaneous lover, untutored songster and sage literateur all in one.

Even Burns has fared better than Shakespeare, of whom there is no authentic biography—but in his day nobody

thought it worthwhile to detail the lives of such small deer as
mere writers for the theatre. Nobody can now make up for
this sad lack. Had Shakespeare been of high birth he might
have had his William Roper (1496–1578). Roper was the
son-in-law of Sir Thomas More, martyr and author of
Utopia. Though emphasizing the saintly qualities of its
subject, Roper's *The Mirrour of Vertue in Worldly Greatnes*,
first published at Paris in 1626, presents a clear portrait of a
great figure of Renaissance England. A complete copy of this
first would be (F).

As a Catholic, More is not included among *The Worthies
of England*, 1662, by Thomas Fuller (1608–61). Here Fuller
deals with Protestant heroes, supplying details about where
they lived and worked. Topographers as well as historians
value this book, the folio first edition of which is (I) or rather
below.

Fuller's contemporary, Isaak Walton (1593–1683), is
associated with *The Compleat Angler*, yet, in its way, his
Lives is of equal merit, written with a sympathy for the
subjects such as would be expected of the author. It is worth
reading even by those who are not deeply concerned with
Donne, Wotton, Hooker and Herbert, the four whom Walton
included in the first collected edition, 1670, grade (b). He
subsequently wrote a life of Bishop Sanderson (1587–1663),
author of the preface to the Anglican *Book of Common
Prayer*. Most modern editions of the *Lives* include the
Sanderson biography.

John Aubrey (1626–97), a younger contemporary of Fuller
and Walton, was a very different kind of biographer. Com-
bining many of the traits of Autolycus and Merlin, he was
described by his friend, Anthony A Wood, as 'a shiftless
person, roving and magotie-headed'. Aubrey was uncommonly
credulous. The only book of his certainly published in his
lifetime was *Miscellanies, A Collection of Hermetic Philosophy*,
1696, probably (a) in the first edition. Throughout the latter
part of his life he snapped up scraps of information and

gossip about his contemporaries and immediate predecessors.

While some of his gleanings were widely known in the intervening years, they were not published as a collection till 1898, when their editor, Andrew Clark, issued them as *Brief Lives* by John Aubrey, in two volumes. Hence the first edition of Aubrey's most important work, graded (h), is the latest and cheapest of his firsts. For the ordinary reader, the best edition is Anthony Powell's *Brief Lives and Other Selected Writings* by John Aubrey, 1949, still lowish in (i). Here it is possible to become fascinated, as Aubrey himself was, with the curious characters of his day. There is, for instance, Judge Walter Rumsey : 'He was an ingeniose man,' writes Aubrey, 'and had a philosophicall head.'

> He was much troubled with flegme, and . . . he took a fine tender sprig, and tied a ragge at the end, and conceited he might putt it downe his throate, and fetch-up the flegme, and he did so. Afterwards he made this instrument of whale-bone. I have oftentimes seen him use it. I could never make it goe downe my throate, but for those that can 'tis a most incomparable engine . . . He wrote a little octavo booke, of this way of medicine, called *Organon Salutis*.

Sure enough, this book, *Organon Salutis. An Instrument to cleanse the Stomach* by W.R., 1657, is sometimes offered for sale. In (H) or (I) it would be a worthy addition to the library of a wealthy collector of medical works. A sophisticated version of Rumsey's 'engine' is still occasionally used by doctors.

Aubrey knew and admired John Evelyn (1620–1706). No two men could have been less alike, except in their possession of inquiring minds. Evelyn was a precise and dignified gentleman, as can be gathered from his *Memoirs*, edited by William Bray, first published in 1818 and now universally known as Evelyn's *Diary*. Evelyn is nowhere so revealingly intimate as Samuel Pepys (1633–1703), the other great diarist of the time. Nevertheless, his literary self-portrait of a serious scholar is fascinating. The first edition in a really good binding is (f), but an acceptable reading copy could be (h). As Pepys's diaries have recently been published in full for the first time and are in print, speculation in early editions would be unwise, except as fine bindings.

Gravity different from that of Evelyn pervades the *Journal* of John Woolman, first edition, 1774. Woolman was a New Jersey Quaker, born in 1720, and an early campaigner against slavery. The *Journal* profoundly affected Charles Lamb. It is quite rare in the first edition and is perhaps (I), but there are later editions to be had in (i).

The Rev James Woodforde (1758–1803) of Norfolk, England, was more worldly than John Woolman, so his *Diary of a Country Parson* in five volumes, edited by John Beresford, 1924–31, makes livelier reading. The original edition is (b), but there is an abridgement, which should cost about £5 ($9.50). Parson Woodforde enjoyed his creature comforts far from the scenes of political intrigue. Those who wish to gain insight into the backroom politics of the end of the eighteenth and the beginning of the nineteenth centuries should turn to the *Creevey Papers*, two volumes, 1903, edited by Sir Herbert Maxwell. The papers are selected from the diaries and correspondence of Thomas Creevey (1768–1838), a prominent Whig MP of his time. The book is presently (g).

The period from the closing decades of the eighteenth century to the Civil War is of prime importance in the history of the USA. Fortunately, good biographies of the great men of those formative years are not too hard to find. A sound first edition of Washington Irving's *Life of George Washington*, five volumes, New York, 1855–9, would not be an impossibility in grade (h). Much more difficult is the quaint *Life and Memorable Actions of George Washington*, written and published by Mason L. Weems about 1800. Weems combined the offices of parson and colporteur, peddling his books in an extensive area centred around Mount Vernon. The seeker of a first edition of Weems's *Washington* may find one in grade (a), but may have to go to (H) for the fifth edition, 1808, the one in which the story of young George Washington and the cherry tree was given to the world for the first time.

North American life and politics in the first half of the last century can fruitfully be studied in the twelve-volume *Memoirs* (d) of John Quincy Adams, the sixth president. These were edited by C. F. Adams and published at Philadelphia between 1874 and 1877. Collectors interested in the Civil War period, besides collecting the wealth of magazine material still available in a great variety of prices, will turn to books about Abraham Lincoln (1809–65). A first of *Lincoln, the True Story of a Great Life* by William H. Herndon and Jesse W. Weik, Chicago, no date, but 1889, should present no difficulty for the purchaser in grade (d). A good deal of Lincolniana is still reasonably priced. Lincoln's *Address delivered at the Cooper Institute*, New York, 1860, *The Political Debates between Lincoln and the Hon. Stephen A. Douglas*, Columbus, Ohio, 1860, and *The Trial of Abraham Lincoln*, New York, 1863, should still be (i), as should Stanley Kimmel's *The Mad Booths of Maryland*, New York, 1940, a biographical study of the brilliant but unbalanced family of actors that included John Wilkes Booth, Lincoln's assassin.

Since Lincoln's time, many politicians and statesmen have written their own memoirs and biographies. It is to be regretted, therefore, that Sir Winston Churchill is not of their number, though he revealed something of himself in several of his books, including *My Early Life*, 1930 (g). The top Churchill item, however, is *Mr Brodick's Army*, first edition, 1903. The last public sale of a copy of this, in cloth, with the original wrappers preserved, was in 1969 when it made £1,500 ($2,850). The price now could be nearly double. By contrast, good sets of Churchill's *The Second World War*, in first editions, 1948–54, would be well down (i).

Sir Winston's various literary works show how difficult it

can be to separate biography from history. Few collectors confine themselves to biography, but venture into history or literature as well. Yet a person who restricted himself to this one subject would have a fascinating field in which to work. Simply by choosing the eminent men and women of a particular period, or famous sportsmen down the ages, or the lives of great failures, he would give himself a lifetime's work.

Building a comprehensive biographical collection of engineers would keep a collector busy for a long time, though he could make a flying start thanks to Samuel Smiles (1812–1904), the biographer first of George Stephenson (1781–1848), the locomotive designer, and then of many other heroes of the Industrial Revolution. His *Life of George Stephenson* was published in 1857, with a revised edition in 1873 that included a memoir of Robert Stephenson, George's son and successor. The *Lives of the Engineers*, three volumes, 1861–2, followed, then came *Industrial Biography*, 1863, *Lives of Boulton and Watt*, 1865, and *Men of Invention and Industry*, 1884. In 1894, Smiles turned his attention to a great pottery manufacturer with *Josiah Wedgwood, His Personal History*. Firsts of all these are (i).

Only the collector who is prepared to browse in bookshops can hope to obtain minor biographies and autobiographies by obscure writers. Here again there is treasure among the dross. The seeker must decide for himself which are the pearls worth sifting.

The border between biography and history is ill defined. The real historian and the serious amateur will want to uncover for himself new facts that may lie hidden in little-known books, not necessarily works of history, and in private papers. If these are obviously important, the owners of such papers rarely do other than entrust their editing to someone academically qualified, or they sell or bequeath them to university or institutional libraries.

It he can keep his eyes about him and his ear to the ground at the same time, the student-collector may turn up useful source material, but he will need just a dash of the Thomas Phillipps to make him willing to comb through old account books, deeds, wills and indentures that may be discarded as waste paper by lawyers, old established business firms and local government officials.

Apart from such gleanings as he may make, the historian will have to obtain certain up-to-date books, chosen from publishers' lists, and some much older authoritative works. The earliest for the English-speaking peoples is the *Anglo-Saxon Chronicle*. The edition most often found in sale-rooms and the lists of antiquarian booksellers is that of 1861, translated by Benjamin Thorpe, grade (h) and satisfactory to work from. Next must come the Venerable Bede's *Historia Ecclesiastica Gentis Anglorum*, written by Bede before AD735. A copy of this, published at Strasburg about 1475–8 would cost above (A) and the first English edition, *History of the Church in Englande*, translated by Thomas Stapleton, Antwerp, 1565, would be (G), but modern translations are available.

The next landmark is William the Conqueror's *Domesday Book*, compiled in 1086. The first complete printed edition, in two volumes, dates from 1783 and is (f). A curious edition appeared ten years later, in two undated volumes with no title-pages and no place of publication stated. This was incomplete and two further volumes were published in 1816, with title-pages supplied for the earlier volumes. The price of the four volumes might be (a). *Domesday Studies*, edited by P. E. Dove, two volumes, 1881–91, should be (i) and would be of more use to the serious student.

The full text of *Magna Carta*, 1215, is not easily found. A fine edition of 1938 is (f). Earlier editions date from 1514, 1527, 1531–2, 1542, 1587 and 1618. An edition, sumptuously printed in gold letters and illuminated appeared in 1816. Two copies were printed on vellum, but even copies on paper could be (G).

The earliest Scottish historian of importance was the

139

Dundonian, Hector Boece (1465–1536), who wisely preferred to live in Aberdeen, as the first principal of the city's older university, King's College. His *Scotorum Historiæ a prima gentis origine* is fabulous—often in the strictest sense of the word. It was translated by John Bellenden as *The History and Croniklis of Scotland* and published at Edinburgh in 1540. Copies are seldom brought forward for sale and would be (D). The edition of 1821, also an Edinburgh publication, is likewise scarce and probably (f).

Boece's unhistorical account of the life of Macbeth was cribbed by Raphael Holinshed (*d*1580), and incorporated in the *Chronicles of England, Scotlande and Irelande*, two volumes, 1577. This book supplied Shakespeare with the basis of his tragedy, *Macbeth*, which is no less a masterpiece for being inaccurate. The two volumes together would be (A).

One of the most informative British histories of the seventeenth century appeared in 1702–4—*The History of the Late Rebellion*, three volumes, by Edward Hyde, Earl of Clarendon, not uncommonly offered in grades (f) to (b). There were many historians in the eighteenth century, including David Hume and Oliver Goldsmith, but their books are obsolete, though quite dear in nice bindings for those who like their libraries to have an air of old-world scholarship. Edward Gibbon (1737–94) was the greatest historian of the period. He looked at the civilization of Rome with a fresh eye and his *The Decline and Fall of the Roman Empire*, six volumes, 1776–88, though it may need correcting and supplementing, cannot be entirely superseded. Despite the decline and fall of classical studies, demand for it makes it (G) as a first edition.

Certain history books are attractive to collectors simply because of their elusiveness. As it was first issued in 1851, *The Fifteen Decisive Battles of the World* by Sir Edward Creasey (1812–78) is sadly out of date. Its reputation as a scarce item in the two-volume first edition gives it an (f) grading.

One of the earlier historians of North America was a Scot, William Robertson, who produced his *History of America*, two volumes, in 1777, while the War of Independence was still raging. This is not a popular work today and the original edition should be (i). Soon after the United States of America came into being, they began to produce able historians of their own. A consulter of T. L. Bradford's *Bibliographer's Manual of American History*, edited by S. V. Henkels, five volumes, 4to, Philadelphia, 1907–10, might be surprised at the number of historical publications that came from the presses of North America in the late eighteenth and early nineteenth centuries.

Before the second half of the century, W. H. Prescott (1796–1859) had produced his *History of the Conquest of Mexico*, three volumes, 1843, and *History of the Conquest of Peru*, two volumes, 1847. Both works as firsts would be (d). John L. Motley (1814–77) was another notable historian, though his interest was not centred on the Americas. His best-known work is *The Rise of the Dutch Republic*, three volumes, 1856, grade (i) and not rising.

In Britain, comparable historians were Thomas Babington, Lord Macaulay (1800–59), and Thomas Carlyle (1795–1881). Neither is feverishly collected, though fine sets of their works sell as library furniture. Macaulay's *History of England*, five volumes, 1849–61, could be (c) in original cloth. His *Lays of Ancient Rome*, 1849, is baffling in the way the prices paid for it vary from (i) to (g). Carlyle's *French Revolution*, three volumes, 1837, may rate (f) and his *Chartism*, 1840, can approach (h), but his other firsts are to be had at ordinary prices, unless they are signed or association copies.

Although John R. Green's *A Short History of the English People*, 1874, was a pioneer work in many ways and is uncommon as a first, it is little collected. It sells for no more than one of the later expanded and illustrated editions, in (i).

Few books by more recent historians have as yet been

raised to the dignity of desired collectors' items. There is, however, great interest in broadsides and pamphlets of historical interest. In the United States the big demand is for broadsides—single printed sheets—connected with the Revolution. A good example is a sheet with Bunker Hill connections, beginning 'This Town was alarmed on the 17th instant at Break of day', and dated 'Boston, 26 June 1775'. A copy, which sold some time ago for $300 (nearly £160), would now be worth $600 (£300) or more. This is about the level for similar proclamations concerning the Jacobite risings of 1715 and 1745. No British broadside, however, could approach in value the premier North American example—the first issue of the *Declaration of Independence*, Philadelphia, 1776, with no date given. The value of a copy must be nearly a million dollars (£526,300).

An inviting aspect of broadsides is to collect the reputed confessions and last dying words of notorious criminals. Some of the confessions were genuine, many were not. They were also issued as broadsheets, which are broadsides printed on both sides, as chapbooks (which are small pamphlets), and occasionally as proper books, in 12mo or 8vo. Prices vary greatly, from grade (i) to (a) and above.

Probably the narratives in Charles Johnson's *A General History of the Pyrates*, 1724, and *A General History of Highwaymen*, 1734, are more authentic than those in the broadsides, etc. Johnson's books are hard to find in good condition as firsts. Without imperfections, they could be (I), but they are more often listed with details of defects and sold *w.a.f.* (with all faults—implying that the seller accepts no responsibility for condition) in grade (g).

Much of Johnson's inspiration for his work on pirates must have stemmed from John Esquemeling's *Bucaniers of America*. As a book originally written in Dutch and first published in Holland, it hardly comes within the purview of this guide. However, an English edition in four parts, usually bound either in one or in two volumes, with part four alone as the second volume, was published at London in 1684 and is (I) if complete. The fourth part is the most highly esteemed, so the first three parts together may be no more than (g).

William Dampier (1652–1715), was both buccaneer and legitimate explorer, so he bridges the narrow gap between history and travel. His three volumes of *Voyages* were published between 1699 and 1703 and show that this coarse and brutal man was also a brilliant navigator and explorer. The three volumes, which may now be (I), take us to the coasts of Australia and many strange places in the old and new worlds. For a sense of adventure, however, Dampier is outclassed by Sir Walter Raleigh in his *Discovery of Guiana*. The accepted first edition, published in 1595, was entitled *The discouerie of the large rich, and bewtiful empire of Guiana. Performed in the yeare 1595*. The second edition, also 1595, had 'empire' in the title altered to 'Empire' and there are slight internal variations. In the same year there was a third edition, this time with 'Empire' replaced by 'Empyre'. These variations naturally affect the price, so that the first could be (B) while the others might be (F). But all are rare and it is hard to predict how high they might rise when next put up for sale.

In the years 1740 to 1744, George, Lord Anson (1697–1762) circumnavigated the globe as a naval captain. His account, *A Voyage Round the World*, 1748, has thrilled readers ever since and is (a).

Beyond journeying between London and Paris, Richard Hakluyt (1552–1616) was no voyager. His fame comes from his collection, *Principall Navigations*, in three parts, 1589, which brought together as stirring a batch of adventures as can be found. Recent prices of the first edition have varied from (I) to beyond (A). The first of the many writers to borrow from Hakluyt was Samuel Purchas (1576–1626), another armchair traveller, who published *Purchas His Pilgrimage* in 1613, at least (g), and *Purchas His Pilgrimes*, four volumes, in 1625–6, probably (D). This latter work, combined with the effects of opium, inspired Coleridge's dream poem, *Kubla Khan*.

Romance and realism go together in *The General Historie of Virginia*, 1624, by Captain John Smith (1580–1631). Though called a history, it is a book of travel and exploration. On two occasions Captain Smith's life was saved by the Indian princess, Pocahontas. The first edition is (a).

In the two centuries after John Smith, the American frontier was pushed ever westwards. Confrontations with the Indians took place deeper and deeper in the interior. The nobility and savagery of the indigenous tribes were recorded by many observers, particularly George Catlin (1796–1872), who lived with the Indians, studying their customs and drawing them in the course of their activities. His *North American Indian Portfolio*, with thirty-one hand-coloured lithographs, was published about 1845, though no date is given. In prime condition, this is certainly a $5,000 (£2,630) book. His other well-known work is *Manners of the North American Indians*, two volumes, 1841. Though less important, it is (I). Even the late Edinburgh reprint of 1926 is (f).

Francis Parkman (1823–93) was another important historian of old America. His *California and the Oregon Trail*, two parts in wrappers, New York, 1849, is still sometimes to be bought at (I).

The story of the development of the West is often one of violence, though popular fiction and film and television drama may have put too much emphasis on this aspect. Those who wish to concentrate on the villains should first arm themselves with Ramon F. Adams's *Six-Guns and Saddle Leather a Bibliography on Western Outlaws and Gunmen*, no date, but 1954, Norman, Oklahoma. Gathering the collectable material it lists and often illustrates should keep them occupied and would sublimate their aggression until their dotage. This still leaves much that is exciting for those with wider interests in the epic of the opening up of the West. The following titles should be in the (e) grade, or below : *An Apache Campaign in the Sierra Madre* by Captain John G. Bourke (a student of

Indian customs), New York, 1886; *Murder and Mob Law in Indiana* by James M. Hiatt, Indianapolis, 1872; *Seventy Years on the Frontier* by Alexander Majors, edited by Colonel P. Ingrahan, Chicago, 1893; *Death Valley in '49* by William Lewis Manly, San José, Calif, 1894; and *Scouting Expeditions of McCulloch's Texas Rangers* by Samuel C. Reid, Philadelphia, 1859. These are only samples of what the modest collector can look for. Dearer and worth individual gradings are: *Hair-Breadth Escapes of 'Grizzly Adams'* by James C. Adams, no place or date, but New York, 1860, (H); *A Plea for the Indians* by John Beeson, New York, 1857, (I); *A Brief History of the New Gold Regions of Colorado Territory* by Edward Bliss, New York, 1864, (H); *Views of Louisiana with a Journal of a Voyage up the Missouri River* by H. M. Brackenridge, Pittsburgh, 1814, (I); *Journal of the Sufferings of Captain Parker H. French's Overland Expedition to California*, Chambersburg, 1851, (A); *Reminiscences of Frontier Life* by Isaac B. Hammond, Portland, 1904, (c); *My Life and Experiences among Our Hostile Indians* by Oliver O. Howard, Hartford, no date, but 1907, (c); *Expedition to the Sources of the Missouri* by Merriwether Lewis and William Clark (both important explorers), two volumes, Philadelphia, 1814, (I); *Fur Hunters of the Far West* by Alexander Ross, two volumes, 1855, (I); and *My Life on the Plains, or Personal Experiences with Indians* by General George A. Custer, New York, 1874, (f).

Canada was being opened up at the same time and owed much to the explorations of Sir Alexander Mackenzie (c1764–1820). His great book is *Voyages from Montreal . . . Through the Continent of North America*, 1801, (G). The turn of the far north came later and brought the gold rush of 1898. There is a whole body of literature on this event. Let Tappan Adney's *Klondike Stampede*, New York and London, 1900, (e) suffice as an example.

Meanwhile back at the settled areas, things were stirring. In the second half of last century the tide of immigration to

North America reached new heights. The immigrants suffered much on their voyages from Europe, crammed into overcrowded ships, but it was not easy going even when they arrived. They were exploited by shady companies and by gangs of 'runners' who offered to help them on their way. Many of the runners were hoodlums who made extortionate charges, stole from and cheated their customers, and beat them up if they refused to pay. One of the most notorious of the runners was John Morrissey, a prizefighter and latterly an apparently respectable senator, whose story is told in William E. Harding's *John Morrissey. His Life, Battles and Wrangles*, published at New York in 1881 as number two of a series, 'Fistiana's Heroes'. It could still be a $10 (£5.25) book as a lucky find.

American enterprise at sea was not confined to the immigrant traffic. It should be remembered that while the clipper ship probably reached its highest development in the British vessels *Thermopylae* and *Cutty Sark*, the basic clipper design was American and American enthusiasts claim their *Flying Cloud* and *Dreadnought* as the equals of the British ships.

Richard Henry Dana (1815–82) had his non-fiction classic, *Two Years before the Mast*, published at New York in 1840. Acceptable firsts should be (c). Joshua Slocum (1844–1909?) was another famous American sailor. In *Sailing Alone around the World*, New York, 1900, he describes his single-handed voyage on board the sloop *Spray*. He disappeared on a second voyage so the date of his death is unknown. *The Cruise of the 'Cachalot' round the World*, 1898, is another great true story of the sea, by the Englishman, Frank Bullen (1857–1915). The Slocum should be (h) and the Bullen (i).

Yorkshireman and honorary Australian, Captain James Cook (1728–79), is the most celebrated circumnavigator of all time, with the possible exception of Ferdinand Magellan (1480–1521), who was in fact killed before he could complete the journey. Cook was of humble origin and rose to the top by sheer merit. Because he knew from experience what life on the lower deck could be like, he was always considerate of his crew. On his first voyage to the Antarctic there was only one death aboard the two ships under his command, the *Resolution* and the *Adventure*. Having regard to the conditions then prevailing, this was as remarkable an achievement as boldly sailing his ships among the icebergs of the uncharted southern seas.

Bibliophiles of varying interests converge when Cook's published works are on sale. His *Journal of a Voyage round the World in HMS Endeavour 1771*, is not too much in (H), nor is his *Voyage round the World in 1772–5*, two volumes, 1781, in (F). Most wanted of all is a set of Cook's first, second and third voyages in nine volumes, including the atlas, issued over the years 1773, 1777 and 1784, probably (B).

Books like *Two Expeditions into the Interior of South Australia*, two volumes, 1833, by Charles Sturt (1795–1869), grade (I) and J. Maclehose's *Picture of Sydney*, Sydney, 1839 (H) or (G) are representative of Australian travel and history items, but they are the caviare. For the general, there are good titbits of information on Australia's early days to be found in minor books, including works of fiction. A rather poor novel, such as J. R. H. Hawthorn's *The Pioneer of a Family*, 1881, can reflect with reasonable accuracy the Australian way of life in the nineteenth century and cost but little. Details of such books are given in E. M. Miller's *Australian Literature, A Bibliography*, revised edition, extended to 1950, edited by F. T. Macartney, and published at Sydney in 1956. The patient bibliophile should be able to collect a representative selection of Australiana at little more than $A10 (£7 or $13.50) a time. At that price *Reclamation of Land at the Head of Wooloomooloo Bay,* two volumes, Sydney, 1857, would be worth having for the title alone.

African travel books are steadily collected. Writings about the continent go back to Roman times, but probably the first sober and enlightening account of African exploration in the English language is *Travels in the Interior of Africa*, 1799, by Mungo Park (1771–1806). The area that this Scottish surgeon-explorer made his own was the Niger valley. As a first edition, the *Travels* would be (b). For little more than £3 ($5.70) the poor scholar could have the informative *Niger: The Life of Mungo Park*, Edinburgh and London, 1934, by Lewis Grassic Gibbon (J. Leslie Mitchell).

Other early books on African travel will be as difficult to find as the Park. James Bruce (1730–94), Scottish wine merchant turned explorer, travelled widely in Abyssinia. His failure to reach the source of the Nile in no way detracts from his *Travels to Discover the Sources of the Nile*, published in five volumes at Edinburgh in 1790. It could be (b). John H. Speke (1827–64) did discover where the Nile rose and told of his adventures in *A Journey of the Discovery of the Source of the Nile*, 1863, (f).

David Livingstone (1813–73) was the most distinguished African explorer. His *Missionary Travels in South Africa* first appeared in 1857, when he was already famous. A large first edition was printed, with a first issue hardly distinguishable from the second and not of greater value. The price of copies in really good condition has risen sharply in the last few years, moving from (h) to (a). Many cheaper copies can be had, but with library labels, entire, scraped or removed. P. H. Muir quotes (*The Book Collector*, volume 2, 1953) a letter by Charles E. Mudie, owner of the celebrated circulating library, written in 1863 and stating that 'the exact number of copies of Livingstone's *Africa* at one time in circulation in the Library was 3,250'. A fair proportion of these must have been firsts.

Everybody, one presumes, links the name of Livingstone with that of Sir Henry M. Stanley (1841–1904). His best-known book is *How I Found Livingstone*, 1872. Its (g) grading is surprisingly low.

Livingstone and Stanley both had a single-minded devotion to Africa. Not so Sir Richard F. Burton (1824–90). His most important African books are *First Footsteps in East Africa*,

1856, (c) and *Abeokuta and the Camaroons Mountains*, two volumes, 1863, (b). His other travel books include *Personal Narrative of a Pilgrimage to El-Medinah and Meccah*, three volumes, 1869, (I) and *Etruscan Bologna*, 1876, (i). Some of the ground covered by Burton on his journey to Mecca was travelled over again by Charles M. Doughty (1843–1926), who described his wanderings in *Travels in Arabia Deserta*, two volumes, with a map in an end pocket, 1888. Though most readers find it hard going it has become a desirable first at (a).

Love of adventure as much as missionary zeal sent George Borrow (1803–81) to Spain in 1835 on behalf of the British and Foreign Bible Society. The result was the classic *The Bible in Spain*, three volumes, 1843, grade (g). Richard Ford (1796–1858) spent nearly four years in Spain just before Borrow's visit, but his *Handbook for Travellers in Spain* did not appear till 1845. This book is as different from the ordinary guide book as chalk is from cheese and the knowing collector would gladly pay in grade (e) for it.

Edward Lear is more famous as a writer of nonsense verse than as a traveller, yet those who know them find his illustrated travel journals as delightful as his verse. The most highly rated is his *Illustrated Excursions in Italy*, two volumes, with fifty-five lithographs, 1846. The landscape illustrations are very fine, so the volumes sell in (a) or (I).

While Lear was travelling in the heat of Italy, Sir John Franklin (1786–1847) was sailing the Arctic seas in command of two famous Royal Navy ships, the *Erebus* and *Terror*, searching for the North-West Passage. He had already explored the waters of the far north and wrote of his findings in *A Journey to the Shores of the Polar Sea*, 1823, now grade (a). Franklin's ships sailed from England in May 1845, and were last seen by a whaler crew two months later. Thereafter all was silence. Many expeditions were sent to find Franklin, but it was the *Fox*, fitted out by Lady Franklin and commanded by F. L. M'Clintock, that sailed to where Franklin and his men lay dead. Sir John had died in 1847 and the rest of the crews not long after—but they had found the North-West Passage. M'Clintock told his story in *The Voyage of the 'Fox' in the Arctic Seas*, 1859. The book was an immediate bestseller, so firsts are not rare and should be (f).

The tragedy of Franklin in the far north resembles that of Captain Robert Falcon Scott (1868–1912) in the Antarctic. Both men succeeded at the cost of their lives. Today, the record of Scott's journey to the South Pole, *Scott's Last Expedition*, two volumes, 1913, edited by Leonard Huxley and containing Scott's own journal, is collected and is grade (i). More highly valued—grade (h)—is Apsley Cherry-Garrard's account of the expedition, *The Worst Journey in The World*, two volumes, 1922. Cherry-Garrard (1886–1959) was himself a distinguished bibliophile.

Like Roald Amundsen, who reached the South Pole ahead of Scott, the first man to get to the North Pole, Admiral Robert E. Peary (1856–1920), survived the homeward journey and wrote a book about his successful expedition—*The North Pole*. The edition favoured by collectors and a true first, is known as the General Hubbard Edition, New York, 1910, (g).

It is but a step from polar exploration to mountaineering. This subject has quite a literature of its own. The classics include *Mountaineering in the Sierra Nevada*, Boston, Massachusetts, 1872, by Clarence King; *My Climbs in the Alps and Caucasus*, 1895, by A. F. Mummery; F. S. Smythe's *The Kangchenjunga Adventure*, 1930; Samuel Turner's *The Conquest of the New Zealand Alps*, 1922; John Tyndall's *Glaciers of the Alps*, 1860; Edward Whymper's *Scrambles Amongst the Alps*, 1871, and *The Ascent of the Matterhorn*, 1880; and Sir F. E. Younghusband's *Epic of Mount Everest*, 1926. All should still be grade (i). Sir John Hunt's *The Ascent of Everest*, 1953 (published in the United States as *The Conquest of Everest*, 1954) is still cheap and plentiful in the first edition and should be secured now. The first important English book on the Scandinavian mountains, by James Forbes (1809–

68), is *Norway and Its Glaciers*, 1853, which, like the Tyndall work above, is partly scientific; it should be (f).

Those who like to do their climbing and travelling vicariously are well catered for in cheap reprints, but they should also look out for volumes of the Hakluyt Society's publications that give accurate and carefully edited versions of many of the world's great travel books. In long runs they could average about £15 (say $30) a copy for the earlier issues and £8 ($15.50) for the later. Odd volumes might be had for slightly less.

8

Topography

Part of the history of North America is written on every map of the continent. Boston, Montreal, San Jose and Petersburg are examples of old names, already familar, given to new places by the first important groups of settlers to arrive : the English in Massachusetts, the French in Quebec, the Spanish in California and the Russians in Alaska. There also remains an abundance of place names used by the indigenous peoples : Indians, Eskimos and Aleuts. Much the same can be said of Australia, though there the names are mainly either British or aborigine.

In like fashion, history can be read from the maps of Britain. Some names, such as Don, occurring as a river in Yorkshire and another in Aberdeenshire, seem to go back to a people whose language is lost, but most are identifiable. England is so called from its take-over by the Angles, a large group of immigrants mainly from the low parts of Germany, who arrived in historic times, and gave the country most of its well-known place names. The same is true of Scotland, named from the Scots, who moved in from Ireland and gave their Gaelic names to the places where they were dominant.

The incomers did not wipe the slate clean. In England, Lincoln and London are examples of settlements where the Angles left well alone, adapting the names already used by the Romans for those towns. For the most part, they also accepted the names of rivers and mountains as they found them. In Scotland, the Scots retained some pre-existing Pictish

Plate 11   This publisher's binding of H. M. Stanley's *In Darkest Africa* was used for the first edition, 1890. It is a typical example of late Victorian pictorial cloth, in exceptionally fine condition.

Plate 12   This 'Exact likeness of the BUFFALO, or Wild Bull' from John Hamilton Moore's *New and Complete Collection of Voyages and Travels*, 1778, is a good example of the copper engravings which enliven many of the travel books of the period.

names, as Pittendreigh and Fetterletter, and some older Celtic names, like Aberfoyle, Lhanbryde and Ecclefechan.

Later, the two countries were infiltrated, to put it kindly, by Norsemen and Danes, who named the places where they settled, in their own closely allied tongues. England, though not Scotland, was then conquered by the Normans, who had their own ideas about the naming of places. In Wales and Cornwall, the early Celtic names largely survived.

As with North America, a look at the map of Britain will show where the different groups of immigrants tended to settle. Norse and Danish names are found all round the coasts, from Dungeness in Kent, northwards up the east coast by Cleethorpes to Wick, and from Skokholm, an island in the Bristol Channel, northwards up the west, by Formby, to Laxford in Sutherland. The Norse 'ay' appears in the endings of the names of several Hebridean islands, and the Danish 'thorp' and 'by' are common in the names of towns through-out eastern England. The scattered Norman influence is seen at Beaulieu, Ashby de la Zouche and Malpas. Truly English names are most plentiful in southern and middle England, where towns and villages in 'ingham', 'ington' and 'borough' abound. This influence extends into Scotland, the capital of which, Edinburgh, has a name of English origin. Of the names of the other large Scottish cities, Glasgow and Dundee are Scots Gaelic, and Aberdeen is old Celtic.

Some names in Britain are of mixed origin. Nantwich, Cheshire, is compounded of the Welsh 'nant', meaning a wooded valley, and the English 'wich', here signifying a place where salt is found. Nantwich, therefore, is 'the salt town in the wooded valley'. Unlike Telford, Shropshire, which com-memorates a great man, and Birmingham, Alabama, which is taken from a much older original, Nantwich has a truly topographical name. That is to say it is descriptive of the place.

Topography, hardly a science, is concerned with the description of places, in more or less detail, so it can cover local and regional history, geography, geology, economics and everything that is germane to a given area. As has been shown, the name of a place, though it may not be descriptive, has much to reveal and is the obvious starting point of topo-graphical inquiry.

Local patriotism most commonly brings a person to topography, with the inescapable consequence—the collecting of topographical books. Some things can be learnt about a place by verbal inquiry and by field work in archaeology, ecology and all the rest, but sooner or later old authorities will have to be consulted via the printed word and no topographer worthy of the name will be content to rely wholly on borrowed books. He will want some of his very own—then more and yet more.

The Nantwich man may regard himself rather as a 'nant' than a 'wich' and go on to explore some of the byways of Welsh language and culture, where we may leave him with William Evans's *New English–Welsh Dictionary*, Carmarthen, 1771, (h). Or he may feel himself strongly 'wich' and devote himself to the important part his town played in the history of Cheshire, thus becoming involved with the life stories of a variety of men, from Hugh d'Avranches to Ludwig Mond, the founder of Imperial Chemical Industries. However narrow his interests may remain, he will want to obtain such important Cheshire books as Daniel King's *The Vale-Royall of England*, 1656, (a) and Raymond Richards's *Old Cheshire Churches*, 1947, (i). Perhaps the close association of Charles Lutwidge Dodgson with the county will make him a Lewis Carroll collector as well as a topographer.

In much the same way, the Ayrshire topographer could become a collector of Burns, who was born in the county, while a native of Concord, Massachusetts, could expand into collecting books by the many literary men associated with his town—Thoreau, Hawthorne, Emerson and others. The reverse, too, could happen. The Burns lover living in Concord might start a general Ayrshire collection and the Ayrshire admirer of Thoreau might become interested in the topography of Concord.

For various reasons, the Cotswold area of England is one that haunts this book, so, moving from Cheshire to Gloucestershire, which contains the major part of the Cotswold Hills, the task facing the Cotswold collector can be examined. He may want to possess some general books on Roman and Saxon England to fill in the early background, but his main collection will extend from the Middle Ages at the time of the Cotswold wool trade, to the present. Cost and scarcity will probably exclude early printed books in original editions, though he will long for a copy of *The Ancient and Present State of Glostershire* by Sir Robert Atkyns, in the first edition of 1712, or the second edition of 1768. Either would be (a), with luck. If his resources are limited he would be advised to turn to less expensive items. For the cost of a copy of Atkyns, he could have a whole run of lesser books, which would be far more informative. To find these he should be prepared to track down every book that has Cotswold (or Cotteswold) in its title, for examination if not for purchase. His best aid would be *The Bibliographer's Manual of Gloucestershire Literature* by F. A. Hyett and W. Bazeley, three volumes, 1895–7, with the supplement in two volumes by Hyett and R. Austin, 1915–16. Failing this, he could try to consult the *Catalogue of the Gloucestershire Collection* of Gloucester Public Library, compiled by R. Austin and issued in 1928. Within this volume there are 15,333 entries of books, pamphlets, magazines, serial publications and individual articles relating to the county.

Not every county is so fortunate, but there are bibliographies that list books pertaining to all British counties. Most of these do not discuss the finer gradings of first and subsequent issues, but the topographer generally concentrates on condition and completeness. He wants the best and most informative edition, whether it be the first or the fifteenth.

British topographical collectors soon learn that one of the

high spots in the field is *Britannia* by William Camden (1551–1623), with its fine maps and useful county surveys. Though they do not despise the first edition of 1586 or later editions up to the sixth in 1607, the seventh edition of 1610 is the one they really covet, as this is the first edition in English (translated by Philemon Holland), the others being in Latin. For this reason and because of the quality of the maps, a good copy of the seventh would be (D), though the earlier ones could be (I). Several editions with fine maps were produced later in the seventeenth century and during the earlier part of the eighteenth. They, too, may not be much cheaper than the seventh edition. However, a new translation by Richard Gough appeared in 1789 and was reprinted in 1806. The text is more easily read than that of the previous editions, though the maps are less quaintly decorative. It used to be fairly cheap but it is now (I) or (H). Though most of the English editions are titled *Britain*, the work is almost always spoken of as *Britannia*. A reprint of the 1695 edition, with maps after Robert Morden and an introduction by Stuart Piggott was recently published in Britain by David & Charles, and in the United States by Johnson Reprint Corporation. *Britannia* is a common victim of the Jack-the-Rippers of the book trade, who ruthlessly destroy good copies so that they can sell the maps.

Many collectors are content merely to dream of owning a copy and concentrate on the reality of obtaining those old county histories that most nearly concern them. Two examples of the many available are *The History and Topographical Survey of the County of Kent* by Edward Hasted (1732–1812), four volumes, Canterbury, 1778–99, (H), and *The History and Antiquities of the County of Dorset* by John Hutchins (1698–1773), two volumes, 1774, (a). In the areas to which they pertain, old county histories are competed for by local people who are neither topographers nor ardent book buyers but who want them for reasons of regional sentiment, thus raising prices. This is equally true of histories of individual towns and villages, which were neglected books at one time.

The rise in value of these can be shown by turning again to the Cotswolds. *The History and Antiquities of Chipping Campden* was published by the author, Percy C. Rushen, in 1899. Though he did not expect to make a profit, Rushen hoped he would recover his costs from sales. Things did not go smoothly. This is what he wrote to one buyer, some months after the book was issued :

> The cost is 5/6 post free, which amount please forward to me as I am publishing the book myself. I have had to abandon the subscription list for lack of subscribers and am therefore offering copies to the general public @ the above price, hoping thereby to dispose of more copies.
>
> As there will be an actual out of pocket loss on the publication, I . . . shall therefore esteem it a favour if you will introduce the work to those of your friends &c. likely to be interested in the subject . . .

In the course of the next decade, a series of events, the chief of which was the establishment of C. R. Ashbee's Guild of Handicraft in the village, brought Chipping Campden out of its decline and raised it to an eminence that it had not enjoyed for 300 years. Rushen was able eventually to sell all the copies and to bring out a second edition in 1911 (undated), revised and enlarged, though poorly printed and bound. It also cost 5s 6d (27½p) a copy, post free, and sold more readily than the first edition.

Today, the demand for Rushen's book, though limited, far exceeds the supply and some people would be willing to pay up to £20 ($38) for a fine copy of the first edition and £10 ($19) for a second edition.

The position is much the same with other similar books of narrow local interest, British or American. When Mark Doolittle wrote his *Historical Sketch of the Congregational Church in Belchertown, Massachusetts* and had it published at nearby Northampton in 1852, it cost only a few cents a copy and showed no appreciable rise in value in the following hundred years. Now, though its appeal is still circumscribed, the few who want it would glady give $30 (nearly £16) for it.

Many local histories, such as Hutchins's *Dorset*, already mentioned, were produced on a subscription basis. This entailed inviting interested people to pay for copies in advance or to guarantee to buy them when they were published. Some writers and compilers went a stage further, particularly in the United States. For extra payments they undertook to feature in the books pictures of the subscribers or of their homes, displaying them with more or less prominence according to the amount of extra money paid. Today, a demand for these books comes from people who are not topographers or local historians, but are nonetheless willing to pay highly for items containing portraits of their great-grandfathers or illustrations of their ancestral homes. Some books so financed contain no more useful and original material than certain modern so-called guide books compiled by firms more interested in revenue from advertisements than in giving fresh information about places.

Among many good local histories that are not overrun with solicited illustrations are: *The History and Antiquities of the City of Dublin* by Walter Harris, 1766; *The History and Antiquities of Shrewsbury* by Thomas Phillips, 1779; *A Description of Matlock Bath* by George Lipscomb, 1802; *The History and Antiquities of the Church and City of Lichfield* by Thomas Harwood, 1806; *Picturesque Memorials of Salisbury* by Peter Hall, 1834; *A Guide to Carlisle* by Samuel Jefferson, 1842; *Historical Memorials of Northampton* by C. H. Hartshorne, 1848; and *A Handbook to Newcastle-on-Tyne* by J. C. Bruce, 1863. Local books of this kind tend to gravitate to bookshops in or near the towns about which they were written because the antiquarian book trade functions that way. However, they will always be scarce and dear, and it is for the buyer to decide how much they are worth to him.

Prices of those listed—and they are typical—could range from (i) to (b).

Often as not, equivalent North American works cover whole counties rather than towns and, generally, belong to a rather later period. The dearest will be those pertaining to areas in the West that were just developing when the books were issued. Here are some typical examples : *Historical Reminiscences of Summit County* by General Lucius Bierce, Akron, 1854, (g); *Guide to Denver* by S. B. Woolworth, Omaha City, 1862, (G); *Upper Mississipi* by George Gale, Chicago and New York, 1867, (g); *History and Directory of Nevada County* by Edwin F. Bean, Nevada, 1867, (d); *Guide to Santa Barbara Town and County* by E. N. Wood, Santa Barbara, 1872, (c); *History of Westchester County* by J. T. Scharf, two volumes, Philadelphia, 1886, (g); and *History of Luzerne County* by H. C. Bradsby, Chicago, 1893, (i). American local history books published in the present century are now almost as important as the earlier ones and the following might be (g); *North Platte and Its Associations* by Archibald R. Adamson, North Platte, no date, but 1910; *History of Custer County, Nebraska* by W. L. Gaston and A. R. Humphrey, Lincoln, 1919; and *History of Natrona County* by Alfred J. Mokler, Chicago, 1923.

Older items of Australian topography are no less in demand and just as difficult to find, and there are far fewer purely local books available. Here are some titles : David Collins's *Account of the English Colony in New South Wales*, two volumes, 1798–1802, (F); Andrew Bent's *Van Diemen's Land Pocket Almanack*, Hobart, 1824, (I); Charles J. Baker's *Sydney and Melbourne*, 1845, (f); William B. Withers's *History of Ballarat*, 1870, (g); and Ernest Favenc's *Western Australia*, 1887, (h). One of the Australian topographical gems is *South Australia Illustrated* by George F. Angas, 1847, which contains sixty hand-finished lithographs of what was then almost virgin territory. A fine piece of work, it is moving up from (B) to (A). A facsimile, produced in 1967, is grade (d).

161

Ties of blood and language no doubt account for the interest taken in British topography by collectors in the other English-speaking countries. Thousands of books about places in England, Wales and Scotland are shipped abroad every year and very few ever return to their native land. This is one reason why supplies of books that were once common are drying up at the sources. For as long as they remained inside Britain, they kept circulating as old collections were broken up and sold and new ones begun. Until the public at large became aware that there could be money in old books—and that is not long ago—scarcity was increased by a desire to have everything new. Books, whatever their content, were treated by the unthinking as twentieth-century disposables. Venerable books, treasured by their earlier owners, were chucked out by misguided heirs. Now the Veneerings of our time have woken up, but too late to bring back some grievous losses.

The wise collector learns to look beyond outward appearances and develops a special kind of visual and mental acuity. For instance, every devotee of the history and topography of the Aberdeen region will have the sense to seize on every book with 'Aberdeen' in its title, but the one who has this cultivated awareness will go further. Virtually nothing about its theme and setting can be gleaned from the name of a forgotten novel of the nineties of last century—*The King of Andaman*, 1895, by James Maclaren Cobban. The title suggests a romance of the Indian Ocean, so only the percipient Aberdeen bibliophile would be drawn to it by noticing the unusual surname of the author and recalling that an Aberdeen printer of the early nineteenth century bore the same name. The bibliophile would hope to find some connection and on examining the book would discover that it was set in a Scottish city called Inverdoon and depicted the lives of depressed weavers in a district called Ilkastane. He would identify Inverdoon with Aberdeen and Ilkastane with Gilcolmston, an area of the city now largely cleared and rebuilt. Much valuable information about the old Gilcolmston could be pieced together from this minor novel and a copy would be worth a place in any Aberdeen collection.

Aberdeen regional collectors are unlikely to become deeply involved with the nineteenth-century novel. George Macdonald is the only notable Aberdeenshire novelist of the time and first editions of his works would be (h) at their highest. Other British counties can boast far grander associations. Dorset and Wiltshire provide the settings for many of the novels of Thomas Hardy and Anthony Trollope. In Hardy, who recreated Wessex as a distinctive part of England, the spirit of place is powerfully felt. Every Wessex child born into a literate family learns at its mother's knee that Hardy's fictional towns and villages have their easily recognized real equivalents. Tolchurch is Tolpuddle, Casterbridge is Dorchester and Melchester is Salisbury—a city which therefore has three aliases, for its old name was Sarum and it is also the Barchester of Trollope, though he added something of Winchester to it.

Collecting regional novels is not strictly a topographical pursuit, but it can have its fascination. The collector could confine himself to one region and set out to acquire all he could connected with it, or he could be more wide-ranging and select representative books from every possible county. He could do quite well in Yorkshire, from the Brontës to J. B. Priestley, perhaps squeezing in Dickens's *Nicholas Nickleby*, 1838–9, (a) in original parts, as it is partly set in Yorkshire. Warwickshire has George Eliot (Mary Ann Cross, *née* Evans), Worcestershire has Francis Brett Young, Manchester, Howard Spring, and Nottinghamshire, D. H. Lawrence, just to make a beginning. London, Dublin and Edinburgh, as great literary centres, have more novelists associated with them than any ordinary collector could cope with to the full.

Some topographers choose to confine themselves to a minute area and within it make themselves mini-Phillippses, collecting every scrap of paper that relates to it. With this approach, a collector can be kept busy. If the chosen little place has, or once had, a railway station then its name must appear, or have appeared, in railway time tables, which can be much more fun than at first appears. If it never had a railway station, then surely it was served by a bus at one time, so that will be recorded in print. The place may be so tiny that its name appears only on maps of the largest scale. Very well, they are available and collectable. At the least, the inhabitants will have a continuous history of eating, drinking, wearing clothes and requiring tools and domestic utensils, so shops will have catered for those needs and kept some written records of their transactions. The most trifling grocers' and drapers' accounts can be the stuff of social history, so they will be looked for and kept carefully when found.

It is surprising how often it transpires that at some time a pamphlet, or even a single sheet, has been published about the most unlikely of places. It is the job of the interested mini-Phillipps to track it down. He may have to work entirely without light, with no bibliography or library record to guide him. Finding a single flimsy piece of paper may take a life-time.

Such pieces are called *ephemera* (Greek: *ephemeros—* lasting for a day). They were not normally intended for posterity, so if they amounted to more than a single sheet they were at best stitched or stapled together with or without paper outer wrappers. The mortality rate of such productions is bound to be high, so they are usually scarce. Misguided collectors often reject important pieces of ephemera because of the prices that may be asked for them. To them, it looks like blatant profiteering for a bookseller to demand £10 ($19), as well he might, for a thin, paper-covered booklet like *Michaelmarsh and its Antiquities* by A. W. (A. Wilkinson), published in 1867 and of Hampshire interest. If a large, handsomely-bound secondhand book can be bought for half that price, the miserable paper thing must be well-nigh valueless. This is a mistaken attitude. Well-bound books were

164

made to survive, ephemera were not.

Many localities—cities, counties and wider areas—have their own historical, antiquarian, archaeological and natural history societies, or societies that combine all or some of these studies. Most of them publish their transactions yearly, or at longer intervals, and some additionally, or instead, produce new scholarly books on aspects of their chosen subjects. Mounting costs have reduced their activities, but many still survive. Few have been established for less than a hundred years, so their publications, despite forbidding outward appearances and often ponderous language, are great repositories of information. Long runs of transactions, in uniformly bound volumes, or original wrappered parts, come on the market from time to time to be bought mainly by university and institutional libraries. The private buyer turns away from them regretfully, thinking of the large amount of shelf space they would occupy. If they are within his means he should nevertheless buy them and find room for them by being really firm for once with the dead wood in his library. If he truly cannot accommodate them he should find out where they are to be consulted so that he may note those parts or volumes that contain articles of particular use to him. He can then look for these as odd copies.

A complete run of *The Proceedings of the Somersetshire Archaeological and Natural History Society* from 1850 to the present time would cost at least £200 ($380), but broken runs would be cheaper in proportion. Single volumes may be quite dear for what they are. Individual articles reprinted from the transactions as separate pamphlets can be had, but the buyer has to pay for the convenience of having only the article he wants, without its contiguous irrelevancies. What is true of the Somerset transactions holds good for the publications of similar societies. It should be remembered, however, that the surviving societies gladly welcome new members and can sometimes supply out-of-print volumes and offprints at prices below those of the general market.

165

Another important source of information is the series of Victoria County Histories, issued by the Oxford University Press for the Institute of Historical Research. The series is by no means complete, though many volumes have been produced from time to time during the past seventy years. One of the first sets to be finished was the *Victoria History of Hampshire and the Isle of Wight*, edited by H. A. Doubleday and others, and issued in six folio volumes between 1900 and 1914. This, like all the others in the series, is excellently illustrated and supplied with many maps. It has been out of print for some time and is probably (H). Others in the series are still in a rather confusing state of preparation and availability. Some, like Hampshire, are complete but in need of supplements, others have certain volumes still in preparation. The position is further complicated in that some early issues have been reprinted in a different sequence. These fine reprints are (h). There has been increased activity of late by the Institute of Historical Research to complete the project, so prospective customers must keep in touch, possibly through the Institute's *Bulletin*, with the latest progress.

At the time when the Oxford University Press became involved with this mighty operation, the Cambridge University Press, was preparing a far more modest issue of topographical works—the Cambridge County Geographies. Almost every British county was covered and the authors were carefully chosen as men with a knowledge of the areas about which they wrote. The standard was high, though some were better than others. *Banffshire*, 1922, by W. Barclay, is obviously written with the author's deepest love, but the neighbouring *Aberdeenshire*, 1911, by A. Mackie, is a curate's egg. The series has risen in esteem since first written about in this book, and copies, though still cheap, can now cost as much as £2 ($3.80).

In a similar class, though probably more popular with collectors, are the Little Guides, published originally by Methuen & Co Ltd. The series began at the end of last century and was extended bit by bit to cover most of England and Wales, with the inclusion of some foreign places as well. The books were made to fit small pockets and bound in green cloth in the early days, but latterly in red. They were well illustrated, with line drawings (many by E. H. New), and photographs. After World War II, they were produced jointly by Methuen and B. T. Batsford & Co Ltd. In the earliest period of their publication they sold for 3s 6d (17½p). Secondhand copies can now be anything between 50p and £2.

Volumes in Macmillan's Highways & Byways series used to be available secondhand almost as cheaply as copies of the Little Guides, but now they are among the stars of their class, though still pretty low in the (i) grade. The series was rather more ambitious than the previous two and artists of the calibre of F. L. Griggs and Hugh Thomson were employed as illustrators. Publication began in 1897 and continued till 1948, when Seton Gordon's *Highways & Byways in the Central Highlands* was published, with illustrations by Sir D. Y. Cameron. The authors were wisely chosen and included Andrew Lang (*The Borders*), Sir Frederick Treves (*Dorset*), E. V. Lucas (*Essex*) and Clement Shorter (*Buckinghamshire*). *Thomas Hardy's Wessex* by Hermann Lea, is different in style internally from the others, but is one of the best. Reprints, revised and pocket editions were produced, but anyone wishing to collect the complete series would be well advised to do so on a first edition basis. All the volumes are dated and it is stated on the versos of the title-leaves whether they are reprints or revised editions. The later volumes were issued in near-white dust-jackets, most of which have gone.

Bibliophiles in every field like to have manuscript and other apposite material in addition to their printed books. This is especially true of topographers. They delight in documents, wills, indentures, old account books, notes of past lectures by antiquarians and village worthies, photographs, maps and prints. The last two raise ethical problems. Hard words have already been written about breakers. Should they be encouraged by collectors who want from various expensive books only the maps and prints pertinent to their own areas?

Since they were never issued in books, old Ordnance Survey maps can always be bought with a clear conscience. They are worth collecting in the first and in the various revised editions, because of the graphic information they give about the changes and developments in Britain's towns and countryside. While nothing can match the feel of ancient authenticity in the originals of the first survey, the collector in a hurry, and bound by economic realism, can opt for the reprints of the original survey issued by the firm of David & Charles. Even the collectors of originals might like to have these for everyday use, keeping the others as a sort of enlightened miser's hoard. Few lovers of Ordnance Survey maps can have welcomed the changes that metrication has brought to the latest maps. For all its disadvantages, the inch is a human sort of measure, which, like much of our heritage, developed naturally and, in its way, has something of the smooth funtionalism of an axe handle. The centimetre is coldly abstract, based on a mismeasurement of a meridianal quadrant. Only a sentimental traditionalist would pretend that metrication has in any way spoilt the maps—but most topographical collectors are unashamed sentimental traditionalists.

Several publishers in North America, Australia and Britain are reprinting important old books and other material on topography and local history. These new issues are a boon to the collector of average means and most booksellers will be happy to give information about available reprints. While old books, originals or not, are essential, it is important to find places for new books in a topographical library. The collector is well advised to make sure that his really new acquisitions are firsts by buying them as soon as they are issued.

The scope of an ideal topographical library is now becoming clear. The topographer who takes a wide view and has ample funds will have a fine array of the classics of his subject. The pride of his British section will probably be a 1610 edition of *Britannia*, paired with a copy of the 1789 edition. His two sets of the first Ordnance Survey maps, originals and reprints, will be set alongside those sheets of later editions that are particularly relevant. They will be supplemented by a copy of such a work as Charles and John Greenwood's *Atlas of the Counties of England and Wales*, 1834, with its key map on the title page and its forty-six coloured maps of counties—an item that is now (F). This may rest beside Samuel Lewis's *Topographical Dictionary of England, Wales, Scotland and Ireland*, 1831–46, in twelve volumes, including two atlases, and now valued (b). There will be room on his shelves for books of topographical engravings of the type dealt with in Chapter 7, and for representative runs of the transactions of at least one local antiquarian society. Books on his home area will be there, and some on other places which interest him. His ephemera, including recent maps and guide books, and possibly postcards dating from Victorian times to the present, will be kept in box files; his individual old maps and prints, if not framed and hung on the walls, will be in portfolios, which he may have made for himself from sheets of cardboard covered with buckram. Deeds and other manuscripts will probably be stowed in drawers, safe from dust and worm.

Some idea of the sort of North American and Australian topographical works likely to be owned by the connoisseur has already been given, but as these are newer countries it is even more difficult to draw the line between topography and travel. He would own many of the books discussed in Chapter 7. Perhaps he would also have some of the following : Arthur Dobbs's *An Account of the Countries Adjoining to Hudson's Bay . . . intended to shew the great Probability of a North West Passage*, 1744, (G); *The American Gazetteer*, three volumes, 12mo, London, 1762, (d); *A Map Exhibiting all the*

169

New Discoveries in the Interior Parts of North America by Aaron Arrowsmith, 1802, (a); D. Appleton's *Northern and Eastern Traveler's Guide*, 12mo, New York, 1854, (h); *Pictorial Illustrations of New Zealand* by J. C. Brees, 1847, (I); *Handbook to Australasia* by William Fairfax, 1859, (I); John Davis's *Tracks of McKinlay and Party across Australia*, 1863, (a); S. T. Gill's *Australian Sketch Book*, undated, but 1865, (G); and Andrew Garran's *Picturesque Atlas of Australasia*, undated but 1886, (c). There are few old North American and Australian books specifically concerned with regional dialects, so the state of Virginia is fortunate in having Bennett W. Green's *Word-Book of Virginia Folk-Speech*, Richmond, Virginia, 1899, (h).

No topographical library concerned with the North American continent should be without *American Scenery* and *Canadian Scenery* by Nathaniel Parker Willis and William Henry Bartlett. Though originally issued in parts, from 1840, these are usually found in two volumes to each title, with 117 American engravings and the same number of Canadian engravings. Between them, they give a remarkable survey of the continent from the eastern seaboard to the frontier. The illustrations are too good to have escaped the breakers, so entire copies are becoming fewer and more expensive. Perhaps each can safely be graded as (H) in fine unfoxed condition.

It would require an average yearly expenditure of about £800 ($1,520) for twelve years to build up an international library to this standard, but a satisfactory topographical collection could be achieved in ten years by spending no more than a keen amateur photographer would pay for equipment and materials over the same period. It should be borne in mind that a topographical library founded on known collectors' pieces and developed according to the collector's own good taste will be a fairly safe investment. A humble collection, with nothing more expensive in it than a run of the Highways & Byways series and containing a few unusual

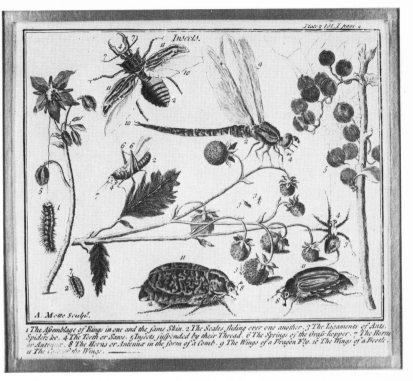

Insects.

A. Motte Sculp.

1 The Assemblage of Rings in one and the same Skin. 2 The Scales sliding over one another. 3 The Ligaments of Ants. Spiders &c. 4 The Teeth or Saws. 5 Insects suspended by their Thread. 6 The Springs of the Grass-hopper. 7 The Horns or Antennæ. 8 The Horns or Antennæ in the form of a Comb. 9 The Wings of a Dragon Fly. 10 The Wings of a Beetle. 11 The Cover of the Wings.

Plate 13 A multiple natural history illustration from *Spectacle de la Nature, or, Nature Display'd*, translated from the French by Mr Humphreys, 2 volumes, 5th edition, 1740. The fine copper plates were the best of this work, which, in the original French, was mocked by Voltaire.

Plate 14 Period charm and historical interest combine in this engraving by Bartlett of 'Rail-Road Scene, Little Falls', from Nathaniel P. Willis's and William Bartlett's *American Scenery*, 1840 (see p. 170).

bargain items such as even the unluckiest of hunters can sometimes pick up, ought to increase in value over the years. It should be remembered, though, that a book like *The King of Andaman* may be worth its weight in gold to an Aberdeen enthusiast as may the *Historical Sketch of the Congregational Church in Belchertown* be to a man from Massachusetts, but they will be worth little far from home.

9

Natural History

Natural history books have always been highly regarded, but never more so than today. Only lately has the wider world come to realize fully what masterpieces are contained within those natural history folios with their magnificent plates, drawn, engraved and coloured by master hands. The artistry of the best of the illustrated books has attracted into this area of collecting many who are not true bookmen. They have little interest in the printed word. They want only to possess and enjoy the beauty of the plates. The bibliophile to whom a book is primarily something to read may be scornful until he, too, is somehow drawn to the books and captivated by the illustrations.

They are like sirens. Allured by them, a victim could spend a fortune in acquiring the mere beginning of a collection. Unless a collector has almost unlimited resources, he must be like Ulysses and tie himself to the mast, as it were, while they work their enchantment. So that he may be forewarned, some of them will be mentioned in this chapter, together with others less bewitching but more likely to be within the grasp of the modest collector.

Botany began as a utilitarian study. Though the word comes from the Greek *botane*, meaning grass or fodder, the early botanists dealt mainly with the identification of medicinal herbs, and in books called herbals, taught how and where they could be discovered. The earliest printed herbal was the *Liber de Proprietatibus Rerum*, by Bartholomaeus

Anglicus, published about 1472, probably at Cologne. Its first English printing was in 1495. It, like the next known herbal, *Das Puch der Natur*, Augsburg, 1475, by Cunrat von Megenberg, often known simply as Konrad, dealt with other matters besides the properties of plants. Though never directly translated into English, *Das Puch* was one of the sources of some later English herbals. It was the first printed book with botanical illustrations, cut in wood. It predates by fifty-one years the first English illustrated herbal, *The Great Herball* of 1526, printed by Peter Treveris, who may have been the compiler as well as the printer, the work being anonymous.

Before the appearance of this illustrated book, another purely English herbal had been published, without a title, as was then common, and known by its opening sentence— *Here begynneth a new mater, the which sheweth and treateth of ye vertues and proprytes of herbes, the whiche is called an Herball*, printed in 1525 by Rycharde Banckes, London, and thought to have been written by Walter Cary. Each of these books is liable to cost over £5,000 ($9,500) if entire, and a mere dozen consecutive leaves could sell at £50 ($95).

The best-known English herbal of Elizabethan times is that of John Gerard (sometimes written Gerarde, but not in the first edition), published as *The Herbal or Generall Historie of Plantes*, 1597, (A). The first printing must have been quite large, for the book is not among the rarest of the period. It quite frequently turns up, usually in imperfect condition. It has become more sought after, so even incomplete copies can be (G). The enlarged edition, edited by Thomas Johnson and printed in 1633, is a more competent work and may cost at least as much as the first. Johnson was the earliest English plant hunter but he did not live to complete his projected English flora.

Nicholas Culpeper (1616–54) was the author of the most popular English herbal ever. Since 1653, when it was first published as *The English Physitian Enlarged, or the Herbal,* his book has run into many editions and has been the main-stay of many a practitioner of cottage medicine. Culpeper had his own ideas about applying astrology to medicine and his book is not much use as a guide to the real properties of plants. The first edition is not all that highly regarded and should be (g).

Copies of early herbals sometimes have hand-coloured illustrations. Unless the work has been done with rare distinction, these copies have no extra value, as the colouring is most probably not contemporaneous with the book. Botanical works issued with coloured plates hardly begin before the eighteenth century as far as England is concerned. John Martyn (1699–1768) is credited with producing the first English book with colour-printed plates other than the primitive attempts of early days. His *Historia Plantarum Rariorum*, issued in parts from 1728, to 1736, is collected by others as well as natural history fans because it is a landmark in book illustration. Though the colour is feeble and the engraving unexciting, the plates point the way to better things. Perhaps non-botanists should be left to pay the £5,000 ($9,500) or more that a set can cost.

Until the nineteenth century, botany was still regarded as a branch of medicine, so we have books like the first English monograph on mistletoe, by Sir John Colbatch, *A Dissertation Concerning Mistletoe: A most Wonderful Specifick Remedy for the Cure of Convulsive Distempers*, 1720. This is one of many treatises on plants of the same period and the modest collector who has to forgo the pleasures of the coloured-plate books can enjoy rounding up a selection of such items at lower cost, though the mere mention of the Colbatch here could well send its price up to (d).

Some of the interest in trees which emerged in the seventeenth century was medical. William Cole, in *Adam in Eden*, 1657, (a) wrote:

Wall-nuts have the perfect signature of the Head : The outer husk or green Covering, represent the *Pericranium*, or outward skin of the skull, whereon the hair groweth, and therefore salt made of those husks or barks, are exceeding good for wounds in the head.

For the most part, the concern was with the uses of timber. John Evelyn, the diarist, wrote of trees as both useful and ornamental in his *Sylva: or, a Discourse of Forest Trees and the Propagation of Timber in His Majesty's Dominions*, issued in two parts in 1664, now usually bound in one volume. The first edition of this commendable early arboricultural study may be (a), but there is also in (d) a fine edition published at York in 1776, with thirty-eight beautiful uncoloured copper-engraved plates.

The most important English botanist contemporary with Evelyn was John Ray (1627–1705), the father of systematic botany, who took the first steps towards establishing a natural method of classifying plants according to families. If the beauty of his books equalled their scholarship they would be beyond price. As it is, his *Flora*, 1665, and *Catalogus Plantarum Angliae*, 1670, are each grade (a) and his greatest work, the *Historia Plantarum*, three volumes, 1686–8 and 1704, is (F).

Robert John Thornton (1768–1837) was a sort of John Ray in reverse. His scholarship was deficient, but his great book is one of the most beautiful of all. Thornton, a doctor, was obsessed with the idea of producing a book as a lasting monument to the genius of Linnaeus, the Swedish natural historian. He engaged some of the most highly qualified artists of his day to paint the original pictures for the plates for his book, with a team of twelve experienced engravers to interpret the paintings. Every plate in mezzotint or aquatint, colour-printed and finished by hand in watercolour, is a masterpiece of its kind.

Thornton, who himself did the illustration of roses, insisted that the flowers in all the pictures should be placed against appropriate backgrounds. There are twenty-eight coloured flower-pieces in the book, besides a portrait of Linnaeus in Lapp costume, and several other engravings. The title of the whole work is *The New Illustration of the Sexual System of Linnaeus* and the section with the coloured plates is *The Temple of Flora*, which was also published separately. The whole work appeared serially between 1799 and 1807, but the priority of the various issues is still in some doubt. A complete early issue of Thornton's book might still be had for under £3,000 ($6,000), but the price keeps rising. In the author's lifetime, each part cost only a guinea and later 25s (£1.25), but sales were poor. Thornton tried to sell some by lottery, but that failed. He lost much money on his life's work and died in poverty.

A more successful illustrated botanical work was begun twelve years before the Linnaeus monument. It was conceived by William Curtis (1746–99), but even he could hardly have imagined that his work would be continued to the present day. In February 1787, the first volume of the *Botanical Magazine* appeared. It was an instant success and brought some much-needed money to Curtis, its originator, writer and editor. In the course of the previous ten years he had produced the two fat folios of the *Flora Londinensis*, 1777 and 1787, (H), which gave illustrations and descriptions of the wild plants growing in and around London. He had given up his work as demonstrator and keeper of the garden of the Society of Apothecaries to prepare this *Flora* and was deeply disappointed when it failed to pay its way. In the *Botanical Magazine* he courted popular support by featuring showy exotic plants instead of the humble natives of the earlier work.

His magazine was in a flourishing condition when Curtis died, so it was willingly taken over by John Sims (1740–1831) and later by Sir William J. Hooker (1785–1865). Sir William was succeeded as editor by his son, Sir Joseph D. Hooker (1817–1911). When Sir Joseph resigned at the age of

87, other editors were found and publication continued to the end of 1920, but by then it was running at a loss. With the last part of volume 146, it looked like the end of the road. However, H. J. Elwes, a keen naturalist, and some friends, bought the copyright and made it over to the Royal Horticultural Society, which capable body has been responsible for publication ever since. It has not appeared with the regularity that it did in Curtis's day and its future is again in doubt. Surely some of the really wealthy collectors who are prepared to spend many thousands on a single book could spare something to help keep alive this beautiful monument to the botanists and horticulturists of England.

The owner of a complete set of the *Botanical Magazine* from 1787 to date would be a man to be envied. Its value could be in the region of £15,000 ($28,500). Building a set would be a long process. Single volumes could cost from £25 to £80 each ($48 to $155), according to age and condition.

There was great botanical activity onwards from the end of the eighteenth century. There are still to be found on the shelves of secondhand bookshops dozens of small books with pleasing coloured illustrations of flowers, native and exotic, some hand-coloured, some printed by the Baxter or other similar process. Alas, they are no longer to be had cheaply. Collecting them is in fashion and even quite insignificant examples are hardly available under £5 ($9.50).

In the 1850s and 1860s, the London publishers, Routledge, Warne & Routledge, produced *Reeve's Popular Natural History*, a series of twenty-four square 16mo books in green, blue or brown bead-grained cloth, intended for young people. Every book contained twenty coloured plates of variable quality. Ten of the twenty-four dealt with botanical subjects. Mention of this series in the first edition of this book helped to increase the demand and the price, so it is no longer true that a complete set could be built up for little more than £24. Nowadays, as much as £15 ($28.50) is asked (not necessarily paid!) for single volumes.

The success of the *Botanical Magazine* encouraged the publication of similar works. S. T. Edwards (*c*1769–1819) was one of the illustrators of the *Magazine*, but in 1815 he set up on his own and brought out *The Botanical Register*, which ran until 1847, by which time thirty-three volumes had been produced, plus an appendix and an index. There are 2,717 hand-coloured plates in the whole work, which sells in the region of £5,000 ($7,600). Conrad Loddiges's *The Botanical Cabinet* blossomed forth in 1817 and ran through twenty volumes, with 2,000 hand-coloured plates, to 1833. It is grade (A).

James Sowerby (1757–1822), the first of a renowned family of naturalist-artists, was also a *Botanical Magazine* illustrator for a time. In 1790 he joined forces with Sir J. E. Smith to issue, by 1814, thirty-six volumes of *English Botany*. He himself did almost all the 2,592 drawings from which the hand-coloured plates were taken. Smith, not Sowerby, supplied the text. This is also an (A) item. The second edition of 1832–46 is considered inferior and is about half the price of the first. A third edition, edited by J. T. B. Syme (later called J. T. Boswell) and published between 1863 and 1892 in thirteen volumes, is (a). James's grandson, John E. Sowerby (1825–70), collaborated with C. P. Johnson to produce *British Wild Flowers*, with ninety coloured plates, in 1860. The first edition is scarce and could be (g), but re-issues are fairly common and are (i).

Between 1837 (though no date is given for the beginning of the work) and 1843, J. Bateman produced a huge folio, *The Orchidaceae of Mexico and Guatemala*. Only 125 copies were issued, all with the set of forty superb hand-coloured lithographic plates. Unremarkably, a copy would cost the buyer at least £4,000 ($7,600) if he could find one for sale. This book belongs to the time when botany was freeing itself from its medical ties and developing into a scientific study in its own right. Sir Joseph Banks (1743–1820) emerged as a patron of botanists and explorers. He gave great encouragement to the brothers Francis and Ferdinand Bauer, who were among the best botanical artists of their day. Though they were Austrian in origin, England was their adopted country. Francis was responsible for *Delineations of Exotic Plants cultivated in the Royal Garden at Kew*, produced between 1793 and 1800, in three parts. Others engraved the thirty hand-coloured plates of flowers from Francis's drawings. A fair price for this work would be £5,000 ($9,500). Ferdinand went with John Sibthorp to Greece and the Greek islands in 1786 to work on the *Flora Graeca*, for which Ferdinand did the drawings of plants. Sibthorp died in 1796, while work on the *Flora* was proceeding. The first part did not appear till 1806 and the series was not completed till 1840. Sir J. E. Smith and, later, John Lindley, were the editors, and James De C. Sowerby, son of the first James Sowerby, prepared the 966 coloured plates from Ferdinand's drawings. Only sixty-five copies were issued. In 1976, a set was sold for £22,000 ($41,800), possibly the highest price ever paid for an English-language printed botanical book.

Soon the era of the plant-hunters had begun in earnest. While Joseph D. Hooker was sailing the southern seas with HMS *Erebus* and *Terror* (later commanded by Franklin, as mentioned in Chapter 7), collecting material for his *Flora Antarctica*, 1844–7, Robert Fortune (1813–80) was preparing his expedition to China, which ended shortly before the publication of his *Three Years' Wanderings in Northern China*, 1847. Fortune was sent to the Far East by the Botanical Society of London and returned with a wealth of information and specimens. His is a worthy book in grade (h). Hooker's Antarctic flora is more likely to be (F). His *Rhododendrons of Sikkim-Himalaya*, edited by his father, Sir W. J. Hooker, and published in parts between 1849 and 1851, with thirty hand-coloured plates, should be (G), but could soon rise to (E). It was the first fruits of the younger Hooker's expedition to the Himalayas, to be followed by *Himalayan Journals* in 1854, (d) and the beautiful *Illustrations of Himalayan Plants*,

1855, with twenty-four coloured plates prepared by W. H. Fitch (1817–92) from Hooker's originals. Hooker's other important plant-hunting book is the *Flora of Australia*, 1859, (a).

Many other plant-hunters have been active since Fortune and Hooker; some will be dealt with in the next chapter, but the attractive work of J. E. Brown should be noted now : *The Forest Flora of South Australia*, folio, the nine parts of which were published at Adelaide between 1882 and 1890, (I).

The fact that he collaborated with James Sowerby and the French botanist, Charles L'Heritier de Brutelle, in producing the *Sertum Anglicum*, 1788, (A) a survey of rare plants at Kew Gardens, enables mention to be made of the Belgian, Pierre-Joseph Redouté (1759–1840), the world's most famous botanical illustrator. He is best known for his books illustrative of roses, which sell for up to £12,000 ($22,800) and will no doubt realize more in the near future. Some of his finest work, however, is to be seen in *Les Liliacées*, Paris, 1802–16. A copy was sold at Sotheby's in 1976 for £19,000 ($36,000).

The arboricultural work of Evelyn was continued last century by P. W. Watson with *Dendrologia Britannica*, two volumes, 1825, and by John C. Loudon (1783–1843) with *Arboretum et Fruticetum Britannicum*, eight volumes, 1838. Both books are (I), with the Watson as the slightly dearer. Though there are 172 coloured plates in *Dendrologia* and 412 in *Arboretum*, those in the latter are inferior in finish. On the other hand, Loudon's book is the more informative, and those who want the work purely for study would do well to seek out the second edition, with uncoloured plates, published in 1844 and probably (f).

One of the most attractive nineteenth-century books on fruit trees is the three-volume *Pomologia Britannica* of John Lindley (1799–1865), with 152 hand-coloured plates, published in 1841. Lindley was a distinguished botanist and horticulturist whose name is commemorated in the fine

Lindley Library of the Royal Horticultural Society. If a present-day admirer of Lindley would like a representative first edition of one of Lindley's works and cannot afford the *Pomologia* at (G), he might find a first of the author's *Ladies' Botany*, 1834, in grade (i).

The earliest printed books on birds dealt with the hunters and the hunted—the hawks and falcons on the one side and the gamebirds and waterfowl on the other, though the hunted then included also a variety of passerines and other small birds. Even when ornithology became scientific, the favourite instrument of the field naturalist was the gun. This, with the wholesale collecting of birds' eggs, was responsible for the temporary extinction of the osprey in Britain and probably hastened the total extinction of other birds in several parts of the world. Salvation came with the high-speed camera which made possible the close observation of birds without the need for killing.

Scientific ornithology can be considered as beginning in 1676 with the posthumous publication of *Ornithologiae Libri Tres* by Francis Willughby, the whole work 'recognovit, digessit, supplevit J. Raius'. This is now at least grade (c), but much preferred is the first English edition of two years later, *The Ornithology of F. Willughby*. Besides being the editor, as of the first edition, John Ray also translated this edition and was probably the author of the 'three considerable discourses' that were added to the book : *Of the Art of Fowling, Of the Ordering of Singing Birds* and *Of Falconry*. This is a grade (H) book.

No other book of such importance to ornithologists was published for more than a hundred years afterwards, but there is much in the interim period for the collector who cannot fly too high. John Moore, a doctor who specialized in treating people for parasitic worms, published *The Columbarium, or the Pigeon House* in 1735. This natural history of tame pigeons is scarce and, although a small book with little eye appeal, is grade (f). A new edition, sometimes in cloth, sometimes in paper covers, was edited by W. G. Tegetmeier and published in 1879. Even that requires a lot of tracking down but might be found for £5 ($9.50) or so. There are some charming and some rather horrific (they used to blind song-birds and slit their tongues) 12mos of the eighteenth century on bird-keeping, for which the collector should keep his eyes open. One example is *The New and Complete Bird-Fancyer*, an anonymous work, undated, but 1784. It and similar books should cost no more than £8 ($15.50) and the collector in a small way can get as much enjoyment from them as his millionaire friends derive from their more magnificent treasures, without having to worry about security, insurance and all the other problems caused by the possession of a priceless collection.

Of some ornithological importance in its time, *A Portrait of Rare Birds, from the Menagery of Osterly Park*, published in two volumes in 1794 and 1799 (the second volume undated), is now more valued for the hundred hand-coloured plates it contains. It was the work of William Hayes, who collected his material at Osterley Park in the former county of Middlesex. The Adam house there was still relatively new and had a flourishing menagerie attached. This two-volume book is (A). In the same period, John W. Lewin was preparing his *Birds of Great Britain* in eight volumes, issued between 1796 and 1801. Although this book is of more interest to the genuine ornithologist, as being the first important avian fauna of Britain to be illustrated in colour—it has 336 hand-coloured plates of birds and their eggs—its market value is only about half that of Hayes's book. Lewin followed his work in Britain with a *Natural History of Birds of New South Wales*, a large folio with twenty-six coloured plates, published in 1822, and much more highly rated, at (C) in fine condition. In the same year Lewin produced *The Natural History of Lepidopterous Insects of New South Wales* (F). His earlier entomological book was a volume of *The Insects of Great Britain*, 1795, with forty-six coloured plates (a). This was intended as the first of a multi-volume work, which was never completed.

The most celebrated bird artists of all time were John James Audubon (1780–1851) and John Gould (1804–81). An American of French origin, Audubon specialized in the birds of his home continent. A copy of the first edition of his *Birds of America* 1827–38, fetched $396,000 (£208,400) at auction in 1977. Other copies have sold for less since, but this one was in superb condition, by all accounts, so a similar copy would presumably rise even higher today. Other early editions of Audubons, though less expensive, are still beyond the ordinary man's reach. A facsimile, with introduction and descriptive text by William Vogt, was published in 1937 and contained 500 coloured reproductions of the original plates, including sixty-five from editions later than the first. This might be found at (h) and a later two-volume facsimile produced in America and Britain in 1966 may be (g).

The Englishman, John Gould, began his long career as a bird artist with *The Birds of Europe*, five volumes, issued between 1832 and 1837. Containing 448 coloured plates, its present value is in the region of £8,000 ($15,200), as is his *Birds of Great Britain*, with 367 coloured plates, issued in twenty-five parts between 1862–73. His *Birds of Asia*, seven volumes, edited by R. B. Sharpe, 1850–83, with 530 coloured plates, is even less accessible to the ordinary collector at something like £12,000 ($22,800), while his *Birds of Australia*, eight volumes including supplement, is in the same class at $A21,000 (£14,000, $26,600). The humble buyer may gain a rough idea of the glories of Gould from a book published by Methuen, London, in 1967 and titled *Birds of Australia: 160 colour-plates from the lithographs of John Gould*, text by A. Rutgers. Since it was remaindered in 1970, its value has risen, but it might be unearthed at £8 ($A12, $15.50).

Among books on the birds of Britain there is sometimes confusion between *British Birds* in six volumes, 1851–7, with many later editions, by the Reverend F. O. Morris, and

British Game Birds and Wildfowl, one volume, 1855, by Beverley R. Morris. The authors and the books are quite distinct. The Reverend F. O. Morris's work has 358 hand-coloured plates and Beverley Morris's has only sixty. At one time the Beverley Morris was considered much the superior and was priced correspondingly. Demand for F. O. Morris's work has lately increased (those breakers!) so that both are (a). Three volumes of *Nests and Eggs*, by the same reverend author and uniformly bound, are sometimes added to the F. O. Morris bird volumes, but these extras are unsatisfactory. The lithographic plates make many of the nests look as if they had been built of seaweed. The price of late editions of the Reverend Mr Morris's books are little lower than of the first and early, but in all cases prospective buyers should look carefully at the plates. The quality of the colouring can vary quite markedly from copy to copy.

This is only a small part of the story of ornithological books. In descriptive ornithology, the first satisfactory standard work was William Yarrell's *A History of British Birds*, three volumes, 1839–43. The black and white illustrations do not attract the attention of the non-naturalist, so copies of the first and subsequent editions are (i). Yarrell's work was the direct ancestor of *The Handbook of British Birds* by H. F. Witherby and others, the present standard work, in five volumes, 1938–41, (d).

Entomologists are not so well served with books of the Audubon and Gould class, which makes things slightly easier for the bibliophile who does not possess a licence to print money. He may be hard pressed, however, if he fancies *The Natural History of the rarer lepidopterous Insects of Georgia*, 1797, by J. Abbot and J. E. Smith, with 104 hand-coloured plates of butterflies and moths of the southern states of America. It could cost him $4,500 (£2,370).

Lewin's two insect books have been referred to earlier in this chapter. John Henry Leech's *Butterflies from China, Japan and Corea*, three volumes, 1892–4, deserves to be mentioned with them and is in (a). William Kirby's *European Butterflies and Moths*, sixty-one coloured plates, 1882, has a standing high enough to put it at (f), but the illustrations are rather disappointing. The same may be said of such books as W. G. Wright's *The Butterflies of the West Coast of the U.S.A.*, 1906, which may be (h), and *The Butterflies of Australia*, Sydney, 1914, by G. A. Waterhouse and G. Lyell, which is (h). Though somewhat quirky in style, the forty-one hand-coloured plates in *The Aurelian*, 1766, by Moses Harris (1731–85) give accurate illustrations of British insects. A similar quaintness is found in E. Albin's *A Natural History of Spiders and Other Curious Insects*, 1736, with fifty-three hand-coloured plates, grade (I). The Quaker, Thomas Say (1787–1834), has been called the father of American entomology. His fame largely rests on his three volumes of *American Entomology*, Philadelphia, 1824–28, (H). A latish work with hand-coloured illustrations is still a standard guide —*The Lepidoptera of the British Islands*, eleven volumes, 1893–1907, by C. G. Barrett, with 504 plates. It could be (a) or (I). As handsome as it is informative, A. A. Lisney's *A Bibliography of British Lepidoptera 1608–1799* was privately printed at the Chiswick Press in 1960. It could be found at (h) and it contains plenty of details to fire the enthusiasm of the collector.

The two important natural history works of Thomas Bewick, already mentioned in Chapter 5, should not be overlooked. *The General History of Quadrupeds* was first published at Newcastle-upon-Tyne in 1790 and *The History of British Birds* at the same place, in two volumes, 1797 and 1804. *The Quadrupeds* is grade (e), but *British Birds* might rise to (H). Other early editions of these will cost little less if the woodcuts are clean and well printed. As they have not the obvious appeal of most of the books already mentioned in this chapter, the Bewicks sell comparatively cheaply for works of genius. An unknown author took his cue from Bewick and produced a *Natural History of Quadrupeds* at Bungay in

187

1796. Though the forty-four plates are hand-coloured, the quality is unremarkable. It is an interesting 'buy' at (h).

A glide down the evolutionary ladder brings us to snakes. Here P. Russell's *An account of Indian Serpents, collected on the coast of Coromandel* is a worthy collector's piece. It was published in 1796, with forty-two hand-coloured plates and followed up with a continuation, also with forty-two plates in colour, which appeared between 1796 and 1809. Together, the two parts should be (H).

Other legless creatures are not well served by fine illustrated books. For fishes, J. Couch's *A history of the Fishes of the British Islands*, four volmes, 1877–8, (a) to (I), is a representative example, and for marine animals there is *Marine Mammals of the North-western Coast of North America* by Charles M. Scammon, San Francisco, 1874, with twenty-seven excellent lithographs, at (d).

One of the most beautiful books containing illustrations of land animals is *The Book of Antelopes*, four volumes, 1894–1900, by P. L. Sclater and O. Thomas. It has one hundred hand-coloured plates and 121 illustrations in the text and is likely to overtop (A). Of the same calibre is William C. Harris's *Portraits of the Game and Wild Animals of Southern Africa*, 1840. In folio size, it has thirty hand-coloured lithographs and is (A). As it contains an illustration of a bison, G. Garrard's book on oxen could be said to stray out of the domestic animal field. It is *A Description of the Different Varieties of Oxen Common in the British Isles*, dated 1800 and issued between that year and 1815. It has fifty-two hand-coloured plates and is another in the (A) grade.

In the science of conchology, which is concerned with shells, the collector can find many lovely little books without having to pay too highly. There are still pleasant volumes, dating from the beginning of last century onwards, with coloured or plain plates, to be had for under £12 ($22.80) each. For those who can pay more there are items like William Swainson's *Exotic Conchology*, 1834, with forty-eight coloured plates, at (a), and *The Genera of Recent and Fossil Shells* by J. and G. B. Sowerby, issued in forty-two parts between 1820 and 1834, though undated and never completed at (H).

This is an example of a book about which we now have accurate information because of work done by competent booksellers. In their new series catalogue No 135, 1976, Wheldon & Wesley Ltd, natural history specialists of Hertfordshire, England, listed a copy, with the following information :

> The number of plates is given incorrectly by the British Museum (Nat. Hist.) as 267, i.e. 279 less 12 not published. This is repeated by Nissen (391). The entry makes no mention of the fact that plates 142 and 161 were not published, which brings the final total to 265.

This information has now been safely recorded and future conchological bibliographies will be corrected. The Nissen referred to is *Die Zoologische Buchillustration* by Claus Nissen, Stuttgart, 1969 and onwards, one of the most important international natural histories of the century.

If God banished mankind from the Garden of Eden, then Darwin banished the Garden of Eden from mankind. In November 1859, Charles Darwin (1809–82) published *The Origin of Species by means of Natural Selection*, thereby striking orthodox religion a blow from which it has not yet wholly recovered. Darwin was a clear thinker and a scientist of genius. Nevertheless, the theory he propounded in his book did not spring Athene-like from his head, nor was he its 'onlie begetter'. He assembled already known facts, arranged them logically and drew the conclusions towards which some of his contemporaries were reaching and from which others were shrinking. For 200 years, geological and biological studies had been moving inexorably towards natural selection as an explanation for the diversity of living forms, and the pace had considerably accelerated in the nineteenth century.

In 1843 and 1846, the remarkable Scottish polymath Robert Chambers published anonymously his two volumes of *Vestiges of the Natural History of Creation, and the Explanation*, (g). Though working without sufficient data, Chambers anticipated Darwin in several particulars. In the chapter that explains his hypothesis of 'the progress of organic creation', Chambers states :

> If it has pleased Providence to arrange that one species should give birth to another, until the second highest gave birth to man, who is the very highest; be it so, it is our part to admire and to submit.

These were brave words for 1843 in Calvinist Scotland, even if the author did not put his name to them.

Working in the remote Malay Archipelago, Alfred Russel Wallace (1823–1913) reached the same conclusions as Darwin, at the same time, but withheld publication of his findings so that Darwin should have the credit that Wallace considered was Darwin's due.

Samuel Wilberforce (1805–73), Bishop of Oxford, became one of Darwin's most trenchant opponents, though many of the clergy and laity of all denominations were equally incensed by the Darwinian theory, which seemed to strike at the roots of Christianity. If the story of the Creation and the Fall was not literally true, the sacrifice of Christ on the Cross and the redemption He offered became meaningless—or so they thought. Most churchmen are now reconciled to Darwinism and are prepared to share Chambers's attitude. Some still find difficulties.

There is no evidence that the depression that caused Hugh Miller (1802–56) to shoot himself was connected with a conflict between his fundamentalist religion and his geological researches, but in his books, *Footprints of the Creator*, 1850, and *The Testimony of the Rocks*, published posthumously in 1857, he seems to be fighting a rearguard action against the

Darwinian testimony of the rocks. Perhaps his intellect pushed him on an evolutionary path which his religion would not allow him to tread. His geological books are (i) or exceptionally (h).

The purpose of this digression is to suggest a field of activity for the natural history collector who cannot afford the high prices of colour-plate books. A collection that records the rise of Darwinism and the concomitant wrangles and attempted refutations should not be too costly to acquire. Even if the most important books in the field are too dear, there is still plenty of good material to be had at low prices.

The centrepiece of such a collection would be a first edition of Darwin's *Origin of Species*. The date on the title-page, 1859, should be sufficient evidence of a first, but it would be as well to check that there is a folding diagram at page 117 and thirty-two pages of advertisements at the end, dated June 1859. The desirable condition is in original green cloth, with half-title. At grade (A), this would be the dearest item in the collection. Next would come Darwin's first book, which has a long title, usually abbreviated to *Journal of Researches*, or *The Voyage of the 'Beagle'*, published in 1839. In the next few years this may well climb above its present (a) grade, while the much later *The Descent of Man* is also liable to be upgraded. This dates from 1871, when it was published in two volumes. Two issues of the first edition are recognized: the first has a list of errata on the verso of the title-page to volume two; the second has no errata, but lists the author's other works on the versos of both title-pages. The first issue should be (b) and the second (c). The rest of Darwin's works could be cheaper. They include *The Variation of Animals and Plants under Domestication*, two volumes, 1868, (b), and *The Expression of the Emotions in Man and Animals*, 1872, (c).

Thomas Henry Huxley (1825–95) was Darwin's great champion and the inventor of the term 'agnostic'. His books may be had for relatively little outlay. The dearest would probably be *The Evidence as to Man's Place in Nature*, 1868, (h). Most of the others would be far down (i), about £10 ($19) each. Huxley was always ready to enter into arguments with the opponents of natural selection and was the subject of many attacks in magazine articles and pamphlets. One such pamphlet was produced after the students of Aberdeen University had elected him their Rector in 1872. It is a small octavo booklet in green paper wrappers and bears the curious title of *Protoplasm, Powheads, Porwiggles; and The Evolution of the Horse from the Rhinoceros*. It was published anonymously at Aberdeen in 1875 and is a satirical diatribe against Huxley and the theory of evolution. The powheads and porwiggles of the title are tadpoles, from which, the author believed, Huxley claimed that men were descended. It was in fact written by the Reverend John Allan, a minister of the Established Kirk in Aberdeen. As literature, science or theology it is worthless. As a piece of Darwinian ephemera, £2 ($3.80) might be its value.

Some of the material in *The Principles of Geology*, three volumes, 1830–3, by Sir Charles Lyell (1797–1875) helped to point the way for Darwin, and Lyell's *Geological Evidences of the Antiquity of Man*, 1863, gave sound support to natural selection. Both are (f). Lyell's scarcer *Elements of Geology*, 1838, would be (e).

The discoveries and controversies of the mid-nineteenth century gave a stimulus to scientific studies, reflected in the increased output of books on geology, zoology and allied subjects. The London publishers Kegan Paul, Trench, Trübner & Co Ltd went some way to meet the demand with their International Scientific Series, begun in 1871 and continued until World War I. The series is distinguished by a uniform binding of fine sand-grained red cloth with bold gilt titling on the spine. Several important works on aspects of biology and other sciences were published for the first time in this series. The recent demands of collectors have raised the price, but the series could be got together in time for under £10 ($19) a volume. The first book was *Forms of Water* by John Tyndall (1820–93), who was a mountaineer, railway engineer and physicist.

Earlier, Sir William Jardine (1800–74) completed his Naturalist's Library, a series of forty volumes by different authors, fourteen of which were on birds, thirteen on mammals, seven on insects and six on fishes. In all, they contained over 1,300 coloured plates and were published at Edinburgh from 1833 to 1843. The small volumes were bound in uniform purplish-brown grained cloth. Some of the plates are indifferent, but others, especially those in the two volumes on parrots (by Edward Lear) and the two humming-bird volumes, are beautifully done. A full set is now (E) and prices are probably still on the upward move. Anybody collecting the volumes one by one has now little hope of cutting costs. He might buy a few individual volumes for under £10 ($19), but double that amount is asked for the best and the scarcest. Now and then extortionate prices are sought for the two humming-bird volumes in the series because they are confused with a special large-paper edition of these which was issued in 1840, in two volumes. These are justifiably (a).

One of the most rewarding of present-day series to collect is Collins's New Naturalist, begun in 1945 and still continuing. Some of the most distinguished naturalists of our time have contributed to the series, every volume of which is well produced, with good colour plates in nearly every case. The green cloth of the covers has a tendency to fade, even under the dust-wrappers, so the books should be shelved away from strong light. Among the best of the series, and so the most difficult to find, are No 9, *A Country Parish* by A. W. Boyd, almost a modern counterpart of White's *Selborne* (see below); No 27, *Dartmoor* by Harvey and St. Ledger-Gordon, and No 29, *The Folklore of Birds* by A. Armstrong. Several monographs have been produced as additions, the most sought-after being James Fisher's monograph No 6, *The Fulmar*. Collectors of flower books should have a special regard for *The Art of Botanical Illustration* by Wilfrid Blunt, No 14 in the general series. Beautifully illustrated in colour, with the facts clearly stated and documented, it is a model for all books of its kind.

Many in the series have been reprinted, but all are worthy of being collected as firsts, preferably in the dust-wrappers, which are among the best in modern commercial book production. Prices will vary from £15 ($28.50) for a fine copy of Fisher's *The Fulmar* to £5 ($9.50) for the least popular titles. Revised editions of some of the titles have been produced and these are just as important as the firsts. Although the series is primarily concerned with Britain, many long runs have found places on the shelves of American collectors.

Some bibliophiles specialize in collecting books on the natural history of selected small areas. The most celebrated work of this kind is *The Natural History of Selborne*, by Gilbert White (1720–93). The first edition, with nine engravings, appeared in 1789, but since then there has been a profusion of others, abridged, enlarged, adapted, edited and annotated; illustrated in colour, with steel engravings, woodcuts, lithographs, photographs and line drawings. Gathering together all these has already been suggested as a pleasant task for admirers of Gilbert White. The vade-mecum here is Edward A. Martin's *A Bibliography of Gilbert White*, preferably in the revised edition of 1934.

John Aubrey wrote the natural histories of two English counties. His *Natural History of Surrey* was published in five volumes in 1719 and is now grade (H). His *Natural History of Wiltshire* was edited for the Wiltshire Archaeological Society by J. E. Jackson and published in 1862, and was reprinted in 1971 by David & Charles. In *The Old English Farming Books*, 1947, G. E. Fussell mentions an earlier edition of this Wiltshire natural history, produced in 1685, during Aubrey's lifetime, under the title of *Memoirs of*

Naturall Remarques in the County of Wilts., but no copies of this are known to exist.

A pattern for all county ornithologies was provided by J. A. Walpole-Bond when he produced *A History of the Sussex Birds*, three volumes, 1938, well illustrated with fifty-three colour plates. It should be (h). The model county flora is *The Flora of Gloucestershire*, 1948, edited by the Reverend H. J. Riddelsdell, G. W. Hedley and W. R. Price, and published by the Cotteswold Naturalists' Field Club. A reprint was issued in 1975 and was immediately swallowed up. Copies of the original or the reprint should be (i). Some other counties and regions are almost as well served, but there are many that lack worthy ornithologies and floras. A collector who has already gathered useful material covering such a region could help to make good the deficiency.

Farming, Gardening, Country Life

Besides singing of arms and the man, Virgil could recline at the court of the Emperor Augustus, with a cup of Falernian wine at his elbow, and sing cheerfully of the joys of country life. So has it been since Adam delved. The cultivator at court and the farmer by the fireside can always take a rosier view than the man who is toiling in the fields. If they lack the poetic gift, they can acquire some books about the country and its pursuits to maintain their euphoria with a little bright reading, as the spirit moves them. Certainly the collecting of books on farming, gardening and country life is one of the pleasantest aspects of bibliophily.

The oldest farming book printed in English is *The Boke of Husbandry*, printed about 1510 and believed to have been translated by Walter of Henley from a thirteenth-century tract ascribed to Robert Grosseteste. It is a robber's rather than a collector's piece as the only known copy is in Cambridge University Library. However, it is available in facsimile in *The Manor Farm*, 1931, by F. H. Cripps-Day, along with a facsimile of *The Boke of Thrift, 1589*, Cripps-Day's book is probably grade (h).

The first undeniably English book on farming is Sir John Fitzherbert's *Boke of Husbandry*, 1523. This is still sometimes catalogued as being by Sir Anthony Fitzherbert, Sir John's brother, and G. E. Fussell (*The Old English Farming Books*, 1947) is an Anthony-ite. But the *Short Title Catalogue* gives Sir John, and most bibliographers follow this ruling. The first edition is so rare that it is unlikely ever to come on the market, but the book was popular for many years and there are a few later editions to be had, probably in grade (H) or above.

In so far as he gave his agricultural advice in verse, Thomas Tusser (1527–80) is entitled to be called the English Virgil. His doggerel hardly matches up to the Latin poet's hexameters, though there is some good sense in its quaintness. Tusser's *A hundredth good pointes of husbandrie* was published in 1557 and must have had some success, for the author followed it sixteen years later with *Five hundreth good Pointes of Husbandry, united to as many of good Huswifery*. Both Tussers are rare and best collected in late editions. A reprint of the *Five Hundreth Pointes*, edited by William Mavor, was published in 1812 and is grade (h) today. E. V. Lucas edited another edition in 1931, bound in leather, and now grade (g). In the same year there appeared *Thomas Tusser, His Good Points of Husbandry*, collated and edited by Dorothy Hartley. This contains a facsimile of *A Hundreth Good Points* from the British Museum copy and the text of the *Five Hundreth Points*, as well as a life of Tusser with his family tree and notes on various editions of the books. There is no reason why this book should cost more than £8 ($15.50) and it should be available for less.

Gervase Markham (1568–1637) is the next agriculturist of importance. He was a prolific writer and a great borrower of other people's material. Presumably he wanted his memorial to be *Markham's Maister-Peece: contayning all knowledge belonging to a Smith, Farrier or Horse-Leech*, 1610. It is certainly a favourite in the salerooms, where it is a familiar grade (D) item. The *Maister-Peece* was reprinted at intervals well into the eighteenth century and some of these later editions are not liable to rise out of grade (f) for some considerable time.

As might be expected of one who served as a captain in Cromwell's army, William Blith's contributions to the literature of farming are soundly practical. He wrote two books, the second being an extended version of the first. *The English Improver* was published in 1649 and *The English Improver Improved* in 1652. In this case, the later book, though sometimes regarded as a second edition, is preferable to the other, covering, as it does, a much wider area of farming. Many of Blith's ideas were ahead of their time and had to wait a hundred years before being fully put into practice. There are still doubts as to the acceptable collation of the 1652 edition. Some copies have three engraved plates, and one such was sold at Sotheby's in 1968, but most copies have only two. The copy from the Britwell Court Library was stated to have the three plates when originally sold, but when put up for sale again in 1966 it was found to contain only two, like most of the others. Was the third plate bound in special copies for a favoured few, or are all those that lack it to be considered defective? Nobody has yet given a definite ruling, so that two-plate and three-plate copies are almost equally desirable and are grade (a).

John Forster's book is another milestone in farming history: *England's Happiness increased: or a sure and easie remedie against all succeeding dear Years; by a plantation of the roots called Potatoes*. Issued in 1664, it is the first important English work on the cultivation of the potato. Andrew Yarranton (1616–84) wrote the wide-ranging *England's Improvement by Sea and Land* which brought him fame when it was published in two parts in 1677–81. It was ultimately less important than his earlier *The Improvement Improved, by a second edition of the great improvement of lands by clover*, published at Worcester in 1663. In this work Yarranton advocated the cropping of clover as is done today, but the idea was allowed to lie fallow for a hundred years. Some agricultural writers mention another book by Yarranton called *The Great Improvement of Lands by Clover*, also with 1663 as the publication date. Fussell (*op cit*) doubts the existence of a book with this title, as he was unable to trace a copy. It is probably the same book as the other 1663 publication, recorded under an abbreviated title.

Before the end of the seventeenth century, the first agricultural journal had been attempted, under the editorship of John Houghton (d1705). It was called *A Collection of Letters for the Improvement of Husbandry and Trade*. The first series ran from 1681 to 1683 and the second from 1692 until 1702. A complete set would probably be graded as (H).

Mentioned rather slightingly by Fussell, the writings of Richard Bradley (d1732) nevertheless give a fair picture of the farming practice of his day. Bradley was not a man of great scholarly attainments and is notorious for having pushed himself into the chair of botany at Cambridge University. He wrote voluminously and his *General Treatise of Husbandry*, 1721–2, grade (f), adequately sums up his ideas on agriculture.

Jethro Tull (1674–1741) is a far more important writer. A barrister turned practical farmer, he was not content to accept the traditional methods of cultivation. As a result of his experiments, he invented a successful seed drill, first used for sowing pulse crops and later applied to turnips and wheat. His method of sowing allowed regular cultivation of the land by means of a horse hoe, which, he maintained, increased the fertility of the soil and largely dispensed with the need for manure. He was wrong on this point, yet his methods of tilling the soil were a great advance. He placed them before the farming public in *The New Horse-Houghing Husbandry, or an Essay on the Principles of Tillage and Vegetation*, printed for the author, 1731. Collectors take this to be a single-edition book, quite separate from *The Horse-Hoing Husbandry*, folio, 1733, but Fussell (*More Old English Farming Books*, 1950) regards this latter as a reprint of the earlier work. Both have much the same price on their heads, well in grade (H).

As the eighteenth century advanced, farming books came thicker and faster from the presses. The agrarian revolution was under way throughout England, keeping pace more or less with the Industrial Revolution. Scottish farming lagged pathetically behind. One of the pioneers of land improvement in that country was Sir Archibald Grant of Monymusk, who is credited with having written *The Practical Farmer's Pocket Companion*, published at Aberdeen in 1756, grade (i). The rapid advance in Scottish farming after that date was to affect the agricultural writing of the next century.

New needs were met in the larger output of farming books. Robert Smith filled a gap in 1768 with his *Universal Directory for Taking Alive and Destroying Rats* (and all other kinds of four-footed and winged vermin). Other days have brought other methods, but this book, in grade (f), is perhaps the only classic in its field.

Before the end of the century, two outstanding farming writers had emerged—Arthur Young (1741–1820) and William Marshall (1745–1818). By all accounts, Marshall was the better farmer, but his literary efforts have not achieved the renown of those of Young. The persistent prompting of Marshall helped to establish the Board of Agriculture in 1793, but it was Young who was appointed its first secretary, much to Marshall's chagrin.

Marshall methodically examined the state of agriculture in various parts of England, then wrote a series of books on his findings. The first was *The Rural Economy of Norfolk*, 1787. Like its successors in the series, it was in two volumes. The *Rural Economy of Yorkshire* was published in the following year, then came *The Rural Economy of Gloucestershire* (with a section on Wiltshire), 1789, *Midland Counties*, 1790, *West of England*, 1796, and *Southern Counties,* 1798. One would hope to find these priced within grade (g), with variations according to condition.

Marshall was prolific and wrote many other books, but for sheer volume of output he cannot compare with Arthur Young, who is credited with 250 books and pamphlets. Some of his earlier works were the products of tours of inspection which he made in various parts of the country, the first being *A Six Weeks Tour through the Southern Counties of England*

and Wales, 1768. The next was *A Six Months Tour through the North of England*, 1770, but best of all was *Travels, during the Years 1787, 1788 and 1789. Undertaken . . . with a view of ascertaining the Cultivation etc. of the Kingdom of France*, which was published in 1792. As such books go, this is not uncommon and should be in grade (d). The others named are (f).

Once appointed secretary of the Board of Agriculture, Young supervised the production of a series of general views of the agriculture of British counties and wrote six of them himself : *General View of the Agriculture of the County of Suffolk*, 1794, *Lincoln*, 1799, *Hertford*, 1804, *Norfolk*, 1804, *Essex* (two volumes), 1807, and *Oxford*, 1809. All were soon reprinted, but all first and early editions are grade (h). Reprints of editions of the Suffolk, Lincoln, Norfolk and Oxford volumes were published by David & Charles, along with others in the series, including *Sussex*, 1813, by the Reverend Arthur Young, son of the great Arthur Young.

Young's works carry agriculture into the nineteenth century, where we meet another travelling agriculturist, the famous William Cobbett (1762–1835). For a time he served as a sergeant-major in the army and brought some of the characteristics of his rank back with him into civilian life. Politically he began as a Tory and ended as a Radical. The work most often linked with his name is *Rural Rides*, first published in book form in 1830, reprinted from his *Weekly Political Register* which ran from 1802 until his death. Cobbett held decided views about most things and did not care whom he offended. In *Rural Rides*, within a few pages, he manages to insult Scotsmen and the Cotswolds, but in a sergeant-majorly sort of way, and as the bark of warrant officers is generally worse than their bite, a Scot who happened to be a Cotswold man by adoption would surely forgive him.

Though classed here as agricultural, *Rural Rides* is also topographical, political and a great deal else besides, well deserving its place as an English classic. Grade (a) is a fair placing for a good first edition, and the fine three-volume edition of 1930, edited by G. D. H. and M. Cole, should be grade (f). There are many other editions and abridgements to be had quite cheaply.

Cobbett was not a modest man, as can be seen from the title of one of his books: *A Treatise on Cobbett's Corn*, 1828. Having seen in America how useful maize could be as a fodder plant, he conceived the idea of popularizing it in England under the name of Cobbett's corn. Climate as much as conservatism thwarted his efforts, but the book is still collected and is grade (g). He was a genuine friend of the poor and in *Cottage Economy*, 1822, he tried to show how cottagers could make the most of the little plots of land at their disposal. It should be grade (h).

Anybody seeking a painstaking survey of world agriculture up to 1825 should find what he wants in John C. Loudon's *Encyclopaedia of Agriculture*, published in that year. Within its 1,226 pages, Loudon packs a staggering amount of information covering agricultural botany, zoology and chemistry, the cultivation of food and forage crops, and the breeding and training of farm animals (including the esculent frog!). Besides giving general surveys of farming in Europe, Asia, Africa and the Americas, the book fits in studies of ancient agricultural methods and provides detailed reviews of the state of farming in most of the British and Irish counties. It concludes with helpful bibliographies of agricultural books in English, French, German and Italian. Loudon was one of Scotland's gifts to England in return for the vital help in land improvement received during the eighteenth century. A copy of the *Encyclopaedia of Agriculture* should not cost more than £20 ($38) today.

In all probability the best agricultural library in Britain is that of the Rothamsted Experimental Station, Harpenden. Its *Library Catalogue of Printed Books and Pamphlets on Agriculture published between 1471 and 1840*, compiled by Mary S. Aslin, was first published in 1926, but appeared in a second, much enlarged edition in 1940, and a supplement was issued in 1949. Few collectors could hope to approach this library in completeness, but many take it as a guide in the formation of their own collections.

After 1840, the number of books on farming published year by year makes it almost impossible to give the collector a lead. For those who combine an interest in Victoriana with farming there is *Breeds of Domestic Animals of the British Islands*, two volumes, folio, 1842, by David Low (1786–1859). The fifty-six coloured plates in the volumes are fine things of their kind. The book is grade (F) for the two volumes. Somebody who would rather have an imposing set of books than Loudon's closely-printed one-volume encyclopaedia might like to acquire *The Rural Encyclopaedia*, in four large quarto volumes, edited by the Rev. J. M. Wilson and first published in 1847. It is prized by industrial/agrarian archaeologists for its illustrations of Victorian farm machinery, and is grade (i).

There is so much of interest to the collector among the plethora of later farming books that he must be highly selective. The period since 1840 has seen the development of mechanical farming and artificial fertilizers. Both were of paramount help in feeding the rapidly growing populations of the last hundred years, but the fertilizers and to some extent the machinery are now being blamed for having contributed to our present-day problems of pollution and erosion. The acquisition of certain key books, such as *Organic Chemistry in its Application to Agriculture and Physiology*, 1840, by Justus Liebig (1803–73), and J. C. Nesbit's *On Agricultural Chemistry and the Nature and Properties of Peruvian Guano*, 1854, could provide the basis for an unusual collection on fertilizers. Neither would be high in grade (i).

Gardening is not always easy to separate from farming and many of the early books on agriculture could well be placed in horticultural collections. One of the first English books exclusively devoted to gardening is *Paradisi in Sole Paradisus Terrestris*, 1629, by John Parkinson (1567–1650). Parkinson seems to have been a cheerful, one might almost say a sunny man, for the title of his book translates as 'Park-in-sun's earthly paradise'—*paradisus* meaning both park and paradise. Although he was an apothecary he was not particularly concerned with the medicinal uses of plants in this book. Its contents may best be summarized by quoting from the title-page :

A Garden of all sorts of pleasant flowers which our English ayre will permitt to be noursed up : with a Kitchen garden of all manner of herbes, ravies, and fruites for meate or sause used with us, and an Orchard of all sorts of fruit-bearing trees and shrubs fit for our Land, together with the right orderinge, planting, and presarving of them, and their uses and vertues.

The book is full of practical advice, a little of which still holds good. The ravies referred to are radishes. Grade (C) is not too high for the first or second (1635) editions, but a facsimile, published in 1904, should cost a good deal less—grade (h).

John Reid produced in 1683 at Edinburgh his *Scots Gardner* which provided for Scotland a book such as Parkinson had given to England. Though the first edition is the dearest, in grade (a), the most interesting is the expanded one of 1766 which contains a 'Gardener's Kalendar', a florist's vade-mecum, a practical bee-master, the Shepherd of Banbury's rules on the weather and the Earl of Haddington's treatise on forest trees. This edition may be found in grade (b) or below.

When John Evelyn, who did much for arboriculture, brought out a translation of J. de la Quintinye's *The Compleat Gard'ner* in 1693, it had long-lasting effects, though English gardens soon modified the ideas of Quintinye, chief

XVIII COURTYARD OF ELM TREE HOUSE, CAMPDEN

1916

Plate 15 The pure line of F. L. Griggs is amply shown in this wood engraving from his *Campden*, 1940 (see p. 108).

Plate 16 R. J. Thornton's own elaborate illustration of roses from his *Temple of Flora*, the production of which ruined him (see p. 177). (see p. 177)

director of the gardens of Louis XIV of France, to suit their own requirements. A copy of this edition should be found in the (d) range. Fussell mentions another translation of this work, brought out by George London and Henry Wise in 1699, probably grade (e), but is silent on the Evelyn edition.

The craze for chinoiserie in the second half of the eighteenth century extended to landscape gardening. The architect, Sir William Chambers (1726–96), used his alleged knowledge of Chinese gardens in drawing up his *Plans of Gardens and Buildings at Kew*, 1763, a folio that is now grade (H). His later *Dissertation on Oriental Gardening*, 1772, has often been ridiculed and has only about a quarter of the value of *Plans of Gardens*, yet it was partly responsible for the willow-pattern look of several gardens of the period. It is a pity that neither Lancelot (Capability) Brown (1715–83) nor William Kent (1684–1748) left behind any substantial works on the landscaping at which they excelled.

John Abercrombie approached gardening from a severely practical angle in *Every Man His Own Gardener*, 1767. The first edition was stated to be 'by Mr. Mawe and other gardeners', but was wholly Abercrombie's work. He was shy about putting his name to the book and paid Thomas Mawe, as a better-known authority, £20 for the use of his name. *Every Man His Own Gardener* was one of the most successful gardening books of all time, running into nearly thirty editions. By 1800 the sixteenth edition had been reached; in 1824 a new edition appeared, edited by R. Forsyth; in 1845 it was revised by W. Gowans. Another new edition was issued in the 1860s, with an added treatise on drawing-room gardening by George Glenny. The final edition was published in 1879. Even then the story was not ended. Several cheap gardening guides of later dates have distinct Abercrombie features and it is still possible to buy new gardening books in which ghostly shadows of the once flourishing perennial can be discerned. A collector who does not mind a certain sameness in his reading matter might specialize in the various editions of *Every Man His Own Gardener*. Some would be rooted out with difficulty, but on average they would cost no more than £8 ($15.50) each.

During the nineteenth century the range of fruits, flowers, trees, shrubs and vegetables was greatly increased and practical books on their cultivation were popular. Some such were considered as suitable reading on railway journeys and were produced as yellow-backs. European plants were taken by emigrants to other parts of the world. Nostalgic gardeners from England who wanted to grow their national flower in Australia were at length catered for by Thomas Johnson's *The Culture of the Rose*, Melbourne, 1866, now worth about $A30 (£20—$38) and in 1871, E. B. Heyne supplied *The Flower, Fruit and Vegetable Garden*, published at Adelaide, for gardeners not solely concerned with roses. It is a grade (h) book. One of the most important early American gardening magazines was *The Horticulturist and Journal of Rural Art*, begun in 1846 and published variously from Albany, Rochester and New York. Though individual volumes might be picked up for under $10 (£5.25), their cost in a fair-sized run would probably average out at $15 (£7.90).

Along with the international and intercontinental circulation of known plants, new plants were being discovered in remote places and brought to the gardens of Europe, America and Australia. Robert Fortune and J. D. Hooker provided exotics from China and the Himalayas, as has already been noticed. American plant-hunters of the past include Humphry Marshall, whose *Arbustum Americanum*, 1785, is grade (a), and Henry Barham, whose *Hortus Americanus*, Kingston, Jamaica, 1794, deals with South American and West Indian plants and is of much the same value as the book previously named. Thomas Nuttall published the *North-American Sylva* at Philadelphia between 1842 and 1854, in three volumes. Recorded prices for this book show big variations, but it could now be placed in grade (e) with some safety.

The plant-hunters of more recent times operated mainly in

Asia, and have added many extraordinarily beautiful flowers to our alpine gardens. The two most important hunters at the beginning of the present century were George Forrest (1873–1932) and Ernest Henry Wilson (1876–1930). Forrest has left behind him plenty for the gardener, but next to nothing for the bibliophile. *The Journeys and Plant Introductions of George Forrest*, edited by J. M. Cowan, 1952, gives an account of his seven expeditions to China, with extracts from his writings (i).

Wilson was much more articulate. He was a Gloucestershire man, born in Chipping Campden, and his early explorations in Asia were undertaken for a British nursery firm. Later he was employed by the Arnold Arboretum of Harvard University. His most important book is *A Naturalist in Western China*, 1913. The American edition appeared in 1929 under the name of *China, Mother of Gardens*. Either copy would be grade (h).

Reginald Farrer (1880–1920) was next on the scene. He was both a practical gardener and an explorer with a love amounting to obsession of alpine plants. Rock gardeners who are also book collectors will give a proud position on their shelves to Farrer's *The English Rock Garden*, two volumes, 1919, which is not far up grade (h). More general collectors will want his *The Rainbow Bridge* and *The Eaves of the World*, both published in 1921, after Farrer's death, and in grade (i).

Frank Kingdon-Ward (1885–1958) was a geographer as well as a plant-hunter and made twenty-two expeditions to China, Assam, Tibet, Burma and Indo-China, between the years 1911–57. His scarcest book is *The Land of the Blue Poppy*, 1913, which must now be graded (g). Of his others, the best are *The Riddle of the Tsangpo Gorges*, 1926, *A Plant Hunter in Tibet*, 1934, and *Burma's Icy Mountains*, 1949. These should be available at under £20 ($38) a copy.

Unaccountably, the books of the later plant-hunters almost never appear at important auctions and this causes book-buyers to believe that they are extremely scarce. They appear quite often, however, in lists issued by dealers specializing in gardening and natural history books.

The supplies of exotics which became generally available as a result of plant-hunting helped to break down the formalism of European and American gardens, as rhododendrons, azaleas and alpine flowers call out for a wild setting. Nineteenth-century exuberance also became the enemy of floral regimentation, as can be seen in an extraordinary book published at Rochester, NY, about 1880, but undated. It was written by Jack Vick and is called *Vick's Flower and Vegetable Garden*. It should be collected by those who are interested in luxuriant Victorian typography—if Victorian is an allowable adjective for an American book. There is no reason why it should cost more than $10 (£5.25) if it can be found.

The apostle of planned informality was William Robinson. His *English Flower Garden*, first published in 1886, had fourteen editions, the last in 1926. None of the editions should cost more than £8 ($15.50), so perhaps the collector should try to obtain the first and the last to illustrate the development of Robinson's ideas and his steadfast faith in woodcut illustrations. He refused to have anything to do with photographic blocks, insisting to the end that they were inadequate for plant illustration. Besides writing other books, Robinson edited *The Vegetable Garden*, translated from the French of Vilmorin-Andrieux and first published in 1885. The first edition is much the best as it deals with a remarkable range of usual and unusual vegetables, including caterpillars and snails—not the creatures, but plants which closely resemble them. These are absent from the later editions. This work should cost no more than the *Flower Garden*.

In her quietly impressive writings, Gertrude Jekyll carried Robinson's ideas much further. Her books are now eagerly collected, have greatly increased in price in the last few years and will keep rising. Buyers have not yet begun seriously to discriminate between the different editions and are prepared to pay as much for a fifth as a first. Miss Jekyll's titles include *Wood and Garden, Home and Garden, Children and Gardens, Wall and Water Gardens* and, with Sir L. Weaver, *Gardens for Small Country Houses.* A fine copy of the last named is climbing to the top of grade (h), but the others may still be around £10 ($19). The same author's *Old English Household Life* and *Old West Surrey* are not gardening books, but studies of bygone cottage furniture, utensils and smallware.

There is a group of writers who are hard to classify. Though they write about nature, they are not naturalists in the strict sense, nor are they agricultural writers or plant-hunters. Their line of descent can be traced back ultimately to Jean-Jacques Rousseau. The outstanding figure in the group is Henry David Thoreau (1817–62). After an unsettled career, he was befriended by Emerson, but subsequently took to the wilderness and lived almost as a hermit. This experience led to his writing *Walden, or Life in the Woods,* published at Boston, Massachusetts, in 1854. A fine first edition of this book would be reasonable if in grade (i) as, indeed, would be firsts of his other works, including the posthumous books, *The Maine Woods,* Boston, 1864, and *A Yankee in Canada,* Boston, 1866.

The English Thoreau is Richard Jefferies (1848–87), a Wiltshire journalist who became a champion of the depressed agricultural workers, then went on to write some carefully observed books on the English countryside and a few novels, which are not entirely satisfactory. His first 'hit' was *The Gamekeeper at Home,* 1878, followed by *Wild Life in a Southern County,* 1879. *The Amateur Poacher,* 1880, *The Life of the Fields,* 1884, *The Open Air,* 1885, and others. He also wrote two books for children, *Wood Magic,* two volumes, 1881, and *Bevis,* three volumes, 1882. *Bevis* is indisputably the better, but both would be grade (h), like most Jefferies firsts.

W. H. Hudson (1841–1922), was a true naturalist as well as an open-air writer and novelist. His novels, *Green Mansions*, 1904, and *The Purple Land That England Lost*, 1885, are not negligible, nor is his *A Naturalist in La Plata*, 1892, but his more general writings are the most rewarding. Because of scarcity, the novels are grade (a), but *A Shepherd's Life*, 1916, should be (g) and is the best Hudson of all.

When Edward Thomas, already mentioned in this book as a poet, wrote his *Life of Richard Jefferies*, published in 1908, he dedicated it to Hudson, thus establishing links between the three. Thomas was forced to do hack work for a large part of his career, but even at their most mechanical, his books are touched with a sincere love of nature. *The South Country*, 1909, contains some of his best prose. When Thomas was killed in World War I, comparatively few people fully appreciated his work. His widow, Helen Thomas, wrote in two parts a moving and intimate biography of her husband, thinly disguising him as 'David'. The two parts were published in one volume in 1931 : *As It Was . . . World Without End*. This undoubtedly brought a wider public to Thomas's works, which are now scarce in first editions, though not highly priced as yet—most are well down in grade (i).

The works of John Burroughs (1837–1921) could be collected for an outlay comparable with that on those of Edward Thomas. Burroughs wrote a number of nature and country sketches from his fruit farm at Riverby, in the state of New York, and has been described as a lightweight Thoreau. With the gradual urbanization of the area about which he wrote, his works are enjoying a revival of interest. They include *Wake Robin*, 1871, *Birds and Poets*, 1878, and *Field and Study*, 1919.

Beekeeping is a pursuit associated with farming, gardening and life in the country. It has a considerable literature of its own, dating, in English, from 1574, when Thomas Hyll's *A Profitable Instruction of the perfite ordering of bees* was published. It is too scarce and expensive—grade (D)—to be pursued by the ordinary collector. If he is able to buy in grade (g), however, he may consider the acquisition of an early edition of *The Feminine Monarchy or a Treatise concerning Bees and the Due Ordering of them*, by Charles Butler (d1647). This book is particularly important in that it was the first to show that the hive is ruled by a queen, not a king as had been previously supposed. The first edition was published in 1609, but the edition of 1634 is more interesting. It is entitled *The Feminin' Monarchi', or the Histori' of Be's* because at the time of its publication the author had become an enthusiast for reformed spelling.

Joseph Warder made use of material from Butler in *The True Amazons: Or, the Monarchy of Bees*, with further contributions from his own observations. He has a delightful way of bursting into verse every now and again, as when, in describing the division of labour in the hive, he writes:

The Burying of the Dead here some contrive,
Some nurse the future Nation of the Hive:
Some feed their Young, whilst others cleanse the Cell,
And some prepare for Winter Hydromel.

His pretensions as an apian palingenesist are impressive until it is realized that bees which are apparently dead may only be comatose. He claims 'I have many hundred Times rais'd dead Bees to Life, tho' not such as have been drowned'. First he describes methods using the heat of his hands, or the warmth from a fire, then he continues:

At other Times, I have taken four or five *Dutch* thin Boxes, and with a Nail (or Bodkin) making Holes in the Covers to give them Air, have gone and fill'd these Boxes with dead Bees, and put them in my Breeches Pockets (that of the Coat or Waistcoat is not warm enough) and so let them remain half an Hour or more; and then opening the Boxes in the Garden, they have all gone Home as before.

This work first appeared in 1726 and is now grade (g). It ran through at least eight editions.

213

Other important bee books are : *The Ordering of Bees* by John Levett, Gent, 1634, *A New Discovery of an Excellent Method of Bee-houses* by John Gedde, 1675, *The Honeybee: its Natural History, Physiology and Management* by Edwin Bevan, 1827, and Thomas Nutt's *Humanity to Honeybees*, 1832. More recent developments in beekeeping have largely stemmed from America and for many beekeepers their Bible is still *The ABC and XYZ of Bee Culture* by A. I. Root and others, published at Medina, Ohio. This publication first appeared in 1877 as *The ABC of Bee Culture*, with A. I. Root as sole author. After running through many editions, it became *The ABC and XYZ of Bee Culture* in 1910, with articles by other contributors. Since then it has been regularly brought up to date. A collection of selected editions would give a useful history of the development of apiculture in the course of about a hundred years.

Go-getters down the centuries have turned to bees for their inspiration; contemplative men have preferred to cast their minds—and other more tangible objects—in the direction of fish. The best-loved dissertation on fishing is Izaak Walton's *The Compleat Angler, or the Contemplative Man's Recreation*. Few books have been so universally popular among the English-speaking peoples. It exists in at least 150 different editions.

The first edition was published in 1653, the second in 1655, the third in 1661 and the fourth in 1668. A complication arises with the fifth edition, 1676. It is normally found as three books in one : Walton's *Compleat Angler*, the second part of the *Compleat Angler*, by Charles Cotton, and *The Experienc'd Angler,* by Colonel Robert Venables. Though this is the fifth edition of Walton's book, it is the first of Cotton's and the fourth of Venables's, which is really quite extraneous. Subsequent editions of the *Compleat Angler* usually contain Cotton's work, but omit the Venables, which, incidentally, was first published in 1662.

A sound first of Walton's book would certainly be grade

(B). A set of the first five editions, the last volume being bound up with the Cotton and Venables as usual, sold in 1968 for £4,600 ($8,750). Some quite early editions have been offered in (e), but in this grade have had defects.

The best of the later editions are identified by the names of their editors—Moses Browne, 1750, Hawkins, 1760, Bagster, 1808, Major, 1823, Nicholas (two volumes), 1836, Marston (two volumes), 1888, Lowell (two volumes), 1889, Le Gallienne (thirteen parts), 1896–7, and so on. There are also the Tercentenary edition in two volumes, 1896, a beautifully printed Nonesuch edition of 1929, and an edition with coloured plates by Arthur Rackham, 1931. The selling prices of all these, as firsts of their own particular editions, range through grades (g) to (I), but there are other quite acceptable editions to be had more cheaply. The Bohn edition of 1856, for example, should be obtainable in original cloth for under £8 ($15.50). On the other hand, there are special copies that rise above the price normally asked for their editions.

The Compleat Angler was by no means the first English book on the sport of fishing. That honour goes to *The Treatyse of fysshynge wyth an angle*, which first appears as an addition to the second edition of *The book of Hawking, hunting and blasing of arms*, 1496 (see Chapter 5). Though this is too rare for any normal collector to hope to possess, there is a facsimile reproduction available, published by Elliot Stock in 1880. With patience it might eventually be hooked, grade (i).

The Experienc'd Angler by Venables, already mentioned, would be grade (I) for a first, but a fine large-paper reprint was issued in 1827 and might be procurable in grade (f).

Though not confined to fishing, *The Gentleman's Recreation*, 1674, by Nicholas Cox, deserves a place in the angler's library, if he can afford it. Its four parts deal with hunting, hawking, fowling and fishing. A first edition would be grade (a), but later editions, to 1721, should scale down to (e).

The eighteenth century produced a few interesting books

on angling, including Robert Howlett's *The Angler's Sure Guide*, 1706, published under Howlett's initials, and Thomas Shirley's *Angler's Museum*, undated, but 1784. However, the great century of fine books for fishermen was the nineteenth, beginning with Charles Smart's *Practical Observations on Angling in the River Trent*, 1801, grade (d), then moving into the period when some of the best angling books were issued with actual fishermen's flies contained in them. Examples of these are W. Blacker's *Art of Angling and Complete System of Fly Making*, 1842, and *A Quaint Treatise on 'Flees and the Art of Artyfichall Flee Making'*, 1876, which provides fly-making materials as well as flies. Both books are roughly equal in value. If the flies and materials are intact, they should be grade (a). With all books which contain flies and materials, these accessories should be examined to make sure they are the originals and not modern substitutes.

Modern angling books deal with so many aspects looked at from so many different points of view that it must be left to the individual collector to decide what he will buy. He might, however, turn his eye to the beautiful angling books produced in limited editions by the Derrydale Press, New York, in the twenties and thirties of the present century and now mostly grade (e). They include Eugene V. Connett's *American Big Game Fishing*, 1935, and Henry Van Dyke's *Travel Diary of an Angler*, 1929. Both are delightful books in their different ways.

From Religion to Railways

Book collectors of bygone ages generally gave pride of place in their libraries to books on religion, philosophy, Greek and Latin classics and ancient history. Few of today's bibliophiles are so high-minded. Yet it is only in the past hundred years that these subjects have fallen from favour. Sir William Robertson Nicoll, who deserted the pulpit to make a solid fortune and an evanescent reputation as a literary man in the early part of this century, detailed his father's bookbuying for a year in a sanctimonious biography, *My Father, An Aberdeenshire Minister*, 1908. In it he reveals that during 1862, out of a miserable stipend, his father bought over 500 books and pamphlets. Of these, about 260 were religious or philosophical works, sixty were classical and almost all the rest were 'improving' in one way or another. The only light relief was provided by Dodd's *Beauties of Shakespere* and Shelley's *Poems*. This one year's haul was typical of the library of 17,000 volumes eventually housed in Nicoll senior's small Scottish manse.

As a Free Kirk minister, Robertson Nicoll's father had austere tastes, but no more so than those of thousands of other nineteenth-century bibliophiles, clerical and lay. Even those whose real inclinations were more cheerful took care to give their libraries an appearance of sobriety by including in them a representative section on religion and philosophy.

The modern book collector feels no obligation to give shelf space to such books and, in relative terms, most of the once favoured moral works have dropped in value. The genuine collector in this area can buy most of what he wants with ease—many booksellers will let him have stacks of meaty nineteenth-century sermons almost for the taking away. However, some parvenu book hunters are impressed by the decayed gentry of the world of letters and spend too much on them in the belief that they are still the collectors' items they long ceased to be.

The most important religious work in the western world is, of course, the Bible. Most old, or reputedly old, English-language Bibles are of little material worth. Those impressive family Bibles, which may be over a hundred years old, will never save their impoverished owners from bankruptcy. They had better keep them and find comfort in their pages than attempt to sell them. Apart from some celebrated editions, such as Coverdale's version of 1537, which could bring in more than £7,000 ($13,300), English Bibles that predate the first Authorized Version of 1611 (the King James Bible) average about £85 (say $165) a copy in the salerooms. The actual first edition of the Authorized Version could be worth over £2,000 ($3,800), but thereafter, with one or two exceptions, prices drop markedly. Certain Bibles, though not valuable as to content in the worldly sense, reach four figures because of their exquisite bindings.

For an outlay of between £800 and £1,000 ($1,500 to $1,900), spread over many years of searching, it should be possible to gather together a representative collection of the strangely named editions, such as the *Printers' Bible*, 1702, where 'printers have persecuted me without a cause' occurs in Psalm 119—'printers' being a misprint for 'princes'—and the *Wicked Bible*, 1632, where the seventh commandment reads : 'Thou shalt commit adultery'. An extensive list of these Bibles is given in Brewer's *Dictionary of Phrase and Fable*.

Testaments, psalters and breviaries are in much the same position. Many can be had quite cheaply, but a few are very expensive. Indeed, one particular psalter, the *Bay Psalm Book*, may be the dearest English-language printed book in the world. As far as is known, this is the first book of any note to have been printed in the erstwhile Anglo-American colonies. It was produced at Cambridge, Massachusetts, by Stephen Daye in 1640 under the title of *The Whole Booke of Psalms Faithfully Translated into English Metre*. Only eleven copies are known, all but two being defective. The last public sale of a copy was at the Parke-Bernet Galleries in New York on 28 January 1947. The item was described as 'a beautiful and perfect copy with the leaf of Errata (L14), "Faults escaped in printing" . . . Tiny portions of eight leaves skilfully repaired, with the addition of a few letters or numerals'. It sold for the then record price of $151,000, the equivalent of £37,750 at that time. This copy may never appear at a sale again, for it is in the Yale University Library. From the names of its various owners, it is known as the Crowninshield-Stevens-Brinley-Vanderbilt-Whitney-Yale copy. If it were to be sold again, its price could be well beyond $1,000,000 (£526,300).

From the first period of printing to the present day, the output of religious, philosophical and moral works has been prodigious. It may be a poor reflection on the twentieth century that the majority are among the least desirable of books, but when it is remembered that so many of them are Protestant denunciations of Catholics, Catholic denunications of Protestants, Calvinist denunciations of Arminians, Arminian denunciations of Unitarians and Quaker scorn for all the warring factions, perhaps their neglect is not so shameful.

The devoted seeker after religious works will probably look for guidance to a higher Authority than this book, but it may help him to know something of the approximate prices of a few. Richard Hooker (1554–1600) played an important part in shaping the constitution of the Church of England and the other Episcopal churches by writing *Of the Lawes of Ecclesiasticall Politie*. The first two volumes alone are (H) and it could cost into (B) to build up a set of all eight volumes in firsts.

Tolerant in theory rather than practice, Jeremy Taylor (1613–67) wrote *The Rule and Exercises of Holy Living*, 1650, and *The Rule and Exercises of Holy Dying*, 1651. They were for long enjoyed by the devout of many persuasions and the two first editions together are (a). Taylor's contemporary, Richard Baxter (1615–91) was a Puritan whose *The Saints Everlasting Rest*, 1650, was formerly much esteemed, but is now (i) or low in (h).

While various divines were wrangling about the outward forms of religion, George Fox (1624–90) was suggesting that people should look to the light within themselves. Fox, founder of the Society of Friends, was a strange man, not altogether sane, perhaps, but with a great fund of piety and love of humanity. Though he wrote and published much while he was alive, his life's work is summed up in his posthumous *Journal*, edited by his friend, William Penn, and published in 1694. A first edition would be (a).

William Penn (1644–1718) was one of Fox's early converts to Quakerism and was the founder of Philadelphia and the state of Pennsylvania. He too, wrote on religion, at a more cerebral level than Fox. His *No Cross, No Crown*, 1669, is grade (g), but his less bulky writings are much more valuable. A two-leaved pamphlet of his, *Information and Direction to Such Persons as are Inclined to America*, no place and no date, but probably 1684, is (A). Robert Barclay (1648–90), an eccentric but highly intellectual Scot, rationalized Fox's beliefs in *An Apology for the True Christian Divinity*, 1679, now (f).

John Wesley (1703–91) was surely the most energetic evangelist the world has ever known. Besides travelling to distant countries, he journeyed the length and breadth of Britain on foot and on horseback and is said to have covered 250,000 miles and preached 40,000 sermons. In addition, he found time to write a great number of books and tracts on all sorts of subjects, from ancient history to medicine, as well as some hymns. His three-volume *Collection of Moral and Sacred Hymns*, Bristol, 1744, and his *Means of Grace*, 1755, are (d). His scarce *Calm Address to Our American Colonies*, undated, but probably 1775, is of particular interest to American collectors and, if found, would be (H) or higher.

The saintly John Henry, Cardinal Newman (1801–90), was as great a figure in his way as Wesley, though quite different in belief and temperament. His most notable work is *Apologia pro Vita Sua*, 1864, which is (g), while his other books are (h).

Though they are often considered together, the only real similarity between *Religio Medici* and *The Anatomy of Melancholy* is the difficulty in classifying them. They are not medical, religious or philosophical, but a mixture of all three, with other elements besides. *Religio Medici* was written by Sir Thomas Browne (1605–82) and officially published in 1643, though it had been preceded by two unauthorized editions in 1642. A fine copy of·the true first could rise above (A), but prices of the unauthorized editions are variable, from (b) to (E). Robert Burton had *The Anatomy of Melancholy* published in 1621. A fine copy of this first could sell for £4,000 ($7,600), though copies with minor blemishes would be much less.

The first great English philosopher was Francis Bacon, Lord Verulam and Viscount St Albans (1561–1626). By forsaking the well-trodden paths of deductive reasoning and developing an inductive system, based on close examination, he helped to lay the foundations of scientific thought. He was also an authority on law. On the flimsiest of evidence, some zealots credit him with having written plays under the name of a well-known man of the theatre. Bacon has recently risen in the world of collecting and firsts are liable to cost a great deal—up to £4,000 ($7,600) for *Two Books of the Proficience and Advancement of Learning*, 1605, and *Instauratio Magna*, 1620.

221

Thomas Hobbes (1588–1679) took a glum view of life. He regarded war and insecurity as the only fruits of man's unguided existence and looked to authority to provide peace and order. His *Leviathan*, 1651, is grade (G) in a verified first issue of the first edition. Points for this include vertical marks on the sword depicted on the engraved title-page and the fact that 'Civil' is spelt with a single 'l' in the full title, which therefore reads *Leviathan or The Matter, Forme and Power of A Commonwealth Ecclesiasticall and Civil*. In the second issue, 'Civill' is so written.

Perhaps John Locke (1632–1704) did not search his soul so deeply as did Hobbes. At any rate, he was more optimistic. His forward-looking *Some Thoughts Concerning Education*, 1693, might be found at a price comparable with that of *Leviathan*, but his *Essay Concerning Humane Understanding*, 1690, is more likely to be (A) in the first issue. George, Bishop Berkeley (1685–1753) followed on from Hobbes in *A Treatise Concerning the Principles of Human Knowledge*, first collected edition, 1734. This might be (a).

David Hume (1711–76) was a clear and original thinker whose scepticism precluded his forming a coherent system of philosophy—he was rather an upsetter of apple carts. As such, his effect on the course of European thought was profound. His *Treatise of Nature*, three volumes, 1739–40, is still a valued work in (I) as a first. Dugald Stewart (1753–1818) was influenced by Hume and, through Lord Brougham and others of his pupils, helped to shape Whig political philosophy in the early nineteenth century. His *Philosophical Essays*, 1810, is (g).

By way of Carlyle, if not directly, something of Stewart's philosophy can be perceived in the writings of Ralph Waldo Emerson (1803–82). Emerson is creeping back into favour, not before time, and firsts of his *The Conduct of Life*, 1860, and of his *Essays*, 1841, are being bought fairly extensively, according to supply. They are moving up to (b).

Following on from Hume, some philosophers of the early

Plate 17 The snowy owl as pictured in J. J. Audubon's *Birds of America*, 1831–4, the world's most expensive bird book (see p. 185).

Plate 18 John Gould's delicate lithograph of Juan Fernandez humming birds from his '*Monograph of the Trochilidae*', 1850–61, a book now worth more than £5000 ($9,500) (see p. 185).

nineteenth century looked on economics as an outlying part of their province, though Adam Smith (1723–90) had fathered economics as a separate discipline in 1776, when he produced the two volumes of his *Inquiry into the Nature of the Wealth of Nations*, a work which is (A) in the first edition.

The developing interest in economics, with the added ferment of the Industrial Revolution, brought fresh problems to the attention of many thinking men. Thomas Malthus (1766–1834) issued his *Essay of the Principle of Population* in 1798, a book that was a bitter pill to swallow in those days and has again come to the fore. Its importance is reflected in its recent rise in price to grade (A). A little earlier, Thomas Paine (1737–1809) had frightened the English establishment with *The Rights of Man*, New York, 1792, with the date misprinted as 1742. Even the American revolutionaries thought Paine had gone too far in this book—currently grade (d)—though they had applauded his earlier *Common Sense: Addressed to the Inhabitants of America*, Philadelphia, 1776. This little book, arguing for independence, could sell as high as $15,000 (£7,000).

In every way, Robert Owen (1771–1858), the Welsh reformer, was a gentler person than Paine, but he was just as firm in his convictions. He wrote against established religion, nonetheless winning the support of some radical churchmen in his bids to alleviate the lot of factory workers. His book, *A New View of Society*, 1813–14, is (I). It sets forth some of the utopian ideas of community living that he later tried to put into practice at New Harmony, Indiana.

Owen was a noble human product of the Industrial Revolution, which was itself developed through many years of investigation, experiment and theoretical writing. The beginnings, as far as the printed word is involved, go back at least as far as the seventeenth century, when there were published books like Cresy Dymock's *A Letter to Mr. Samuel Hartlib Concerning an Invention of Engines of Motion*, 1652. This should be (G).

Much more was written on practical mechanics and technology in the eighteenth century, but the ordinary collector interested in the Industrial Revolution and industrial archaeology turns to the nineteenth century for books he can afford. As an example there is *An Essay on Wheels, Comprehending the Principles and Their Application in Practice to Mill-work*, 1808, by Robertson Buchanan and Peter Nicholson. Patient work should eventually bring the collector a copy at (f).

Less difficult, but still involving patience, would be the acquisition of some volumes of *The Mechanics' Magazine*, begun in 1823. Odd volumes might cost no more than £6 ($11.50) apiece, with longish runs averaging about £8 ($15.50) a copy. It is an unhappy thought that many runs of magazines of this kind have been thrown out as rubbish. There may still be other runs doomed to this fate unless the collector happens to be present at the chucking-out.

One of the best reviews of the industrial progress of the first half of the nineteenth century is given in the five volumes of the *Official Catalogue* of the Great Exhibition of 1851, a grade (f) item. A similar American review, slightly later, is J. S. Ingram's *The Centennial Exposition*, no date, but published at Philadelphia in 1876, and in (g).

Many important links in the chain of industrial expansion are described in a scarce and unusual book produced early this century—*Old Time Invention in the Four Shires* by Percy C. Rushen. No date or place of publication is given, but it is identifiable as a reprint in book form of a series of articles written by Rushen for the *Evesham Journal and Four Shires Advertiser*. There are no signatures, but the book collates as a small quarto, cased in green cloth.

The four shires of the title are Gloucestershire, Worcestershire, Warwickshire and Oxfordshire, so that the particulars of inventions given include those of the iron-founders, the Darbys of Coalbrookdale, and of James Watt, during his long association with Birmingham. When dealing with inventions concerning the cotton industry, the author steps beyond the bounds of the four shires to mention devices evolved in other parts of the country. The descriptions given are taken from the details supplied when the patents were granted. The first invention recorded in the book dates from 1693 and the last from 1810.

Probably the book was not published in the ordinary way; it is certainly uncommon. It is surprising that so useful a work is still largely ignored by industrial archaeologists. The paper and printing are poor, the style is dry, but the information is invaluable. An interested collector might value it at £8 ($15.50) or more.

The nineteenth century was the great era of railway development, so essential a part of the Industrial Revolution. Old railway items used to sell cheaply. Now everybody is only too well aware of their value. Not so long ago, Thomas Hill's *Treatise upon the Utility of a Rail-way from Leeds to Selby and Hull*, Leeds, 1827, would have been priced about £6 ($11.50). This essay of thirty-two pages could now cost four or five times as much.

Some well-known items have always been expensive and are more than holding their market value. Thomas Talbot Bury's *Views on the Liverpool and Manchester Railway*, in two wrappered volumes, 1831, is well into (A) and *Views of the Opening of the Glasgow and Garnkirk Railway*, 1832, is at (G).

Collecting early editions of *Bradshaw's Railway Guides* and other timetables can be enjoyable. Charles Lamb would have put these in his class of 'books that are not books', but they are not just dull lists of times. They are full of poetry. They record branch lines such as the one that ran from Uffington to Faringdon. Repeat 'Uffington to Faringdon' several times and you have a perfect picture of the little train puffing its way through the green English countryside. Timetables are worth the prices now asked. The first issue of the first *Bradshaw*, dated 19 October 1839, is likely to be (b) if complete and in good order. Reprints of some of the significant editions can be found at more reasonable prices. John C. Bourne's *History of the Great Western Railway*, 1846, is (F), but a recent reprint would be much cheaper.

T. G. Cumming's *Descriptions of Iron Bridges of Suspension*, 1824, though pre-dating railway development, is so closely bound up with the subject that a railway enthusiast with the money would want it at (g). Nor would he neglect Edwin Clark's *The Britannia and Conway Tubular Bridges*, 1850, an octavo volume of text and folio of plates, in (c) as a pair. Perhaps he might also hope to get John Roebling's *Long and Short Span Railway Bridges*, New York, 1869, a single folio with thirteen folding or double-page plates, in (f). More in his direct line is R. Armstrong's *An Essay of the Boilers of Steam Engines*, 1839, (g).

Zerah Colburn helped the development of the locomotive in two continents. With A. L. Holley, he published at New York in 1858 *The Permanent Way and Coalburning Locomotive Boilers of European Railways*, and with D. R. Clark, at Glasgow in 1860, *Recent Practice in the Locomotive Engine*. Both are (f).

Though they began to appear rather later than the British books, there are many works illustrative of the growth of railroads in North America. A. C. Morton's *Report on the St. Lawrence and Atlantic Rail-road*, is quite early, being first published at Montreal in 1847. It is hard to locate, even at (g). Exera Brown's *Gazetteer of the Chicago Northwestern Railway*, Chicago, 1869, is for the collector who can make the (H) grade, but the *Business Directory of the Northern Central Railway*, Syracuse, 1874, by Andrew Boyd, is typical of several similar items at (h). Eugene V. Smalley's short *History of the Northern Pacific Railroad*, New York, might be had in (i).

Collecting Australian railway material is still in its childhood and few titles have yet come into prominence. One of the best known is George Phillips's *Pioneer Railways for*

Queensland, Brisbane, 1892, which should be (h).

Some railway collectors specialize in old showcards, posters, leaflets, guide books and miscellaneous railway publications. There is enormous scope here. With a good 'nose' for such things and a willingness to pay fair prices, keen searchers should still do well. The late Roger Wilson's book, *Go Great Western*, Newton Abbot, 1970, shows what can be done.

If the railways offer an exceptionally colourful range of ephemera, they are at least equalled by the theatre, of which the ephemera can capture much of the glamour of the stage and rouse the imagination of collectors. Modern material is just as acceptable as old. Some include cinema posters and stills in their theatrical collections, others keep them apart.

Really old playbills take the palm for romance and for humour that is often unconscious. At one time the bills served the double function of programme and poster, so they were crammed with information, given in a wild assortment of eye-catching types. The metropolitan bills carry famous names and record historic performances, but those from remoter places have their own charm.

In the early nineteenth century, Aberdeen was the northern-most outpost in Britain of the regular professional theatre. The town's Theatre Royal was founded in 1795 by Stephen Kemble, the fattest and least talented of a famous family of actors that included John Kemble and Mrs Sarah Siddons. His reign was a short one and was followed by a line of actor-managers who seem to have lived on the 'tick and shift' system. By 1810, the management was in the hands of a Mr Beaumont and his wife. A surviving playbill of 1810, in the author's collection, announces the performance of 'the Grand Drama of the Castle Spectre' but much more space is given to 'the beautiful, musical After-piece (NEVER PERFORMED HERE) called PAUL and VIRGINIA'.

'A negro dance, a grand chorus and procession' is promised in Scene 2, and in Scene 4, set on a rocky coast with a view of the sea:

A tremendous Storm of THUNDER and LIGHTNING—
the Sea violently agitated—the perilous Situation of the Ship,
on board of which Virginia has been conveyed, which at
length takes Fire, and is dashed to Pieces upon a Rock.
Virginia seen FLOATING on the Waves. The brave but
unsuccessful Attempt of Paul to save her, which at last is
effected by the daring Intrepidity of Alambra—forming
altogether the most awful and interesting Picture ever
brought forward upon the Stage.

The Machinery invented and executed by Mr DUFFUS,
Machinist to the Theatre.

How did the performance match this billing? Perhaps the
procession was quite large, made up of extras recruited for
the occasion and tastefully blackened with burnt cork. More
probably it was small and made to look impressive by being
marched round the back of the stage and on again several
times.

What of the storm and the agitated sea? A metal sheet
provided the thunder, no doubt, and the lightning was
supplied by candlelight reflected from a mirror that was
moved quickly (stage lightning from lycopdium powder did
not arrive till 1836). The sea was probably a large sheet of
painted canvas spread over rollers, which Mr Duffus was able
to rotate from off stage. The effect was probably not up to
Covent Garden or Metropolitan standards, but some years
later a lover of the Aberdeen theatre wrote that 'the stage,
though by no means extensive, could be made effectively
accommodating'.

With imagination and a slight knowledge of the old ways of
the theatre, it is possible to see in the mind's eye stage performances of long ago from the details given on playbills.
They can also be aids to investigating theatre history. The
Aberdeen playbill lists in the cast of *Paul and Virginia*:

Diego   Mr POWER

Officer   Mr POWER junr.

This Mr Power junr could well have been Tyrone Power I, great-grandfather of Tyrone Power, one of the dashing stars of the great days of the cinema. In 1810, the Mr Power junr of the bill would not have been adjudged too young to play a minor role as an officer, even if he had been only in his early teens, as Tyrone I would then have been. In those days, acting was not an overcrowded profession, so it is unlikely that another family of Powers was engaged in it. Some time later, Tyrone I, known to have been the son of a strolling player, emigrated to the United States, where he became a famous actor. His son did not follow the profession, so Tyrone II, his grandson, was father of Tyrone III, the film star.

This one example illustrates the great fascination of collecting old playbills. They can be bought from booksellers and print shops at anything from £5 ($9.50) to £50 ($95) or more, according to age and content. Until the collector has made himself an expert on the subject, he should buy only from reputable sources. The many fakes and forgeries in circulation are not always easy to detect. However, bills may be looked for in other places. They are still sometimes found in the storerooms of old-established shops that at one time exhibited the bills in return for free tickets.

The collecting of old plays has been dealt with in chapter three, with mention of the earliest English dramatists from Norton and Stevenson, by way of the Elizabethans and the Restoration wits, to Goldsmith and Sheridan. So far, no modern playwrights other than Wilde and Shaw have been considered. Among the many Irish writers for the theatre of the present century, John M. Synge and Sean O'Casey promise to be the most durable. Synge's *The Well of the Saints*, Dublin, 1905, is possibly (g) and would be the dearest single item, as it was edited by W. B. Yeats and is also collected by his followers. The other individual plays should be (i) or (h), and the first collection of his works, 1910, would be (d). Most of O'Casey's plays—*The Plough and the Stars*, 1926, *The Silver Tassie*, 1928, and others—are in (i), but his

Two Plays, 1925, may be (h). It contains *Juno and the Paycock* and *The Shadow of a Gunman*.

James Joyce wrote only one play, *Exiles*, 1918, a first of which could be (g). Though Samuel Beckett, a disciple of Joyce, is Irish, he has written most of his plays in French, then translated them into English. The first English editions are (i), as with his *Endgame*, 1958.

Among the uncollected English dramatists are Somerset Maugham and Sir Noel Coward. Maugham's later plays are noted for their irony and almost all Coward's work is light-hearted, though the satire can be telling. His targets were the manners and follies of the English upper-middle classes between the wars. In the future they will be valued as social documents and for sheer theatrecraft if not for their pro-fundity. Signed books by Maugham and Coward could cost up to (g), but ordinary firsts would be below today's average price for a new book.

Eugene O'Neill, Arthur Miller and Tennessee Williams are the obvious representative US dramatists of the twentieth century. O'Neill will be the most expensive, with his *The Hairy Ape*, undated, but New York, 1922, and *'Anna Christie'*, New York, 1932, in (g), and his signed limited editions considerably higher. A first of Tennessee Williams's *The Glass Menagerie*, New York, no date, but 1945, and of Arthur Miller's *Death of a Salesman*, New York, 1949, would be nearing the top of (i).

The theatre in English-speaking countries seems to be settling down after a period of turmoil, so it may be worth while to collect representative plays by our younger writers and try to appraise them anew. They should still be found in firsts at ordinary out-of-print prices.

12

Hunting and Caring for Books

A sensible book collector once said that although he would never get farther from the surface of the earth than on a charter flight across the Atlantic, he would never tire of looking at close-up pictures of the moon and reading about those who had been there. Every true bibliophile shares his feelings. Many know that they will never be able to possess those fine and costly books that go to the wealthiest collectors and the best-endowed institutional libraries, but they love to hear about them and to have them described. Somehow this enhances rather than detracts from their own pursuit of 'charter-flight' books. In the preceding chapters an attempt has been made to balance the naming and description of some of the greatest treasures among English-language books with consideration of their lowlier kindred—the sort that are within the reach of all who seriously take up bibliophily.

Some beginners feel there is a price level below which there can be nothing worth collecting. They set this level according to their own means and inclinations. It has already been stated that it is always worth while to sift through the dross, but low price is not necessarily the indicator of what is dross. Up to the early sixties, and for longer in some corners, good clean copies of books in the King Penguin series, published during World War II and for some years afterwards, by Penguin Books, could be had for 2s (10p, roughly 20c). This was a reasonable second-hand price for books which had originally cost 3s 6d (17½p, roughly 30c). The

King Penguins were attractive little books in pictorial or decorated boards, with texts by knowledgeable writers and, for the price, excellent colour plates. It dawned on some people that they were worthy of a place in any respectable library, so they set to work to collect the whole series of seventy-six titles. The lucky pioneers had comparatively little trouble in finding all they wanted and acquired full sets for about £10 ($19). As more collectors entered the field it became apparent that some titles were scarce, so prices for them edged upwards. As they became more valuable, they drew the attention of collectors who measure desirability by price, so that now £2 ($3.80) is reasonable for a copy of one of the more plentiful books in the series. Scarcer titles can cost a good deal more—£16 ($30.40) is not out of the way for *Magic Books from Mexico,* No 64 in the series, published in 1953.

A complication attaches to this title. When the Olympic Games were held in Mexico in 1968, a special reprint was brought out in Mexico City. It had the same format as the original, with the same decorated boards. The title-page was headed '*Magic Books from Mexico*' with, underneath, 'Ediciones Lara, Villalongin 32/Mexico 5, D.F.' On the verso it was stated 'First published by Penguin Books 1953/ Reprinted by permission from Penguin Books Ltd, in 1968'. Its series number did not appear. This reprint is no easier to find than the original, and, as an unnumbered reprint, is not an adequate substitute. However, it is a rather special item, which deserves a place of honour in any King Penguin collection.

A fine set of King Penguins, with the Mexican extra, could have a value of about £200 ($380). Dross, indeed! It is hard to believe that a series comparable to this one is waiting on the bargain shelves for its apotheosis, but there are certainly plenty of neglected series that the wise collector could raise in status by acquiring in their entirety. Among the innumerable children's books brought out in the past twenty years

234

there are many that are poorly illustrated and printed on nasty paper, many more that are pleasant, neat, acceptable and no more, but there are some that have never attracted the attention of the critics, child experts and educationists but that nevertheless have real distinction. They, surely, deserve attention.

In adult literature there is the unregarded Reader's Library, sold in Britain through the F. W. Woolworth Co from 1924 to about 1941. The volumes in this series were hardbacks, produced to sell at 6d (2½p, 5c). Under the dust-wrappers, of which few now exist, there were the hard covers, sometimes in cloth, more often of compressed paper. They had the appearance of small 8vos, but most were really 16mos, not sewn in sections, but trimmed into individual leaves and stuck together with glue, rather in the way of gutta-percha bindings. The paper was of the sort that easily yellows and the type was small and sometimes a bit grey or muzzy. They hardly contribute to the dignity of a library.

There are two good reasons for collecting them—cheapness and interest. With their undistinguished appearance, no book-seller would dare to charge highly for them, and among them there are some remarkable books, including a number of unusual 'books of the films'. For example, No 249 is *The Singing Fool* by Hubert Dail and contains eight illustrations of stills from the film, the first 'talkie' to be generally shown in Britain. Other film books in the series have illustrations of Norma Shearer, Greta Garbo, Lillian Gish, Emil Jannings and others in action. Edgar Wallace wrote a few stories and novels specially for the series, so these are undoubted firsts. Classics like *Tom Brown's Schooldays* and *Les Misérables* are also represented.

In the previous edition of this book it was stated that it would be possible to find a copy of John Masefield's *Sard Harker*, in the first edition of 1924, during the course of a day's tour of English bookshops, priced at under 80p ($1.50). This is still true, as it is of similar novels by authors of

235

some standing, so the collector of good readable fiction can still build up his library at small cost. Other authors he may consider, if he likes a more sensational kind of novel, are Bram Stoker (1847–1912), the creator of Dracula (*Dracula*, 1897; *Dracula's Guest*, 1914, etc), Sax Rohmer (Arthur S. Wade, 1883–1959), the creator of Fu Manchu (*The Book of Fu Manchu*, 1929, *The Bride of Fu Manchu*, 1933, *Daughter of Fu Manchu*, 1931, etc); E. Phillips Oppenheim (1866–1946) (*The Avenger*, 1908, *The Devil's Paw*, 1920, etc) and J. S. Fletcher (1863–1935) (*Bonds of Steel*, 1902, *The Borgia Cabinet*, 1932, etc). These authors are already collected to some extent and several of their books are unaccountably scarce in first editions, but they provide good sport for the hunter. Many titles will be found round about the £2 ($3.80) mark, but as ever, the scarce ones will have to be paid for. Books of the late nineteenth century, with pictorial cloth covers, in fine condition, are now widely collected and can be dear when the content is good, as with H. M. Stanley's *In Darkest Africa*, two volumes, 1890, (h).

The English bookshops that can have so much to offer are not always easy to find. In any given town, ask an inhabitant how to get to the nearest butcher, baker or boutique and he will give you directions easily enough, but inquire where the nearest antiquarian bookseller is, and he will look either puzzled or shocked—as if he had been asked for directions to a *balneator* or a brothel.

Help can come from one or other of the guides to antiquarian booksellers: *A Directory of Dealers in Second-hand and Antiquarian Books in the British Isles*, Sheppard Press, PO Box 42, Russell Chambers, Covent Garden, London WC2E 8AX, and the *Directory of Booksellers in the British Isles specialising in Antiquarian and Out-of-Print Books*, published by The Clique Ltd, 75 World's End Road, Handsworth Wood, Birmingham B20 2NS. Both give essential information about almost all British and Irish antiquarian booksellers—if and when their premises are open to the public, the subjects in which they specialize, and whether they issue lists and catalogues. The Sheppard Press also publishes *Bookdealers in North America* and *European Bookdealers*. Representation of the Sheppard Press in the United States is by Standing Orders Inc, PO Box 183, Patterson NY 12563.

In some areas, booksellers combine to produce give-away leaflets listing the shops within the area. Besides providing the information that makes productive tours a possibility, the guides are useful to the stay-at-homes, for they enable collectors to make contact and do business with the dealers who conduct a postal trade. Many issue their catalogues free, but will soon stop sending them to unresponsive clients. Those booksellers who make a small charge will continue to send their catalogues as long as they are paid for.

Though they may present other difficulties, the more elaborate catalogues will be almost free from abbreviations; other lists may be full of them. Anyone of ordinary intelligence and patience should be able to translate most of the contractions with ease, but a list of them is given at the end of this book. Here is a catalogue entry showing some typical abbreviations :

Dickens (Charles). *A Christmas Carol*, trial issue of first t.p. and hf.t. in red and green; cold. plts. and wdcts. by Leech; 12mo, orig. brown cl., a.e.g., yellow e.p.s., mco-bkd. c.; Lond., Chapman & Hall, 1844; top of sp. nicked, front cvr. sltly. rubbed, mild foxing on fp., o/w v.g. copy of excessively rare item.   £500

This translates as :

DICKENS (Charles). *A Christmas Carol*, trial issue of first edition, title-page and half-title in red and green, coloured plates and woodcuts by Leech; duodecimo; original brown cloth, all edges gilt, yellow end-papers; morocco-backed case; London, Chapman & Hall, 1844; top of spine nicked, front cover slightly rubbed, mild foxing on frontispiece, otherwise very good copy of an excessively rare item.   £500

Booksellers' contractions have never been completely stand-ardized. Title-page, written in this entry as t.p., often appears as title-p. and is sometimes shortened to 'title', while hf.-title is often used for half-title. An alternative to mco.-bkd. is mor.-bkd. and c. is more often used for *circa* (about) than for case, usually written in full. Frontispiece can appear as front. and frontis.

The subject of the entry is described as excessively rare and, with qualifications, as a very good copy. 'Excessively rare' is a phrase seldom met with outside booksellers' catalogues. It is just allowable in the entry, for few copies of the item exist, but it is a dubious superlative at best, some-times used with more enthusiasm than veracity. 'Very good' usually means what it says, but there are booksellers who have a great repertory of descriptions of condition, with 'very good' some way down from the top, as : 'mint' (or 'as new'), 'very fine', 'fine', 'near fine', 'exceptionally good', 'extremely good', 'very good', 'really good', 'good', 'quite good', 'goodish', 'fairly good', 'fair', 'rather worn', 'worn', 'very worn' and 'poor'. The collector ordering by post should not let these descriptions worry him. He should accept them for what he thinks they are worth and if the books fail to come up to his expectations, he should send them back with a request for the return of any money paid. If he acts promptly, no decent bookseller will demur. If a dealer is found to be consistently unsatisfactory—all can make genuine mistakes—the collector will drop him, and vice versa if the collector is continually niggling.

An elaborate catalogue may contain an entry (imaginary) like this :

CALDBORNE (Geffray or Geoffrey). *Here begynneth the boke of the merie gest of Pope Jehanne*, 4to; J. Rastell, 1524 : sole edition; blind-tooled seventeenth-century panelled calf with raised bands; signatures A–L^4 (unnumbered); A$_1$ and L$_4$v blank, text A$_2$–L$_3$; colophon L$_4$r; wormhole from A$_1$ to D$_3$ scarcely affecting text; K$_2$–L$_4$ heavily damp-marked. Not in S.T.C.   £4,000

Most of the terms used have already been explained, so the main difficulty is in interpreting the symbols. L^4 signifies a four-leaf gathering signed L, while L_4 denotes the fourth leaf of such a gathering. The recto (upper page of a leaf) is denoted by r and the verso (second or lower page) by v. The meaning of signatures $A-L^4$ is that there are gatherings in fours signed consecutively from A to L, making eleven gatherings in all, with the normal omission of J. 'A_1 and L_4v blank' means that nothing is printed on the first leaf of the book, nor on the second side of the last leaf. The text runs continuously from the second leaf (A_2) to the penultimate leaf (L_3). The colophon, a note giving such details about the book as its author, printer and place and date of printing, is on the first side of the final leaf. The pages are unnumbered, so the extent of the wormhole is explained in signatures—it runs from the first leaf of the book through to the fifteenth. Similarly, the damp-marking affects the last seven leaves. The book has no title-page and no proper title, as would be expected of a book published in 1524. No place of publication is given, but Rastell is known to have been a London printer of the time.

The collector who buys mostly through catalogues should visit bookshops whenever he can. None of his wants may be on the shelves of the shops he visits, but he can learn simply by looking through what is displayed. Most booksellers are happy to let customers inspect their stocks at leisure and while they are not given to taking umbrage if a browser buys nothing, they think more highly of him if he makes a token purchase, be it no more than a tired paperback.

As the wise woman maketh a friend of her physician, so does the bibliophile make an ally of the bibliopole. This is the advice John Carter gave (*Taste & Technique in Book-Collecting*, Cambridge University Press, 1948):

No bookseller resents a reasoned scepticism in bibliographical matters, nor an honest difference of opinion as to the value

239

of a book. Indeed, a good bookseller respects, appreciates and is glad to profit by both, when they are backed by knowledge and experience. What he does resent is a collector who regularly assumes that he is about to be deceived and automatically regards a marked price as something to be reduced. He will sell to such a one reluctantly and with a sour heart. For though booksellers are destined always to be parting from books, they have a liking for them and a pride in their own stock. The grocer who sells a pound of butter cares nothing who eats it. But the bookseller who has a fine thing to dispose of would rather sell it to someone who will appreciate it . . . A sale is a sale, even if it is made with a sigh. But the customer who prides himself on being 'tough' would be surprised if he knew how often a book which he wants, and is known to want, has been kept in a drawer during his visit, to be sold, sometimes for a smaller profit, to another in whose collection the bookseller has been encouraged to take a personal interest.

Collectors should put in an appearance wherever there are books to be had—jumble sales, junk shops and charity gift shops. Some enthusiasts have been known to throw dignity to the winds and inspect dustbins or trashcans for possible finds.

Attendance at important book auctions in the leading salerooms should be a part of every collector's education. It has been shown in Chapter 9 how a bookseller's catalogue can provide new information about a book. The catalogues of the top auctioneers can also be wonderful sources of knowledge. When William Harvey's copy of the *Opera Physica Anatomica* by Geronimo Fabrizio was put up for sale at Sotheby's, London, in 1970, this note was given in the catalogue:

William Harvey left his library to the College of Physicians in his will of 1652 and his books were probably deposited there before his death by himself. The library was destroyed by fire in 1666 and all Harvey's books were lost. However, a few books were rescued by Dr Christopher Merrett and Sir Geoffrey Keynes lists three surviving books belonging to Harvey (Life of William Harvey, p 403): Falloppius, Opera, 1584, with annotations, still in the College library; Galenus, Opuscula, Goulston's edition, 1640, with annotations, in the British Museum; Sylvius, De febribus commentarius, 1555, with Harvey's signature, in the Dr Waller library, Upsala. He also refers to the present book, but he had not seen it. A fourth book is in the Dr Pybus library now in the University of Newcastle on Tyne.

The present book is particularly interesting, as its author was, of course, Harvey's teacher in Padua. The annotations are fairly extensive, they occur on 19 pages, in several cases they have his characteristic initials W H added to them; a few are in pencil. Furthermore, there are very many underlinings on almost every page and numerous pencil marks by him in the margins drawing attention to passages in the text. It is quite clear that Harvey studied this work with the greatest care and in great detail.

It is needless to stress that the appearance of a famous book closely connected with the greatest figure in modern medicine is not only entirely unexpected but an event of considerable historical importance.

The sale of this book (it went for £12,000—then $28,800) was truly a historic occasion, marked, among other things, by this classic catalogue entry which gives the story of the book in a nutshell. Attendance at some sales, with the printed catalogues, where such books are auctioned is as good as a course of lectures in bibliography.

Before attempting to bid more than small amounts at these events, the beginner should familiarize himself with what goes on and should bear in mind that some of the most successful collectors find it better to commission an expert to bid for them than personally to enter the arena. Completely to avoid book sales, however, is to be imperfectly educated and to miss one of the great thrills of the game.

The time has gone when auctioneers handling unimportant house sales regarded books as a nuisance and knocked down large miscellaneous lots quickly to anybody who was rash enough to make an offer. If they appear to be of any possible value, the books are listed prominently in the auctioneers' catalogues, which are then sent to a wide circle of dealers.

The private collector must be sensible at these small sales if he is to make any good buys. He can occasionally go one bid higher than the dealer, who has to think of reselling at a profit. It is wrong to assume, however, that the dealer can always be safely outbid. He may bear a commission from a client prepared to pay any amount for an item particularly desired, or he may set out deliberately to break any private opposition. In such a circumstance he purposely forces up the prices of the early lots and buys them with a dissembled air of satisfaction at having so easily bagged them. If this does not shake off persistent rivals, he will continue to force the pace, but, by using his skill and experience in bidding, drop the lots on his opponents at the inflated prices. Unless his rivals are wildly reckless, they will realize he is making them pay too much and will leave him a clear field.

Though illegal in Britain, and members of the Antiquarian Booksellers' Association are pledged not to participate, a dealers' 'ring' may still operate at some sales. To allay suspicion, two or three of the participating dealers will make the bids on behalf of the ring, using a breaking technique on the opposition if necessary. As a rule, the ring will acquire most of the best lots. When the sale is over, the members of the consortium will bid for the pooled purchases at a second auction, known as the 'knock-out'. Here the bidding on most lots will be higher than at the real sale and the extra money made will be shared out as a dividend among the participants at the end of the second sale. Sometimes the workings of the ring are even more complicated.

It is popularly believed that these illegal arrangements depress prices at sales. This is not always true. There have been occasions when booksellers in the ring have deliberately pushed up prices at sales where there have been good books available, but few bidders. They realise that it is bad for their business if they let the prices of certain items fall below a respectable level.

242

In the United States, where the laws governing auctions may vary in the different states, rings scarcely exist. The university buyer, the individual collector and the dealer bidding on commission tend to dominate the sales, leaving little room for a booksellers' combine to operate.

Everybody who attends sales regularly is sure to obtain a good bargain sooner or later and is entitled to tell the world about it. It is just as legitimate to take pride in non-bargains of the right kind. For a collector to have desired a book so strongly that he has been prepared to pay a record price for it is something of a feather in his cap. What he should keep quiet about is a mistake, like paying up to the hilt for what he took to be a scarce first edition but which proved later to be a second impression.

A collection is as complete as the collector wants it to be. At no point can he say that he has every scrap of material available about an individual subject or author. A Kipling devotee may have every listed item written by his favourite. But can he be quite sure that nothing has escaped? That his author did not at some time write a letter, or an anonymous article for some obscure newspaper, in Britain, America or India; or something else that has not yet come to light? He can never dot the 'i' in 'collection'.

Then there is the case of John Galt (1779–1839). A collector may have first editions of all his novels, but how does he rank *The Last of the Lairds*, published at Edinburgh in 1821? Though it is the first, it is an edition very different from what Galt intended. The author was a cheerful realist who wrote his humorous books in a solemnly pawky style, detailing with frankness the foibles of his characters. A good deal of the writing in *The Last of the Lairds* was unacceptable to the publishers, and a minor literary figure of the day, Dr D. M. Moir, who wrote as 'Delta', was given the job of bowdlerizing the text. He made a thorough job of this, so that Galt later all but repudiated it. Only in 1976 did the Scottish Academic Press publish the true version, edited from the original manuscript by Ian M. Gordon. Incongruous as it may look in its modern dust-jacket over its sober black covers, this, the real first edition, must be put with the old Galt editions in original boards.

Book-collecting is a pursuit in which few ever achieve final contentment. Most go on scouring the bookshops, attending all the best sales and scanning the catalogues of dozens of dealers yet finality eludes them still. Further help can come to them through booksellers who can advertise their wants in the trade press. *The Clique* is issued weekly from Birmingham and is given over almost entirely to such advertisements and lists of books for sale. *The Bookdealer*, another weekly from London, by Fudge & Co Ltd, also carries both wants and sales lists.

The Antiquarian Bookman, published weekly at Clifton, New Jersey, USA, though likewise listing wants and sales, gives more space to news of books of all kinds—old, new, specialist and out-of-print. A *Bookman's Yearbook* is issued annually by the same company. The *Antiquarian Book Monthly Review*, published at Oxford, is roughly equivalent to the American *Antiquarian Bookman*.

All these publications circulate on both sides of the Atlantic, as do two important annuals : *Book Auction Records* and *American Book Prices Current*. *Book Auction Records*, often abbreviated to BAR, covers important sales in Britain, the United States, Australia, Canada, Belgium, France, Germany, Holland, Italy, South Africa and other countries. It gives notes on the more important books sold, with prices, and is a useful tool for the bookman, but is by no means beyond criticism. *American Book Prices Current* is better on the descriptions of books, but does not cover world sales as BAR does.

Both these publications must be used with caution. They do not give full details of condition. The apparent sudden drop in the price of a book one year may be due to a copy's poor condition, not to any falling off in demand. Slavish adherence to the recorded prices would also drive every antiquarian bookseller out of business. Sellers may approach a dealer with a book and quote the price as £50, according to the last BAR figure. If he buys at that price, the dealer must then face the customer who will argue that the selling price must be £50, as that was the last recorded price at an important sale.

The Book Collector, a London quarterly, has a well-earned international reputation, containing articles of the highest standards, mostly written by distinguished bibliophiles and bibliographers. Over the years, this magazine has shed much light on puzzles and problems that beset both beginners and experts. The *American Book Collector*, issued from Chicago, is slightly less rarefied than the English publication, but may be of even greater help to the beginner whose interest is mainly in American books, though it, too, is international in outlook. *The Private Library*, the quarterly journal of the Private Libraries Association, issued from London, is no less informed and erudite and may be the best of all for the beginner.

Besides seeking external help, the collector should develop the kind of awareness that comes from knowledge and familiarity with the wide world of books. A collector of nineteenth-century guide books, in combing through the shelves of a small bookshop, noticed a fine copy of W. B. Yeats's *Poems*, 1906, with an extra something, at a remarkably low price. He bought it and asked the bookseller why it was so cheap. The bookseller said he could not charge more, because somebody had spoiled the copy by doodling on the title-page. It was the doodle that had attracted the buyer. It was a lovely thumbnail watercolour sketch, signed with the tiny initials, 'J.B.Y.' The buyer had realized that it was the work of Jack B. Yeats, the artist brother of the poet. He was able to sell it later at a good profit which gave him extra funds for collecting in his own field.

Some bookmen give the impression of being clairvoyant in

the way they can tell without opening a book whether or not it is 'right'. The first general edition of T. E. Lawrence's *Seven Pillars of Wisdom* was published in July 1935. The second and third impressions were issued in August of the same year. All have apparently exactly similar bindings in brown buckram, yet there are some dealers who are so familiar with the book that they can often pick out a first impression from the others without looking inside. They would not score 100 per cent in a prolonged test, but would do much better than the 33.33 per cent that chance could earn them.

The importance of collecting books in the best possible condition has already been emphasized. What should the collector do if a sub-standard copy is all that he can find or afford? Throughout the English-speaking world, bibliophiles are agreed that he should try to leave it as it is, giving it the best protection possible. This is done by putting it in a case, cardboard or leather, that has been specially made for it. The case should not be too tight fitting, for if the book has to be pulled out with force it will wear more quickly than if placed naked upon a shelf. The most impressive type of case, made to look like a book, is called a soleander, but a careful amateur can make his own adequate, if less elaborate case.

Where the original binding of a book is in really desperate straits, rebinding is advisable. If it is an important book, this should be done as finely as the owner can afford. To case-bind some rare seventeenth-century book in serviceable grey cloth is little short of criminal. If it cannot be given the full treatment in leather, it were better that it should be left to disintegrate rather than suffer such humiliation. It is a matter of personal taste whether an old book should be bound in modern style or after the fashion of its own time. Some book-binders can design so that the finished product does not look like a fake antique, yet harmonizes with the old text.

Where the spine of a leatherbound book has gone, but the sides have survived, the book can be rebacked, that is, given a new spine. This is a difficult job, which should be left to an expert, who will probably charge almost as much as for a complete rebind.

As regards minor repairs and restorations, it is difficult to state where the border lies between the acceptable and the unacceptable. Soap and water can be used to wash the grime from some types of old cloth covers, but the attempt usually ends in disaster. There are several liquid 'book restorers' available. They remove grime and certain stains quite effectively. When their distinctive odour has gone, there is nothing left to show that they have ever been used—if they have been applied judiciously. Before applying them to valuable books it is as well to try them out on unconsidered volumes.

Where there is a tiny fray at the corner of a cover, little harm is done by touching it with a spot of latex gum. If the titling-pieces of leather books have come loose, they should be restuck with ordinary starch paste, not with patent glues or gums. Centuries of experience have shown that starch has no deleterious effect on leather, but as yet there is no way of knowing what effect modern adhesives may have after a hundred years or so—an important consideration when it is remembered that nobody is ever the absolute owner of a good book; he is merely its guardian during his lifetime, or until he transfers the responsibility by sale or gift.

Leather books are often polished with shoe cream. Those who do so may say that the cream 'feeds the leather'. As leather has no digestive system, it cannot be fed. What is meant is that the surface of the leather can be clogged up with heaven knows what sort of stuff, which may do as much damage as good in the long run. Unreadable books in conventional nineteenth-century calf or morocco bindings may be so doctored, but really valuable old bindings should not suffer this abuse. Frequent gentle handling with clean hands and an occasional rub with a silken cloth ought to keep them in good order.

If leather becomes at all brittle it may be given a dose of castor oil. A soft rag should be lightly smeared with the oil and rubbed gently over the leather, which is then wiped with a dry rag. Similar applications can be made on successive days until the oil has been absorbed below the surface without the leather's becoming saturated. If the book has unavoidably to face harsh conditions, paraffin wax should be added to the oil. This is done by shredding a little wax into the oil then heating till the wax melts. In *Bookbinding and the Care of Books*, 1901, and subsequent reprints, Douglas Cockerell suggests that the wax should be a quantity weighing about half as much as the castor oil. This may be a little too much. Beeswax can be used instead, but it costs more and is no better for the purpose.

A little book called *The Preservation of Leather Bookbindings* by H. J. Plenderleith is published by the Trustees of the British Museum. It gives the recipe for the British Museum leather dressing, based on anhydrous lanolin, cedarwood oil and beeswax, with details of where it may be obtained, ready for use. Anybody who has to care for large numbers of leatherbound books should have this publication.

Bookworms, which can do a great deal of damage, are just as likely to attack new books as old. They are the larvae of several species of beetle belonging to the genus *Anobium*, the commonest being *Anobium domesticum*. They are identical with woodworms, though it appears that certain races are better adapted to a diet of paper than others. Some bookworms are the grubs of *Xestobium tessellatum*, the notorious death-watch beetle, but fortunately, this is rarely the case.

Worming of books often begins at a corner of the spine, where the eggs are laid. When the grub hatches, he eats out a tunnel through the leaves and finally escapes as a mature beetle, having spent an intermediate period as a fat pupa, cosily wrapped in a cocoon. The perfect insect has wings and can fly quite a distance to cause infestation elsewhere. Books can be wormed by grubs, which start life in the wood of shelves and continue their tunnelling from the wood to the books.

Treatment is lengthy, but fairly simple. An infested book should be examined and all living grubs removed. It should then be put in a sort of gas chamber consisting of an airtight box in which there have been placed some pieces of cotton wool soaked with ether. The soaked cotton should not be allowed to touch the book. Twenty-four hours in the closed box will kill off any grubs or developed insects, but not the eggs and possibly not the pupae. The book should be left for a week or more for the eggs to hatch, then the treatment should be repeated. If this is done twice more, the book will be free from pests.

The procedure is also effective against the booklouse, *Atropos divinatoria*, a tiny insect that can be seen scuttling merrily among old books and documents, often in large gangs. It has an Epicurean regard for glue and paste and in course of time can seriously weaken bindings.

Library hygiene is essential if infestations of such pests are to be avoided. Books and shelves should be dusted and examined regularly. If the wood shows signs of recent worming it should be given appropriate treatment and pieces of camphor or naphthalene should be placed in suitable corners of the shelves to discourage further attacks. At one time potassium cyanide was employed as a fumigant. It is a deadly poison and should never be used—it is no more effective than ether.

Sunlight is another enemy to be warded off. Bookcases and shelves should never be placed where direct sunlight can fall on them. If this is not possible, they should have curtains to keep the devastating rays off the books and prevent their becoming faded. Dust-wrappers are not sufficient protection. Under continued exposure to sunlight, the design of the wrapper can be photographed on the cloth cover of a book.

Human beings are among the worst despoilers of books, so the bibliophile is careful not to let any Tom, Dick or Harry handle his treasures. Tom may drag a book from the shelf by placing a finger at the top of the spine and pulling hard; Dick, on finding that a tightly-bound book does not easily open, may seize the covers and double them back till they meet, thus cracking the binding; Harry may be an inveterate finger-licking fumbler with a genius for rucking up leaves.

The collector with the easiest mind is he who does all his own dusting. He brushes the outsides of his books lightly and goes through the leaves to make sure that no dust has lodged between them. If it has, he flicks it away with a feather duster, trying to use it as a fan instead of letting it touch the paper and cause smearing. Few things horrify the book-lover more than the sight of books being dusted roughly—perhaps by the cruel method of taking a volume in either hand and bashing the two together as if they were a pair of cymbals.

Human ill-treatment of books does not end with handling and cleaning. The amateur repairer can inflict serious wounds on books. It sometimes happens that one of the covers, usually the front, of an old leatherbound volume becomes detached. The would-be book cobbler re-affixes it by means of several strips of transparent cellulose tape, or sometimes a glue-soaked strip of cloth. If the book is ever to be reinstated the tape or cloth has to be removed and a proper repair done—and the removal can cause damage. There is no harm in using cellulose tape, inside or out, on the worn tenth or later impression of an inferior modern paperback. It should not be applied to any book of the slightest value. Repairs should be entrusted to a qualified person, or the collector should take a course in bookbinding and become proficient in the work himself.

One of the worst crimes committed against books is the removal or mutilation of endpapers. Fear of black magic seems to linger in the minds of many apparently civilized people. When they come to sell books on which their names have been written, they are so terrified lest the names fall into the hands of sorcerers who will work evil against them that they tear out the endpapers that carry the names. The result is not only unsightly but makes the book incomplete and weakens it. Sometimes only the part of the endpaper bearing the name is cut out, or an ink solvent is applied. These mutilations are equally deplorable. There is no dishonour in selling a book with its original owner's name on it. Rather is it a privilege to have one's name discreetly written in a book destined to form part of some cherished private or public collection.

Conversely, there are stuffy collectors prejudiced against books that carry a former owner's name as evidence of a perfectly legitimate defloration. This preoccupation with the maidenly state does no honour to an old book. If it has every sign of being *virgo intacta*—unread and unloved—after fifty or a hundred years, that is a poor commendation for a book deemed worthy of a place in a collection. Bibliophily would be a more warmly human activity if there was general agreement that every owner of a book should write his name in it, the first making a start at the top left corner of the front free endpaper and the others following in order. In time, the book would carry its own history with it instead of being just any old copy.

A well-designed bookplate, neatly affixed to the front pastedown endpaper, should also be looked on as an enhancement. It is possible to buy mass-produced bookplates incorporating a more or less appropriate design and reading 'Ex libris . . .' or 'From the library of . . .', and the owner is expected to write his name on the dotted line. These are all very well, but they lack individuality. The collector should have his own personal bookplate or equivalent. Not everybody can afford to commission an artist of standing to design his plate, but rather than settle for an inferior design, the collector should seek out a capable printer to supply him with a personal book label, distinguished by its typographical excellence. In time, the front paste-down endpapers of a book can become a sort of palimpsest as one owner's plate is pasted over the one before.

Bookplates are legitimately stuck into books—nothing else is. Sometimes the listed details of a book from a dealer's catalogue are cut out and pasted on an endpaper. The proper place for such a cutting is in a dated scrapbook. Other compulsive cutters-out stick photographs, extracts from newspapers or fragments of information from dustwrappers into books. These, too, are more at home in a scrapbook, though if they are not of sufficient bulk to put a strain on the covers, they may be loosely inserted, as may other relevant material —authors' letters and the like.

Older authorities maintained that since the dust-wrapper was not an integral part of a book it could be discarded. This is not now acceptable, particularly when a printed note inside the book states 'wrapper designed by J. Smith', or when a photograph printed on the wrapper is included in the list of illustrations. Yet wrappers are fragile things and however well cared for will become frayed and worn in time. The collector must either resign himself to this, or he can remove the wrapper and file it, substituting a loose brown-paper jacket of his own making or leaving the book unclothed on his shelves.

A somewhat similar problem arises with certain books published in the early part of this century. They were bound in cloth or boards, but instead of being titled directly on the spine, paper titling pieces were used. Realizing that these labels would wear or discolour, the publishers provided duplicate labels with the books, lightly stuck on one or other of the back endpapers. Is a book of this type complete if the original label has been discarded and replaced by the duplicate? The question has often been asked, but no pundit has yet given a ruling.

There is little need for the collector to concern himself with thermometers and hygrometers in his library. Books should be maintained at an even temperature and should not be allowed to become too dry or too damp. A room temperature that is comfortable, if coolish, for ordinary living, in an atmosphere with a pleasant sense of being neither too moist nor too dry, is ideal for books. They enjoy a bit of a breeze now and again. This can be supplied by reversing the action of a vacuum cleaner. The stream of air blows away the dust and is alleged to prevent the paper from becoming brittle.

Books must be kept in an upright position on the shelves. They should neither be packed too tightly nor allowed to flop at an acute angle. It is dangerously easy to shelve books reasonably tightly yet slightly keeled over. Once books have acquired the obliquity that this position imposes it becomes almost impossible to straighten them out again. Where a shelf has to be left unfilled, verticality can be maintained by the use of a metal book-rest.

Old Sir Thomas Phillipps has been popping up throughout this book like King Charles's head in Mr Dick's history. This greatest of bibliomaniacs derived from a family long established in the Cotswold country between Chipping Campden and Broadway, and it was at Middle Hill, in the parish of Broadway, that he made his home and built up his library. A really dedicated bibliophile might wish to buy, in (f), A. N. L. Munby's five volumes of *Phillipps Studies*, 1951–60, which according to their author, 'abound in a mass of detail relating to the history of palaeography, bibliography, bookselling, auctioneering, scholarship, librarianship and archive administration'. But even in those pages, the content of the Phillipps library can only be hinted at. Sir Thomas himself produced a *Catalogus Librorum Manuscriptorum in Bibliotheca D. Thomae Phillipps, Bart, A.D. 1837* (sold in 1976 for £2,400—$4,560), which goes only a little way towards listing what he collected. If Phillipps had stopped to make a full catalogue, he would have lost much precious collecting time, but would have had a library of more manageable proportions.

This is the dilemma faced by all collectors. How much time and trouble should they spend on cataloguing their possessions? Various elaborate schemes have been and still are recommended. They can profitably be ignored. A man intelligent enough to become a book collector should have the wit to devise his own author and title card-index system. Even if it is an ill-favoured thing, it will be his own and he will know how to use it. If he puts reference numbers on the cards, he will also write them on the front endpapers of the books to which they pertain, lightly, in pencil, so that they can be erased if necessary. If he tries to shelve the books in a strictly logical order he will find he has often to partner fat folios with slim duodecimos so that his library will look like a frozen Hal Roach comedy, with incongruous Laurels and Hardys gazing down from every shelf. Logicality must sometimes give way to common sense. In any case, if he is truly a book-lover he will seldom have to consult his catalogue : he will know where in his library his friends are to be found, even if they ultimately be numbered by the thousand.

Besides keeping a card index, he will have an accessions book into which he will enter every acquisition as it is made, with details of how and where it was obtained and the price paid. More should be given than bare statements of fact. The accessions book will make better reading in the future if it is written up in anecdotal style. As already mentioned, a scrapbook is also worth keeping. It will contain informative cuttings from many sources about books and bookmanship, and anything else the compiler considers to be worthy of inclusion.

The most important thing of all is for the collector to enjoy and use his library. Some bibliomanes become so absorbed with points, priorities and variants that they cease to look on a book as something to be read. They have the snaffle and the bit all right, but forget about the bloody horse. They buy good books that have long remained unopened in the technical sense and refuse to take the paperknife to them. They invest in first editions so fine that they never dare to lay a finger on them except to dust them. A few fanatics maintain two libraries— one in which the books are regarded as inviolable and the other in which they may grudgingly be consulted and read. Eccentricities of this sort must never be allowed to develop, nor will they if the book collector exercises his common sense at all times and adds to it the closely allied senses of proportion and humour.

Glossary of Terms used in Book Collecting

This list gives only a few of the terms that the book collector is liable to meet. For the best list ever compiled, he should consult John Carter's delightful *ABC for Book Collectors*.

Ana Written and printed material about a particular author or subject, often added to the name of the author or subject to make a new word. In combination it usually takes the form *iana* or *eana*, as Sussexiana, Whitmaniana, Coleridgeana, etc.

Antiquarian books A loose term. When a dealer states that he sells 'antiquarian, secondhand and out-of-print books', 'antiquarian' can be taken to mean 'old and desirable', 'secondhand' to mean 'old and not very desirable' and 'out-of-print' to mean 'recent, but longer available from publishers' stocks'. However, an antiquarian bookseller may specialize in first editions of the present century, which, desirable though they may be, are not old.

Association copy A copy of a book having special links with the author, with somebody else associated with the book, or with some other important person. Henry Irving's copy of *Dracula*, for example, would be an Irving association item.

Biblio- A prefix denoting 'book' or 'books' when compounded with other words derived from Greek.

Biblioclast A destroyer of books.

Bibliomane, bibliomaniac While the two words are really synonymous, bibliomane is more often used of a book collector who is wildly enthusiastic and bibliomaniac of one who is a hopelessly abandoned fanatic.

Bibliopegist A bookbinder or a collector of fine bindings.

Bibliophily The love of books. Used as a synonym for book collecting, as bibliophile is used for a book collector.

Bibliopole A bookseller in his Sunday best.

Binder's cloth A single copy of a book that has been specially bound in cloth is in binder's cloth as distinct from the original cloth met with in the normal copies of an edition. The term 'binder's leather' is never used.

Black letter. This is commonly used for English 𝔊𝔬𝔱𝔥𝔦𝔠 types, though it correctly pertains only to a special type of Gothic. In late years typographers have come to use 'Gothic' for type faces without serifs. Bibliographers reject this usage.

Blind-tooled Decorated with impressions from bookbinders' tools, but not gilded. If the impressions have been made from blocks, a book cover is said to be blind-stamped.

Boards The outermost parts of a book. The boards may be paper-covered or overlaid with leather or cloth. When no covering other than paper is used, the book is described as being in boards; otherwise it is said to be in leather or cloth.

Bookplate A label bearing an engraved device, specially printed to show the ownership of a book and normally pasted on the front inner cover. Where there is no engraving, the equivalent is a book label.

257

Bookworm A devourer of books, human or insect. Slight worming in old books is to be expected and hardly counts as a defect, provided the holes do not seriously affect the text or illustrations. A surprising number of worms are obliging enough to make meals only of the margins. As a rule, human bookworms do not literally eat books.

Breaker A biblioclastic bookseller who breaks books to sell the plates individually. A book considered suitable for his purpose is also called a breaker or a breaking copy.

Broadsheet An unfolded sheet of paper with printed matter on both sides. The term is applied mainly to sheets of ballads and street songs sold by pedlars until quite recently, but it is also used of proclamations, news items, etc similarly produced on single sheets. It is sometimes applied to a broadside.

Broadside An unfolded sheet of paper with printed matter on one side only, otherwise agreeing in every respect with the broadsheet. While theatrical playbills are technically broadsides, they are usually considered and collected separately. See *The Broadside Ballad* by Leslie Shepard, 1962.

Calf A smooth, hardwearing leather tanned from calfskin, used for leather bindings from early days to the present. Natural calf is a pale fawnish colour, but the leather is usually dyed in some shade of brown or in other colours. Tree calf is highly polished and bears a design supposed to resemble a tree. Sprinkled and mottled calf have little flecks of different colours on them, and diced calf is embossed with an allover design of small lozenges. A book described as in antique calf will probably be a modern rebind in old style.

Calligraphic Should mean beautifully handwritten. It is often used of any kind of handwritten material in a printed book, as 'a calligraphic title tipped in takes the place of the missing printed title-page'.

258

Called for A bookseller's term meaning that such-and-such is necessary for the completeness of a book, according to some good authority.

Cancel A substitute leaf introduced after the sheets of a book have been printed and folded (*folium cancellans*).

Cancelland An unacceptable leaf that has to be removed (*folium cancellandum*).

Cap The headcap and tailcap are the shaped tops and bottoms of spines of books bound in leather in the traditional way.

Casing A method of fitting covers to a book without lacing the cords to the boards. Most books in cloth are cased.

Chapbook Single sheets as for broadsheets could be folded to make small booklets, often 8vos and 16mos, but also in other formats. Like broadsides and broadsheets, they could contain ballads, but the subjects ranged widely, from folk tales, by way of reports of murders, to accounts of the lives of famous and notorious people. 'Omnibus volumes' exist, made from several chapbooks sewn together and bound in boards. The books were hawked in the streets and from door to door by chapmen, from the seventeenth to the nineteenth centuries. A chap, meaning a fellow, is a shortening of chapman.

Chromolithography A technique of colour-printing from stone. Many early chromolithographs were hand-finished to supply the finer gradations of tone.

Collate To examine the pages of a book to check that all is in order and complete. It can also mean to compare one copy with another known to be correct in all particulars.

Colophon A paragraph giving details of printer, author, date and place of printing etc, at the end of a book. Early books had no title-pages and bore colophons instead; some, slightly later, have both. Many printers used to put their trademarks with the colophons and when these marks later came to be printed on title-pages they were still sometimes called colophons.

Colour(ed) plates Can be hand-coloured or printed by one of various processes. There is a tendency to refer to those done by hand, or one of the older printing methods, as coloured plates and those produced by modern methods as colour plates.

Cropped A book that is shaved (qv) may suffer only slight damage to the text, but when it is described as cropped, or cut into, it may be assumed that the damage is serious.

Disbound Short, integrated pieces of printing, broken from a parent volume, are so described when sold separately.

Doublure The ornamental lining, often with gold-tooled edges, found on the immediate inside of a finely-bound book.

Dust-wrapper The paper jacket put round most modern books for additional protection—also called a dust-jacket.

Editio princeps The first printed edition of a work already in existence as a manuscript book before the introduction of printing. The term is most commonly applied to the first printed editions of Greek and Latin classics, but is equally applicable to books in other languages. It is sometimes grandly but mistakenly used of any important first edition.

Endpapers Blank leaves at the front and back of a book. The paste-down endpaper is stuck to the inside of the cover, so its next neighbour is the free endpaper. Blank leaves at the fronts or backs of books other than these are called fly-leaves.

Ephemera Pamphlets, broadsides, handbills and the like produced without thought of their being preserved for posterity.

Errata slip A slip of paper pasted in, usually at the beginning of a book, noting errors in the text. Corrections are generally given also, in which case the slip is more correctly headed *errata et corrigenda*, meaning 'errors made and needing correction'. Errata are sometimes noted on a preliminary leaf bound in the book.

Ex-library A book that has identifiably been at one time an item in a lending library, but not a private library, is so described.

Extra-illustrated See grangerized.

First printing Has two meanings. It is used as an alternative for 'first impression' and is also applied to the first appearance in print of a work later issued in another form. The first printing of Rudyard Kipling's poem 'The Absent-Minded Beggar' was in the *Daily Mail*, 31 October 1899. Its first separate issue came later that year, when it appeared as a three-leaved folder published by the newspaper. It was first collected in Volume XXII of the 'Bombay' edition of Kipling's works, 1915, limited to 1,050 copies.

Fore-edge painting The fore-edge (sometimes pronounced 'forridge') of a book is the edge opposite the spine. A fore-edge can be slightly and evenly opened out and held fast while a painting is applied to it. When the book is firmly closed and the whole edge gilded, the painting cannot be seen, but when the edge is splayed out again, the picture is revealed. Thus a dull book can become a sophisticated and expensive toy, enjoyed by collectors who are not fond of reading. The technique was popular in the late eighteenth and early nineteenth centuries—Moore's *Lalla Rookh* seems to have been a favourite subject—but the art is still practised, mainly on old books.

Format Refers to the number of times each whole sheet has been folded to provide the leaves of a single gathering for a book. The names of the different formats are given in Chapter 1.

Foxing Marked with brown spots and blotches, often caused by the action of dust on certain chemicals in paper.

Gathering The unit for sewing a book together, formed when the printed sheet has been folded the number of times required by the format. As a gathering normally carries a signature, it is often called a signature.

Gauffered, goffered Describes the edges of books that have been embossed with ornamental designs.

Grangerized A book that has had a number of extra illustrations bound or tipped in is said to be grangerized, after James Granger, an eighteenth-century publisher who issued a history of England with blank leaves on which the owners could paste illustrations of their own choice. Where a large number of extra leaves has been tipped in after the book has been bound, great strain is put on the binding, which may soon break. Grangerized books should be professionally rebound after the insertion of the extra leaves. An alternative term is extra-illustrated.

Gutta-percha binding An unfortunate substitute for a sewn binding invented about 1840 by Thomas Hancock. A caoutchouc binding is virtually the same thing.

Half binding A binding where the leather covers little more than the spine of a book, with triangular pieces of matching leather at the outer corners. A leather half binding is often described as being in half leather. Half bindings in cloth are sometimes seen. Half bindings with a generous allowance of leather are often called three-quarter bindings.

Half title The leaf in front of the title-page, carrying the name of the book and little or nothing else. It is sometimes called a 'bastard title', but this is not because its absence or presence in some cases can be a source of irritation to bibliographers.

Headband A protective band sewn inside the top of a spine. The equivalent at the base is a tailband, but both may be spoken of as headbands. Many modern headbands are stuck on instead of being sewn in.

High spot An author's high spot is the book widely accepted as his best. Some collectors devote their energies exclusively to acquiring first edition high-spots of a select number of authors. A slightly different use of the term is seen in 'Audubon's *Birds of America* is one of the ornithological high spots', meaning that it is one the finest bird books ever produced.

Historiated Decorated with figures of people or animals, more or less in action. It is used of the marginal decorations and more particularly of the enriched initial capitals of illuminated books.

Hornbook A leaf of paper, parchment or vellum bearing some rudimentary educational memoranda (the alphabet, the numbers one to ten, and the Lord's Prayer, perhaps), slipped between a thin layer of clear horn and a wooden backing fitted with a handle so that it looks like a small square looking-glass. Genuine examples from the sixteenth, seventeenth and eighteenth centuries are rare, but 'manufactured' specimens are not unusual. Andrew W. Tuer's *History of the Horn-Book*, the best work of reference on the subject, published in 1896, should contain two replicas of hornbooks in packets at the end.

Impression An impression is the complete number of books of an edition printed at one time. The first edition of the collector is normally the first impression.

Imprimatur An official licence to print, issued by church or state authorities. It ordinarily appears on one of the preliminary pages of a book.

Incunabula Books from the earliest period of printing, up to 1500. Incunable is widely used as the singular, with incunables as an alternative plural.

Issue The issue of a book is the total number published at one time. This may be only part of an impression, so there can be first, second, etc issues of a whole impression.

Juveniles In the antiquarian book trade, children's books, particularly those of the Victorian era and earlier.

Kern The overhanging part of a letter such as 'f', awkward to print when followed by certain other letters. The difficulty is got over by using ligatures, combinations of letters cast in type as one—'ff', 'fi', etc.

Large-paper A term applied to books printed on leaves bigger than those of the normal edition. Large-paper copies were made either for presentation or for selling at a higher rate to those willing to pay. Sometimes the page proportions are horribly wrong, so that the text looks like a postage stamp stuck in the middle of a huge envelope. Booksellers may price up large-paper copies, but they should be bought according to their real merit.

Limited edition An edition of a book confined to a given number of copies. Where the limitation is over a thousand, it ceases to have much significance. Where it is unstated it raises a big question.

Miniature books Books collected because of their dwarfishness. John Carter suggested that any volume less than $2 \times 1\frac{1}{2}$in (50x37mm) should qualify for the title.

Modern face Printing types where the difference between the thick and the thin strokes is strongly marked are modern face types. They were truly modern in 1815, but went out of vogue later last century, when old-face types again took over. Some fine modern faces have been designed in recent years, so the style is back in use.

Monograph A book that deals exclusively with one subject or one part of a subject.

Morocco An attractive grained leather derived from goatskin, often dyed red, but also common in other colours. Levant and Niger are types of morocco; crushed morocco is a variety with the grain pressed flat but still discernible and a favourite with the best binders of the arts and crafts movement.

Nice For various reasons some books wear badly in their original bindings—the first edition of *Moths*, three volumes, 1880, by Ouida (Louise de la Ramée, 1839–1908), is a notorious example—so when a dealer comes across such a book in unusually good condition he describes it as 'nice'. The word is seriously overworked by some who lack discrimination and is sometimes applied to books in far from good condition.

Old face Printing types of the styles popular up to the end of the eighteenth century showed no marked contrast between thick and thin strokes. When they were revived in the nineteenth century they were referred to as old-face types.

Oleograph A picture or illustration printed in oil colours, as in the Baxter process.

Parchment A material much like vellum (qv), but got from sheepskin. Inferior parchment is sometimes called forel.

Part-issue The issue of a book in serial parts. Until the appearance of *The Pickwick Papers* only inferior fiction, important illustrated books and some works of reference were issued in parts. The term is used of the regular numbers of Addison's and Steele's *The Spectator* and similar magazines, but these were not conceived of as building up to a single unified book.

Pigskin Leather from the pig, when properly processed, provides an extremely hardwearing if unattractive covering for books.

Pirated edition An edition of a book produced without the consent of the author or owner of the copyright.

Points The features such as misprints, corrections, advertisements, etc used as guides to distinguish one issue or edition of a book from another.

Presentation copy A copy of a book clearly presented by the author, or possibly the illustrator, and not merely signed by him. A copy of Darwin's *The Origin of Species*, presented by T. H. Huxley to Herbert Spencer, would be a valuable association copy, not a presentation copy.

Printing An alternative word for impression, as in 'second printing'. See 'first printing'.

266

Private press A privately owned press usually devoted to the production of fine books or those unlikely to succeed in the ordinary way of trade.

Provenance The history of a book's ownership. This can be determined by bookplates, by the owners' names written in the book, or by information obtained from old sale catalogues or booksellers' lists.

Publisher's cloth If an entire issue, impression or edition has been bound by or for a publisher in uniform cloth, the books are said to be in publisher's cloth.

Quarter binding A binding where the leather or other material for backing covers the spine with some overlap on either side, but with no protective corners of the same material.

Raised bands The binding cords of a book when their presence shows on the leather of the spines as decorative ridges. A book may have false raised bands.

Rebacked When only the spine of a book has been renewed, it is said to be rebacked. Where possible, portions of the old spine are retained and overlaid on the new to preserve as much as possible of the original binding.

Reversed leather Some books are bound with the underside of the leather, treated to give it a suede-like appearance, on the outside. They are said to be in reversed calf, sheep, etc as the case may be.

Roxburghe binding A superior type of quarter binding, depending on its excellence of finish rather than decoration for its effect; named from the third Duke of Roxburghe, who favoured bindings of this type.

267

Rubricated Having the text supplied with red letters where appropriate and often with borders of red lines. Rubrication is found in Bibles, prayer books, almanacs, etc.

Russia Russia leather is prepared from cowhide and somewhat resembles calf, though it is blander to the touch. It has been little used for books for the past 150 years.

Section An alternative word for gathering—booksellers' rather than bookbinders' jargon.

Shaved A book whose edges have been severely trimmed without actually having been cropped.

Serif The fine cross-stroke seen at the ends of roman and italic letters. Printing types that lack these are called sans-serif types.

Sheep Sheepskin leather, termed 'sheep', is not ideal for book-binding as it tends to peel in strips. When new it looks very like calf.

Signature The letter or other sign printed on the lower margin of the first and, sometimes, subsequent leaves of a gathering. A whole gathering is often spoken of as a signature.

Signed copy This is taken to mean a copy of a book signed by the author and/or the illustrator and not by anybody else, however notable.

Slip case A cardboard, cloth-covered or leather case into which a book can fit snugly, with the spine showing. Slip cases provide good protection if they are not too tight.

State The different states of an issue are the variations arising from changes made before any portion of an edition was published. It is sometimes hard to distinguish between a state and an issue.

Sugar paper A soft, rather coarse paper, often grey-blue, but found in other drab colours. It is so named for its being the material traditionally used in Britain for making small sugar bags. In the eighteenth and early nineteenth centuries, when it was also used for covering the plain boards in which books were originally issued, it was normally a laid paper, which is one made on a wire mesh with the wires set parallel so that they leave their marks on the finished paper. The marks show when the paper is held to the light. Nowadays, the marks can be imitated on paper which is a *wove,* not a real laid paper, like most modern machine-made papers.

Sunned When the covers of a book have been more or less bleached by sunlight, booksellers euphemistically describe them as sunned.

Three-decker A book in three volumes, but the term is used almost exclusively of Victorian novels in this form.

Ties Ribbons or strips of leather attached to the front edges of the covers of some books and intended to be tied together when the books are not in use. They have little more than nuisance value as they serve no discernible purpose except to reduce the price of the book when they inevitably become worn and fall off.

Tipped in Plates, maps and other illustrative material separately printed on single leaves are generally gummed along their inside edges and placed in position between two of the sewn leaves of a book at appropriate places. They are then said to be tipped in. Such extra leaves may alternatively be given wide inner margins to provide a folded overlap, allowing the leaf of illustration to be sewn in with the others.

Titling piece The thin leather label on the spine, bearing the title of a book. Titling pieces, or lettering pieces, were tooled

269

in situ as the gold would have rubbed off in the course of sticking the label to the spine. Some books bound in materials other than leather have paper titling pieces.

Top edge gilt Describes a book with the top edge cut and gilded. Books may have top and fore-edge gilt, or all edges gilt.

Trimmed All books that have their leaves opened and their edges cut smooth are trimmed. Some people apply the term to books that have had the work rather roughly done.

Unbound Not in a binding. Applied to a book or pamphlet that has never been bound.

Uncut A book that is uncut has all the edges of its leaves in the rough state. An uncut copy is *not* one in which the leaves have not been slit apart.

Unopened An unopened book is one in which the leaves are still joined at the folds. Some books that have survived in this condition for 200 years and more seem condemned to remain unread for ever, as few collectors would have the courage to take the paperknife to them after so long.

Vellum The inner side of calfskin, cured, but not tanned, to produce a very durable material, nearly white and smooth enough to be written upon. If not subjected to extremes of dampness or dryness it will outlast leather as a covering for books.

Vignette A small illustration or decoration on a title-page or at the beginning (headpiece) or ending (tailpiece) of a chapter or portion. Any small illustration not contained within a border is equally entitled to the name.

Woodcut An illustration printed from a block of wood on which a design has been cut. The best authorities say that a woodcut is cut along the grain of the wood and a wood engraving is graved on a cross-section. Bewick woodcuts are undoubted wood engravings and the mid nineteenth-century pictures in the *Illustrated London News* are indisputable woodcuts proper. But in many cases—eg, the later work of some of Bewick's pupils—it is almost impossible to tell without examining the original blocks.

Wrappers Generally the paper covers in which books, periodicals and pamphlets were originally issued.

Xylography The art of wood engraving.

Yapp edges The limp leather overlapping edges of the covers of some Bibles and other books, mainly devotional. They are named from a Mr Yapp, a London bookseller who introduced books so edged in the 1860s.

Yellow backs Cheap books published mainly for sale at railway bookstalls during the nineteenth century, bound in pictorial or decorated boards, generally yellow in colour.

Zincograph An illustration printed from a zinc plate engraved by a special process. Zincographs were much used between 1860 and 1880 for illustrating books on antiquities and local history.

Abbreviations used in Booksellers' Catalogues

Such abbreviations have never been completely standardized. There is a growing tendency to omit the stops and write 'ads', 'aeg', etc, but they are given in this list as they are still retained in most catalogues.

ads., advts., adverts. advertisements

a.e.g. all edges gilt

A.L.S., A.L.s. autograph letter, signed. The second form is preferable

app. appendix

bd. bound

bdg., bg. binding

bds. boards

bkd. backed, as 'mor.-bkd. bds.' for 'morocco-backed boards'

bk.-pl., bk.-plt. bookplate

b.l. black letter

buck. buckram

b. & w., b.w. black and white (of uncoloured illustrations)

c. case, *circa* (about)

cf. calf

cl. cloth

col(d). colour(ed)

cond. condition

cont., contemp. contemporary

contr. contraction

contr. contributor, contribution

dblr. doublure

dec., decor. decorated, decoration

ded. dedicated, dedication

disbd. disbound

d.w. dustwrapper

ed. editor, edited

ed., edn. edition

eng., engr. engraved, engraving

endp., e.p. endpaper

ex-lib. ex-library

facs. facsimile

fig. figure

fp., front., frontis. frontispiece

g., gt. gilt

hf. half, as 'hf. bd.' for 'half bound'

h-m-p., h.m.p. hand-made paper

h.t. half-title

ill., illust. illustrated, illustrtion

imp. imperial (size of paper)

imp., impr. impression
impft. imperfect
inscr., inscrip. inscribed, inscription
jt. joint
intro., introd. introduction
leath. leather
lge. large
L.P., l.p. large-paper
ld., ltd. limited (of an edition)
lf. leaf
ll. leaves
marb. marbled
marg. margin, marginal
m-b-c., m.b.c. morocco-backed case
mco., mor. morocco
n.d. no date
n.p. no place, no publisher, or no printer
o.p. out of print
or., orig. original
p., pp. page, pages
p.d. paste-down, as 'p.d. e.p.' paste-down endpaper
pict. pictorial
pl., plt. plate
pol., pold. polished
port. portrait

P.P., p.p. privately printed
pres. presentation
pt. part
ptd. printed
pub(d). published
qtr. quarter
remd., removed, as 'e.p. remd.' for 'endpaper removed'
repd. repaired
reprod. reproduced, reproduction
rev(d). revised
rub. rubricated
ser. series
sig. signature
sigd. signed
sm. small
sp. spine
tabs. tables
t.-label title-label
T.L.s. typewritten letter, signed
trans. translated, translation
unb(d). unbound
v.d. various dates
vell. vellum
vig. vignette
vol. volume
w.a.f. with all faults
wraps. wrappers

The contractions 'r' for 'recto' (front side) and 'v' for 'verso' (back side) are found in descriptive bibliography more than in booksellers' catalogues.

A Short Bibliographical Guide
for Collectors

A comprehensive bibliography suitable to the needs of collectors of every kind would fill many large volumes. This list is intended as a foundation on which collectors can build their own personal bibliographies of the books they want to pursue. Many of the items listed are exceedingly hard to find, but a really determined collector should be able to track down copies for consultation, if not for buying.

GENERAL WORKS

Aldis, H. G. *List of Books Printed in Scotland before 1700*, reprint, National Library of Scotland, Edinburgh, 1970

Bateson, F. W. (ed). *The Cambridge Bibliography of English Literature*, 5 vols, Cambridge University Press, 1957 (see also under Watson)

Besterman, Theodore. *World Bibliography of Bibliographies*, 4th edn, 5 vols, Geneva, 1965–6

Binns, Norman. *An Introduction to Historical Bibliography*, reprint, Association of Assistant Librarians, London, 1962

Block, Andrew. *The English Novel 1740–1850*, reprint, Dawsons Pall Mall, London, 1967

Brussel, I. R. *Anglo-American First Editions*, 2 vols, Constable, London, 1935–6

Carter, John. *Binding Variants in English Publishing*, Constable, London, 1932

———. *Publishers' Cloth, 1820–1900*, Constable, London, and Bowker, New York, 1935

———. *Taste and Technique in Book-Collecting*, reprint, Private Libraries Association, Pinner, 1974

274

————. *ABC for Book-Collectors*, 4th edn, Hart-Davis, London, 1968

Chapman, R. V. *Cancels*, Constable, London, 1930

Collier, J. Payne. *Bibliographical Account of the Rarest Books in the English Language*, London, 1865

Collinson, R. L. *Bibliographies Subject and National: A Guide to Their Contents, Arrangements and Use*, 3rd edn, New Librarianship, London, 1968

Duff, E. Gordon. *Fifteenth Century English Books*, Bibliographical Society/Oxford University Press, 1917

Esdaile, Arundell. *A List of English Tales and Prose Romances Printed before 1740*, Bibliographical Society, London, 1912

Ghosh, Jyotish C. and others. *Annals of English Literature 1475–1950*, Oxford University Press, 1961

Halkett, S. and Laing, J. *Dictionary of Anonymous and Pseudonymous Literature of Great Britain*, ed by J. Kennedy and others, 9 vols, Oliver & Boyd, Edinburgh and London, 1926–62

Howard-Hill, T. *Bibliography of British Literary Bibliographies*, Oxford University Press, 1969

Keynes, Geoffrey. *Bibliotheca Bibliographici*, Trianon Press, London, 1964

Kunitz, S. J. and Haycraft, E. *British Authors of the Nineteenth Century*, New York, 1936; *British Authors of the Twentieth Century*, with supplement, 2 vols, New York, 1956–9

Lowndes, W. T. *The Bibliographer's Manual of English Literature*, 4 vols, new edn by Henry G. Bohn, G. Bell & Sons, 1857, reprint in 8 vols, Pordes, London, 1968

McKerrow, Ronald B. *An Introduction to Bibliography*, reprint, Oxford University Press, 1948

————. *Printers' and Publishers' Devices in England and Scotland 1485–1640*, Bibliographical Society/Oxford University Press, Oxford, reissue, 1949

Muir, Percy H. *Points, 1874–1930; 1866–1934*, 2 vols, Constable, London, 1931–4

Northup, C. S. *A Register of Bibliographies of the English Language and Literature*, Yale University Press, New Haven, 1925

Pollard, A. W. and Redgrave, G. R. *Short-title Catalogue 1475–1640*, 2 vols, Bibliographical Society/Quaritch, London, 1926 (revised edition in progress)

Riches, Phyllis W. *Analytical Bibliography of Universal Collected*

Bibliography: Comprising Books Published in the English Tongue in Great Britain and Ireland, and the British Dominions, London, 1934

Rosner, Charles. *The Growth of the Book Jacket,* Sylvan Press, London, Harvard University Press, Cambridge, Mass, 1954

Sadleir, Michael. *Excursions in Victorian Bibliography,* Constable, London, 1922

———. *The Evolution of Publishers' Binding Styles,* Constable, London, 1930

———. *XIX Century Fiction,* 2 vols, Constable, London, and California University Press, Los Angeles, 1951.

Smith, F. Seymour. *An English Library,* revised and enlarged edition, Deutsch, London, 1963

Taylor, A. and Moser, F. J. *The Bibliographical History of Anonyms and Pseudonyms,* University of Chicago Press, 1951

Wing, Donald, *Short-Title Catalogue 1641–1700,* 3 vols, Columbia University Press, New York, 1945–51, index vol, Charlottesville, Va, 1955 (second edition in progress)

Watson, George. *The Concise Cambridge Bibliography of English Literature, 1600–1950,* Cambridge University Press, 1958

AERONAUTICS (EARLY)

Brockett, Paul. *Bibliography of Aeronautics,* Washington, DC, 1910

AGRICULTURE

Aslin, Mary S. *Rothamsted Experimental Station, Harpenden, Library Catalogue of Printed Books and Pamphlets on Agriculture 1471–1840,* 2nd edn, Harpenden, 1940, supplement, Harpenden, 1949, *Catalogue of Serial Publications,* Harpenden, 1953

Fussell, G. E. *The Old English Farming Books,* Crosby Lockwood, London, 1947

———. *More Old English Farming Books,* Crosby Lockwood, London, 1950

Loudon, J. C. *An Encyclopaedia of Agriculture,* Longman, Hurst, Rees, Orme, Brown & Green, London, 1825.

Perkins, W. F., *British and Irish Writers on Agriculture,* 3rd edn, London, 1939

AUSTRALIA

Ferguson, J. A. *Bibliography of Australia*, 7 vols, Sydney, 1941–69

Miller, E. M. *Australian Literature, A Bibliography*, revised edn extended to 1950, ed by F. T. Macartney, Sydney, 1956

Spence, S. A. *Bibliography of Selected Early Books and Pamphlets Relating to Australia 1610–1880*, Spence, Mitcham, Surrey, 1952

BEES

Scottish Beekeepers' Association. *Catalogue of the Moir Library*, Scottish Beekeepers' Association, Edinburgh, 1951

BIRDS

Anker, Jean. *Bird Books and Bird Art*, Copenhagen, 1938

Harting, J. E. *Bibliotheca Accipitraria*, London, 1891 (falconry)

Irwin, Raymond. *British Bird Books: A Guide to Modern British Ornithology*, London, 1952

Mullens, W. M. and Swann, H. K. *A Bibliography of British Ornithology from the Earliest Times to the End of 1912*, with supplement, Witherby, London, 1917–23

Nissen, Claus. *Die Illustrierten Vogelbücher*, reprint, Stuttgart, 1975

Sitwell, S., Buchanan, H. and Fisher, J. *Fine Bird Books*, Collins, London, 1953

Zimmer, J. T. *Catalogue of Edward E. Ayer Ornithological Library*, Chicago, 1926

BOTANY

Arber, Agnes. *Herbals, Their Origin and Evolution*, 2nd edn, enlarged, Cambridge University Press, 1938

Blunt, Wilfrid. *The Art of Botanical Illustration*, New Naturalist series No. 14, Collins, London, 1950

Dunthorne, G. *Flower and Fruit Prints of the Eighteenth and Early Nineteenth Centuries*, London, 1938

Henrey, Blanche. *British Botanical and Horticultural Literature before 1800*, 3 vols, Oxford University Press, 1975

Jackson, B. D. *Guide to the Literature of Botany, Including Nearly 6,000 Titles not in Pritzel*, Index Society, London, 1887

Pritzel, Georg A. *Thesaurus Literaturae Botanicae Omnium Gentium*, Brockhaus, Leipzig, 1872, new edn, ed by Dr C. Jesson, Milan, 1950

Render, Alfred. *The Bradley Bibliography. A Guide to the Literature of the Woody Plants of the World Published before the Beginning of the Twentieth Century*, 5 vols, Arnold Arboretum, Harvard University, Cambridge, Mass, 1911–18

Sitwell, S. and Blunt, W. *Great Flower Books 1700–1900*, Collins, London, 1956

CANADA

Peel, Bruce B. *Bibliography of the Prairie Provinces*, Toronto, 1956

Staton, F. M. and Tremaine, Marie. *Bibliography of Canadiana*, 2 vols, Toronto, 1959–65

CHILDREN'S BOOKS

Darton, F. J. H. *Children's Books in England*, Cambridge University Press, 1932

Gottlieb, Gerald. *Early Children's Books and Their Illustrations*, Pierpont Morgan Library/Oxford University Press, 1975

CRICKET

Gaston, A. J. *A Bibliography of Cricket*, London, 1895

Taylor, Alfred D. *Catalogue of Cricket Literature*, London, 1906, reprint, E. P. Group, East Ardsley, Yorks, 1972

DRAMA AND THEATRE

Arnold, J. F. and Robinson, J. W. *English Theatrical Literature 1599–1900*, Society for Theatrical Research, London, 1970 (based on *A Bibliographical Account of English Theatrical Literature*, by Robert W. Lowe, 1888)

Baker, Blanch M. *Dramatic Bibliography*, New York, 1933

Brown, T. Allston. *History of the American Stage*, New York, 1870

Genest, Rev. J. *Some Account of the English Stage 1660–1830*, 10 vols, published by the author, Bath, 1832

Greg, Sir W. A. *Bibliography of the English Printed Drama to the Restoration*, 4 vols, Bibliographical Society/Oxford University Press, Oxford, 1939–59

Harsage, Alfred. *Annals of English Drama 975–1700*, London and Philadelphia, 1940

Haskell, Daniel C. *List of American Dramas in the New York Public Library*, New York Public Library, New York, 1916

Hill, Frank P. *American Plays Printed 1714–1830, A Bibliographical Record*, Stanford University Press, Palo Alto, California, 1934

Loewenberg, Alfred. *The Theatre of the British Isles, Excluding London: A Bibliography*, London, 1950

McGuire, Paul. *The Australian Theatre*, Sydney, 1949.

Nicoll, Allardyce. *A History of Early Eighteenth Century Drama*, and *A History of Late Eighteenth Century Drama*, Cambridge University Press, 1925 and 1927

Ward, Sir A. W. *A History of English Dramatic Literature*, 5 vols, London, 1899

FISH AND FISHING

Dean, Bashford. *A Bibliography of Fishes*, 3 vols, American Museum of Natural History, New York, 1916–23

Hampton, J. F. *Modern Angling Bibliography*, Herbert Jenkins, London, 1947

Westwood, T. and Satchell, T. *Bibliotheca Piscatoria*, W. Satchell, London, 1883

GENEALOGY

Harrison, H. G. *A Select Bibliography of English Genealogy, with Brief Lists for Wales, Scotland and Ireland*, London, 1937

GEOLOGY

Challinor, John. *The History of British Geology: A Bibliographical Study*, David & Charles, Newton Abbot, 1971

GYPSIES

Black, G. F. *A Gypsy Bibliography*, Gypsy Lore Society, London, 1914

HISTORY

Bibliography of British History, 5 vols, various compilers, American Historical Association/Royal Historical Society/ Oxford University Press, Oxford, 1959–75

Bradford, T. L. *Bibliographer's Manual of American History*, ed. S. V. Henkels, 5 vols, Philadelphia, 1906–10

Scott, John. *Bibliography of Works Relating to Mary Queen of Scots*, Edinburgh, 1896

ILLUSTRATION

Abbey, J. R. *Life in England in Aquatint and Lithography 1770–1860, from the Library of J. R. Abbey*, privately printed, 1953 (reprinted by Dawsons Pall Mall, London)

Bennett, Whitman. *Practical Guide to American 19th Century Color Plate Books*, New York, 1949

Bland, David. *A History of Book Illustrations*, Faber, London, 1969

Darton, F. J. H. *Modern Book-Illustration in Great Britain*, London, 1951

Hamilton, Sinclair. *Early American Book Illustrators and Wood Engravers*, New York, 1958

Levis, Howard C. *A Descriptive Bibliography of the Most Important Books in the English Language Relating to the Art and History of Engraving*, Ellis, London, 1912

Weber, Carl J. *Fore-Edge Painting*, Harvey House, New York, 1966

INSECTS

Lisney, A. A. *A Bibliography of British Lepidoptera, 1608–1799*, privately printed, Chiswick Press, London, 1960

IRELAND

Bradshaw Collection. *Catalogue of Irish Books in the University Library, Cambridge*, 3 vols, Cambridge University Press, 1916

LAW AND CRIME

Beale, Joseph H. *A Bibliography of Early English Law Books*, Harvard University Press, Cambridge, Mass, 1926

Cumming, Sir J. *A Contribution towards a Bibliography dealing with Crime and Cognate Subjects*, London, nd

MEDICAL AND SCIENTIFIC

Bolton, H. C. *A Select Bibliography of Chemistry*, Washington DC, 1893, Kraus Reprint Corp, New York, 1965

Garrison, F. H. and Morton, L. T. *Medical Bibliography*, 3rd edn, Deutsch, London, 1970

Knight, D. M. *Natural Science Books in English 1600–1900*, Batsford, London, 1972

Osler, Sir William. *Incunabula Medica*, London, 1923

Zeitlinger, H. and Sotheran, H. C. *Bibliotheca Chemico-Mathematica: A Catalogue of Works in Many Tongues on Exact and Applied Science*, 2 vols and 3 supplements, Sotheran, London, 1921–41

MUSIC

Day, C. L. and Murrie, Eleanore B. *English Song Books, 1651–1702*, Bibliographical Society, London, 1940

Dean-Smith, Margaret. *A Guide to English Folk Song Collections, 1833–1952*, Liverpool University Press/English Folk Dance and Song Society, Liverpool, 1954

Scholes, P. A. *A List of Books about Music in the English Language*, London, nd

NAVAL AND MILITARY

Cockle, M. J. D. *Bibliography of English Military Books up to 1642*, 2nd edn, Holland Press, London, 1957

Manwaring, G. E. *A Bibliography of British Naval History*, reprint, Conway Maritime Press, London, 1970

POLITICAL ECONOMY

McCulloch, J. R. *Literature of Political Economy: A Classified Catalogue*, 1845, reprint, London School of Economics, London, 1938

PRINTING, BINDING AND PRIVATE PRESSES

Barker, Nicholas. *The Oxford University Press and the Spread of Learning*, Oxford University Press, 1978

Bigmore, E. C. and Wyman, C. W. H. *Bibliography of Printing*, 2 vols, 2nd edn, New York, 1945

Craig, Maurice. *Irish Bookbindings, 1600–1800*, Cassell, London, 1954

Duff, E. Gordon. *Early English Printing*, London, 1896

Duff, E. Gordon. *William Caxton*, Chicago University Press, 1905

Fletcher, W. Y. *English and Foreign Bookbindings*, 2 vols, London, 1895–6

Franklin, Colin. *The Private Presses*, Studio Vista, London, 1969

Gaskell, P. *A Bibliography of the Foulis Press*, Hart-Davis, London, 1964

Isaac, Frank. *English and Scottish Printing Types*, 2 vols, Bibliographical Society, London, 1930–2

Matthews, Brander. *Bookbindings, Old and New*, G. Bell & Sons, London and New York, 1896

Mitchell, William S. *A History of Scottish Bookbinding, 1432–1650*, for Aberdeen University by Oliver & Boyd, Edinburgh and London, 1955

Roberts, W. *Printers' Marks*, G. Bell & Sons, London and New York, 1893

[Sandford, C., Rutter, O. and Sandford, A.] *Bibliography of the Golden Cockerel Press, 1921–1949*, 3 vols in 1, Dawsons, Folkestone,and Alan Wofsy, San Francisco, 1975

Tomkinson, G. S. *Select Bibliography of Principal Modern Presses*, First Edition Club, New York, 1928

Weale, W. H. J. and Taylor, L. *Early Stamped Bookbindings in the British Museum*, for the British Museum, London, 1922

(See also under Cobden-Sanderson, Morris and Whittinghams in the individual author section.)

RAILWAYS

Cotterell, S. *Bibliography and Priced Catalogue of Early Railway Books*, David & Charles, Newton Abbot, 1969

RELIGION, PHILOSOPHY ETC

Barlow, T. H. and Moule, H. F. *Historical Catalogue of Printed Editions of the Holy Scripture in the Library of the British and Foreign Bible Society,* 2 vols in 4, 1903–11, reprint, Kraus Reprint Corp, New York, 1963

Gillett, Charles R. *Catalogue of the McAlpin Collection of British History and Theology, 1500–1700,* New York, 1927–30

Louttit, C. M. *Handbook of Psychological Literature,* Indiana College, Bloomington, Indiana, 1932

Rand, Benjamin. *Bibliography.of Philosophy, Psychology and Cognate Subjects,* New York, 1905

SCIENCE FICTION

Briney, R. E. and Wood. *Science Fiction Bibliographies,* Chicago, 1972

TRAVEL AND TOPOGRAPHY

Anderson, John P. *The Book of British Topography: A Classified Catalogue of the Topographical Works in the Library of the British Museum,* W. Satchell, London, 1881

Chubb, Thomas. *Printed Maps in Atlases of Great Britain and Ireland,* 1927, reprint, Dawsons Pall Mall, London, 1966

Cox, E. G. *A Reference Guide to the Literature of Travel, Including Voyages, Geographical Descriptions, Adventures, Shipwrecks and Expeditions,* 4 vols, University of Washington Press, Seattle, 1935–49

Garling, A. *Bibliography of African Bibliographies,* African Studies Centre, Cambridge, 1968

Gross, Charles. *Bibliography of British Municipal History,* New York, 1897, reprint. Leicester University Press, 1966

Hancock, P. D. *Bibliography of Works Relating to Scotland,* 1916–50, Edinburgh University Press, 1971

Humphreys, A. L. *A Handbook to County Bibliography,* London, 1917

Mill, H. R. *Catalogue of the Library of the Royal Geographical Society,* Royal Geographical Society, London, 1895

Taylor, C. R. H. *Pacific Bibliography,* Wellington, NZ, 1951, 2nd edn, Oxford University Press, 1965

Wagner, H. R. *The Plains and the Rockies: A Bibliography of*

Original Narratives of Travel and Adventure 1800–1865, ed C. L. Camp, privately printed, Columbus, Ohio, 1937

UNITED STATES OF AMERICA

Adams, Ramon F. *Six Guns and Saddle Leather: a Bibliography on Western Outlaws and Gunmen*, Norman, Okla, nd but 1954

Blanck, Jacob. *Bibliography of American Literature*, 6 vols, Yale University Press, New Haven, Conn, 1955–73

Brown, J. C. *Bibliotheca Americana*, 3 parts in 5, New York, 1961–3

Cowan, R. E. and R. G. *Bibliography of the History of California 1510–1930*, 3 vols, San Francisco, 1933, new edn, 1952

Evans, Charles. *American Bibliography*, 14 vols, Chicago and Worcester, Mass, 1903–34–55

Hargrett, Lester. *Bibliography of Constitutions of the American Indians*, Harvard University Press, Cambridge, Mass, 1947

Hill, F. P. and Collins, V. I. *Books Printed at Newark N.J.*, privately printed, Newark, 1902

Peterson, C. Stewart. *Bibliography of County Histories of the 3,111 Counties in the Forty-Eight States*, revised edn, Johns Hopkins University Press, Baltimore, 1946–50

Sabin, Joseph. *A Dictionary of Books Relating to America*, 29 vols in 15, Bibliographical Society of America, Amsterdam, 1961 (also available in a Readex Microprint with magnifying glass, New York, nd)

Smith, Charles W. *Pacific Northwest Americans*, 3rd edn, ed by Isabel Mayhew, Portland, Oregon, 1950

Streeter, Thomas W. *Bibliography of Texas*, 3 vols, Harvard University Press, Cambridge, Mass, 1955–6

Wickersham, James. *Bibliography of Alaskan Literature*, Cordova, Alaska, 1927

BIBLIOGRAPHIES OF INDIVIDUAL AUTHORS

AINSWORTH: Harold Locke *Bibliographical Catalogue of the Published Novels of William Harrison Ainsworth*, London, 1925

ARNOLD: Thomas B. Smart *The Bibliography of Matthew Arnold*, London, 1892

AUDEN: B. C. Bloomfield and E. Mendelson *W. H. Auden:*

A Bibliography 1924–69, University of Virginia Press, Charlottesville, Va, 2nd edn, 1973

AUSTEN: Geoffrey Keynes *Jane Austen: A Bibliography*, Nonesuch Press, London, 1929

BACON: R. W. Gibson *Francis Bacon: A Bibliography*, 2 vols, Scrivener Press, Oxford, 1950–9

BALLANTYNE: Eric Quayle *R. M. Ballantyne: A Bibliography of First Editions*, Dawsons Pall Mall, London, 1968

BARRIE: B. D. Cutler *Sir James M. Barrie: A Bibliography*, New York, 1931

BEAUMONT & FLETCHER: S. A. Tannenbaum *Beaumont and Fletcher: A Concise Bibliography*, New York, 1938

BECKFORD: G. Chapman and J. Hodgkin *A Bibliography of William Beckford of Fonthill*, Constable, London, 1930

BEERBOHM: A. E. Gallantin and L. M. Oliver *Max Beerbohm: A Bibliography*, Hart-Davis, London, 1953

BELLOC: Patrick Cahill *The English First Editions of Hillaire Belloc*, published by the compiler, London, 1953

BERKELEY: Geoffrey Keynes *A Bibliography of George Berkeley, Bishop of Cloyne*, Oxford University Press, 1976

BEWICK: S. Roscoe *Thomas Bewick: A Bibliography Raisonné*, Oxford University Press, 1953

BLAKE: Geoffrey Keynes *A Bibliography of William Blake*, Grolier Club, New York, 1921, reprint, Oxford University Press, 1931

BORROW: T. J. Wise *A Bibliography of the Writings in Prose and Verse of George Henry Borrow*, London, 1914, reprint, Dawsons Pall Mall, London, 1966

BOSWELL: F. A. Pottle *The Literary Career of James Boswell, Esq., Being the Bibliographical Materials for a Life of Boswell*, Oxford University Press, 1929

BRIDGES: G. L. McKay *A Bibliography of Robert Bridges*, 1933, reprint, Dawsons Pall Mall, London, 1964

BRONTËS: T. J. Wise *Bibliography of the Brontë Family*, 1917, reprint, Dawsons Pall Mall, London, 1964

BROOKE: Geoffrey Keynes *A Bibliography of Rupert Brooke*, Hart-Davis, London, 1954

BROWNE: Geoffrey Keynes *A Bibliography of Sir Thomas Browne*, revised edn, Oxford University Press, 1968

BROWNING, E. B.: W. Barnes *A Bibliography of Elizabeth Barrett Browning*, University of Texas Press, Austin, Texas, 1969

BROWNING, R.: L. N. Broughton, C. S. Northup, R. Pearsall *Robert Browning: A Bibliography, 1830–1950*, Cornell University Press, Ithaca, N.Y., Cumberledge, London, 1954

BUNYAN: F. M. Harrison *A Bibliography of the Works of John Bunyan*, Bibliographical Society, London, 1932

BURNS: J. W. Egerer *A Bibliography of Robert Burns*, corrected reprint, Oliver & Boyd, Edinburgh and London, 1964

BURTON: N. M. Penzer *Annotated Bibliography of Sir Richard Francis Burton*, 1923, reprint, Dawsons Pall Mall, London, 1967

BYRON: T. J. Wise *A Bibliography of the Writings in Verse and Prose of George Gordon Noel, Baron Byron*, 2 vols, reprint, Dawsons Pall Mall, London, 1965

CARLYLE: I. W. Dyer *A Bibliography of Thomas Carlyle's Writings and Ana*, Portland, Maine, 1928

CHAUCER: E. P. Hammond *Chaucer: A Bibliographical Manual*, New York, 1933

CHURCHILL: F. Woods *A Bibliography of the Works of Sir Winston Churchill*, Vane, 1963, Kaye & Ward, London, 1969

COBDEN-SANDERSON: A. W. Pollard and Edward Johnston *Cobden-Sanderson and the Doves Press*, reprint, *In Usum Bibliophili*, Wymerveer, Holland, 1964

COLERIDGE: T. J. Wise *A Bibliography of the Writings in Prose and Verse of Samuel Taylor Coleridge*, 1913 and supplement, Bibliographical Society, London, 1919

CONRAD: T. J. Wise *A Bibliography of Conrad*, 2nd edn, 1921, reprint, Dawsons Pall Mall, London, 1964

COOK: Sir M. Holmes *Captain James Cook: A Bibliographical Excursion*, Francis Edwards, London, 1952

COPPARD: G. H. Fabes *The First Editions of A. E. Coppard, A. P. Herbert and Charles Morgan*, Myers, London, 1933

COWPER: Norma Russell *A Bibliography of William Cowper to 1837*, Oxford University Press, 1963

CRANE: Gertrude C. E. Masse *A Bibliography of the First Editions of Books Illustrated by Walter Crane*, London, 1933

DARWIN: R. B. Freeman *The Works of Charles Darwin: An Annotated Bibliographical Handlist*, revised and enlarged edition (1,806 entries), Dawsons, Folkestone, 1977

DIBDIN: William A. Jackson *An Annotated List of the Publications of the Rev. Thomas Frognall Dibdin*, Harvard University Press, Cambridge, Mass, 1965

DICKENS: Thomas Hatton and H. H. Cleaver *A Bibliography of the Periodical Works of Charles Dickens*, Chapman & Hall, 1933; J. C. Eckel *The First Editions of the Writings of Charles Dickens*, revised edn, Maggs Bros, London, 1932

DODGSON: S. H. Williams and F. Maden *The Lewis Carroll Handbook*, revised and brought up to 1970 by Roger Lancelyn Green, Dawsons Pall Mall, 1970

DONNE: Geoffrey Keynes *A Bibliography of Dr John Donne*, 4th edn, Oxford University Press, 1973

DOYLE: H. Locke *A Bibliographical Catalogue of the Writings of Sir Arthur Conan Doyle 1879–1928*, London, 1929

DREISER: D. Pizer, R. W. Dowell and F. E. Rusch *Theodore Dreiser: A Primary and Secondary Bibliography*, Boston, Mass, 1975

DRUMMOND: R. H. MacDonald *The Library of Drummond of Hawthornden*, Edinburgh University Press, 1971

DRYDEN: Hugh MacDonald *John Dryden: A Bibliography*, reprint, Dawsons Pall Mall, London, 1967

EDGEWORTH: Bertha C. Slade *Maria Edgeworth 1767–1849*, London, 1937

ELIOT: Donald Gallup *T. S. Eliot: A Bibliography*, new edn, Faber, London, 1969

EVELYN: Geoffrey Keynes *Bibliography of John Evelyn*, new edn, Oxford University Press, 1968

FITZGERALD, E.: W. F. Prideaux *Notes for a Bibliography of Edward Fitzgerald*, London, 1901

FITZGERALD, F. S.: Matthew J. Bruccoli *F. Scott Fitzgerald: A Descriptive Bibliography*, University of Pittsburgh Press, Pittsburgh, 1972

FORSTER: B. J. Kirkpatrick *A Bibliography of E. M. Forster*, Hart-Davis, London, 1965

FROST: W. B. S. Clymer and C. R. Green *Robert Frost: A Bibliography*, Amherst, Mass, 1937

GALSWORTHY: H. V. Marrot *A Bibliography of the Works of John Galsworthy*, London, 1928

GALT: Erik Frykman *John Galt's Scottish Stories*, University of Uppsala, 1959

GIBBON, E.: J. E. Norton *A Bibliography of the Works of Edward Gibbon*, Oxford University Press, 1970

GIBBON, L. G.: Ian S. Munro *Leslie Mitchell: Lewis Grassic Gibbon*, Oliver & Boyd, Edinburgh and London, 1966

GILL: E. R. Gill *Bibliography of Eric Gill*, reprint, Dawsons Pall Mall, London, 1973

GOLDSMITH: T. Scott *Oliver Goldsmith Bibliographically and Biographically considered*, New York, 1928

GRAY: C. S. Northup *A Bibliography of Thomas Gray*, Yale University Press, New Haven, Conn, 1917

HAGGARD: J. E. Scott *Bibliography of the Works of Sir Henry Rider Haggard*, London, 1947

HARDY: R. L. Purdy *Thomas Hardy: A Bibliographical Study*, reprint, Oxford University Press, 1968

HAZLITT: Geoffrey Keynes *A Bibliography of William Hazlitt*, Nonesuch Press, London, 1931

HEMINGWAY: A. Hanneman *Ernest Hemingway: A Comprehensive Bibliography*, Princeton University Press, 1967

HENTY: R. L. Dartt *G. A. Henty: A Bibliography*, Dar-Web Inc, Cedar Grove, NJ, J. Sherratt & Son, Altrincham, 1971

HOBBES: H. Macdonald and Mary Hargreaves *Thomas Hobbes: A Bibliography*, Bibliographical Society/Oxford University Press, Oxford, 1952

HOPKINS: Tom Dunne *Gerald Manley Hopkins: A Comprehensive Bibliography*, Oxford University Press, 1976

HOUSMAN: John Carter and John Sparrow *A Bibliography of A. E. Housman*, Hart-Davis, London, 1952

HUDSON: G. F. Wilson *A Bibliography of the Writings of W. H. Hudson*, reprint, Bailey Bros & Swinfen, Folkestone, 1968

JAMES: Le Roy Phillips *A Bibliography of the Writings of Henry James*, New York, 1930

JOHNSON: W. P. Courtney and D. N. Smith *A Bibliography of Samuel Johnson*, 1925, supplement by R. W. Chapman, 1939, reprint, Oxford University Press, Oxford, 1968

JONSON: S. A. Tannenbaum *Ben Jonson: A Concise Bibliography*, New York, 1938

JOYCE: John H. Slocum and H. Cohoon *James Joyce: A Bibliography*, Hart-Davis, London, 1953

KEATS: J. R. Macgillivray *Keats: A Bibliography*, University of Toronto Press, 1949

KIPLING: Flora V. Livingstone *A Bibliography of the Works of Rudyard Kipling*, New York, 1927, supplement, Harvard University Press, Cambridge, Mass, 1938

LAMB: J. C. Thomson *A Bibliography of the Writings of Charles and Mary Lamb*, Hull, 1908

LAWRENCE, D. H.: Warren Roberts *A Bibliography of D. H. Lawrence*, Hart-Davis, London, 1963

LAWRENCE, T. E.: F. A. Clements *T. E. Lawrence: A Reader's Guide*, David & Charles, Newton Abbot, 1973

LEWIS: G. Handley-Taylor and T. d'A. Smith *Cecil Day Lewis: A Bibliography*, St James Press, London, 1968

LONDON: D. L. Walker and J. E. Sisson *The Fiction of Jack London*, Texas Western Press, El Paso, Texas, 1972

MACDIARMID: K. D. Duval and S. G. Smith (eds) *Hugh MacDiarmid: A Festschrift*, with checklist by William R. Aitken, Duval, Edinburgh, 1962

MANSFIELD: Ruth E. Mantz *The Critical Bibliography of Katherine Mansfield*, New York, 1931

MARLOWE: S. A. Tannenbaum *Christopher Marlowe: A Concise Bibliography*, New York, 1937, supplement, 1947

MAUGHAM: R. Toole Stott *A Bibliography of the Writings of W. Somerset Maugham*, B. Rota, London, 1956

MEREDITH: M. B. Forman *A Bibliography of the Writings in Prose and Verse of Meredith*, with supplement, Bibliographical Society, London, 1922–4

MILLAY: Karl Yost *Bibliography of the Works of Edna St Vincent Millay*, New York, 1937

MOORE: E. Gilcher *A Bibliography of George Moore*, North Illinois University Press, Dekalb, Illinois, 1970

MORRIS: H. B. Forman *The Books of William Morris*, 1897, reprint, Holland Press, London, 1976

MUIR: E. W. Mellown *A Bibliography of the Writings of Edwin Muir*, N. Vane, London, 1966

NEWTON: G. J. Gray *A Bibliography of the Works of Sir Isaac Newton*, 1907, reprint, Dawsons Pall Mall, 1967

O'NEILL: Barrett H. Clark *A Bibliography of the Works of Eugene O'Neill*, New York, 1931

POPE: R. H. Griffith *Alexander Pope: A Bibliography*, 2 vols, Holland Press, London, 1962

POTTER: Jane Quinby *Beatrix Potter: A Bibliographical Check List*, published by the author, New York, and Sawyer, London, 1954
POUND: Donald Gallup *A Bibliography of Ezra Pound*, Hart-Davis, London, 1969
POWYS, J. C.: Derek Langridge *John Cooper Powys, A Record of Achievement*, Library Association, London, 1966
POWYS, T. F.: Peter Riley *A Bibliography of T. F. Powys*, R. A. Brimmell, Hastings, 1967

RAY: Geoffrey Keynes *A Bibliography of John Ray*, Faber, London, 1951
RICHARDSON: W. M. Sale *Samuel Richardson: A Bibliographical Record of His Literary Career*, Yale University Press, New Haven, Conn, 1936
RUSKIN: T. J. Wise and J. P. Smart *Complete Bibliography of the Writings in Prose and Verse of John Ruskin*, 2 vols, 1889–93, reprint, Dawsons Pall Mall, London, 1964

SCOTT: J. C. Corson *A Bibliography of Sir Walter Scott 1797–1940*, Oliver & Boyd, Edinburgh and London, 1943
SHAKESPEARE: W. Ebisch and L. L. Schueking *A Shakespeare Bibliography*, Oxford University Press, 1931, supplement, Oxford University Press, 1937; T. Howard-Hill *Shakespearian Bibliography and Textual Criticism*, Oxford University Press, 1971; William Jaggard *A Shakespeare Bibliography*, Jaggard, Stratford-on-Avon, 1911, reprint, 1913
SHAW: Geoffrey H. Wells *A Bibliography of the Books and Pamphlets of George Bernard Shaw*, London, 1928
SHELLEY: T. J. Wise *A Shelley Library*, Dunedin Press, Edinburgh, 1924
SITWELLS: R. Fifoot *A Bibliography of Edith, Osbert and Sacheverell Sitwell*, 2nd edn, Oxford University Press, 1971
SPENSER: F. R. Johnson *A Critical Bibliography of the Works of Edmund Spenser, Printed before 1700*, Johns Hopkins University Press, Baltimore, 1933, supplement by Dorothy F. Atkinson, Johns Hopkins University Press, Baltimore, 1937
STEVENSON: George L. McKay *Catalogue of a Collection of Writings by and about Robert Louis Stevenson Formed by Edwin J. Beinecke*, 6 vols, Yale University Library, New Haven, Conn, 1951–64; W. F. Prideaux *A Bibliography of the Works of Robert Louis Stevenson*, new edn, London, 1917

SWIFT: H. Teerink *Bibliography of the Writings of Jonathan Swift*, 2nd edn, ed by A. H. Scouten, University of Pennsylvania Press, Philadelphia, 1963

SWINBURNE: T. J. Wise *Bibliography of the Writings in Prose and Verse of Algernon Charles Swinburne*, 2 vols, privately printed, London, 1919–20

TENNYSON: J. C. Thomson *Bibliography of the Writings of Alfred Lord Tennyson*, reprint, Pordes, London, 1967

THACKERAY: H. S. Van Duzer *A Thackeray Library*, privately printed, New York, 1919

THOMAS: J. A. Rolph *Dylan Thomas: A Bibliography*, Dent, London, 1956

THOREAU: F. H. Allen *Bibliography of Henry D. Thoreau*, Boston, Mass, 1908

TROLLOPE: Michael Sadleir *Trollope: A Bibliography*, Constable, London, 1928

VAUGHAN: E. L. Marilla *A Comprehensive Bibliography of Henry Vaughan*, University of Alabama Press, University, Alabama, 1948

WALLACE: W. O. G. Lofts and D. Adley *The British Bibliography of Edgar Wallace*, H. Baker, London, 1969

WALPOLE: A. T. Hazen *A Bibliography of Horace Walpole*, Yale University Press, New Haven, Conn, 1942; A. T. Hazen and J. P. Kirby *A Bibliography of the Strawberry Hill Press*, Yale University Press, New Haven, Conn, 1942

WALTON (Izaak): P. Oliver *A New Chronicle of the Compleat Angler 1655–1936*, New York, 1936

WELLS: M. Katanka *Comprehensive Bibliography of H. G. Wells*, Katanka Ltd, Edgware, Middlesex, 1968

WHITE: E. A. Martin *A Bibliography of Gilbert White, the Naturalist and Antiquarian of Selborne*, revised edn, Halton, London, 1934

WHITMAN: E. F. Frey *A Bibliography of Walt Whitman*, Bailey Bros & Swinfen, Folkestone, 1967

WHITTIER: T. F. Currier *John Greenleaf Whittier: A Bibliography*, Harvard University Press, Cambridge, Mass, 1937

WHITTINGHAMS: Arthur Warren *The Charles Whittinghams, Printers*, Grolier Club, New York, 1896

WILDE: C. S. Millard ('Stuart Mason') *Bibliography of Oscar Wilde*, 1914, new edn, B. Rota, London, 1967

WISE: G. E. Haslam *Wise after the Event: A Catalogue of Books, Pamphlets, Manuscripts and Letters relating to Thomas James Wise*, Manchester Central Library, Manchester, 1946; William B. Todd *Thomas J. Wise: Centenary Studies*, University of Texas Press, Austin, and Edinburgh, 1960

WOOLF: B. J. Kirkpatrick *Bibliography of Virginia Woolf*, Hart-Davis, London, 1957

WORDSWORTH: T. J. Wise *Bibliography of William Wordsworth*, Bibliographical Society, London, 1916

YEATS : Allan Wade *A Bibliography of the Writings of W. B. Yeats*, 3rd edn, revised Alspach, Hart-Davis, London, 1968

Index

Illustrations are indicated by italic figures

293